Palgrave Macmillan Memory Studies

Series Editors: **Andrew Hoskins** and **John Sutton**

International Advisory Board: **Steven Brown**, University of Leicester, UK, **Mary Carruthers**, New York University, USA, **Paul Connerton**, University of Cambridge, UK, **Astrid Erll**, University of Wuppertal, Germany, **Robyn Fivush**, Emory University, USA, **Tilmann Habermas**, University of Frankfurt am Main, Germany, **Jeffrey Olick**, University of Virginia, USA, **Susannah Radstone**, University of East London, UK, **Ann Rigney**, Utrecht University, Netherlands

The nascent field of Memory Studies emerges from contemporary trends that include a shift from concern with historical knowledge of events to that of memory, from 'what we know' to 'how we remember it'; changes in generational memory; the rapid advance of technologies of memory; panics over declining powers of memory, which mirror our fascination with the possibilities of memory enhancement; and the development of trauma narratives in reshaping the past.

These factors have contributed to an intensification of public discourses on our past over the last thirty years. Technological, political, interpersonal, social and cultural shifts affect what, how and why people and societies remember and forget. This groundbreaking series tackles questions such as: What is 'memory' under these conditions? What are its prospects, and also the prospects for its interdisciplinary and systematic study? What are the conceptual, theoretical and methodological tools for its investigation and illumination?

Aleida Assmann and Sebastian Conrad (*editors*)
MEMORY IN A GLOBAL AGE
Discourses, Practices and Trajectories

Aleida Assmann and Linda Shortt (*editors*)
MEMORY AND POLITICAL CHANGE

Brian Conway
COMMEMORATION AND BLOODY SUNDAY
Pathways of Memory

Richard Crownshaw
THE AFTERLIFE OF HOLOCAUST MEMORY IN CONTEMPORARY LITERATURE AND CULTURE

Astrid Erll
MEMORY IN CULTURE

Anne Fuchs
AFTER THE DRESDEN BOMBING
Pathways of Memory 1945 to the Present

Irial Glynn and J. Olaf Kleist (*editors*)
HISTORY, MEMORY AND MIGRATION
Perceptions of the Past and the Politics of Incorporation

Yifat Gutman, Adam D. Brown and Amy Sodaro (*editors*)
MEMORY AND THE FUTURE
Transnational Politics, Ethics and Society

Amy Holdsworth
TELEVISION, MEMORY AND NOSTALGIA

Jason James
PRESERVATION AND NATIONAL BELONGING IN EASTERN GERMANY
Heritage Fetishism and Redeeming Germanness

Emily Keightley and Michael Pickering
THE MNEMONIC IMAGINATION
Remembering as Creative Practice

Mikyoung Kim and Barry Schwartz (editors)
NORTHEAST ASIA'S DIFFICULT PAST
Essays in Collective Memory

Philip Lee and Pradip Ninan Thomas (editors)
PUBLIC MEMORY, PUBLIC MEDIA AND THE POLITICS OF JUSTICE

Erica Lehrer, Cynthia E. Milton and Monica Eileen Patterson (editors)
CURATING DIFFICULT KNOWLEDGE
Violent Pasts in Public Places

Motti Neiger, Oren Meyers and Eyal Zandberg (editors)
ON MEDIA MEMORY
Collective Memory in a New Media Age

Anna Saunders and Debbie Pinfold (editors)
REMEMBERING AND RETHINKING THE GDR
Multiple Perspectives and Plural Authenticities

V. Seidler
REMEMBERING DIANA
Cultural Memory and the Reinvention of Authority

Evelyn B. Tribble and Nicholas Keene
COGNITIVE ECOLOGIES AND THE HISTORY OF REMEMBERING
Religion, Education and Memory in Early Modern England

Forthcoming titles:

Owain Jones and Joanne Garde-Hansen (editors)
GEOGRAPHY AND MEMORY
Exploring Identity, Place and Becoming

Palgrave Macmillan Memory Studies
Series Standing Order ISBN 978–0–230–23851–0 (hardback)
978–0–230–23852–7 (paperback)
(outside North America only)

You can receive future titles in this series as they are published by placing a standing order. Please contact your bookseller or, in case of difficulty, write to us at the address below with your name and address, the title of the series and the ISBN quoted above.

Customer Services Department, Macmillan Distribution Ltd, Houndmills, Basingstoke, Hampshire RG21 6XS, England

---

The Mnemonic Imagination

Remembering as Creative Practice

Emily Keightley
Senior Lecturer in Communication and Media Studies, Loughborough University, UK

and

Michael Pickering
Professor of Media and Cultural Analysis, Loughborough University, UK

palgrave
macmillan

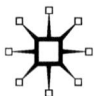

First published 2012 by
PALGRAVE MACMILLAN

Palgrave Macmillan in the UK is an imprint of Macmillan Publishers Limited, registered in England, company number 785998, of Houndmills, Basingstoke, Hampshire RG21 6XS.

Palgrave Macmillan in the US is a division of St Martin's Press LLC, 175 Fifth Avenue, New York, NY 10010.

Palgrave Macmillan is the global academic imprint of the above companies and has companies and representatives throughout the world.

Palgrave® and Macmillan® are registered trademarks in the United States, the United Kingdom, Europe and other countries.

ISBN 978–0–230–24336–1

This book is printed on paper suitable for recycling and made from fully managed and sustained forest sources. Logging, pulping and manufacturing processes are expected to conform to the environmental regulations of the country of origin.

A catalogue record for this book is available from the British Library.

A catalog record for this book is available from the Library of Congress.

10 9 8 7 6 5 4 3 2 1
21 20 19 18 17 16 15 14 13 12

Printed and bound in Great Britain by
CPI Antony Rowe, Chippenham and Eastbourne

In memory of
Cyril George Keightley (1908–2008)
and Harry Pickering (1916–2002)

Contents

Acknowledgements

In the Communication and Media Studies section of the Department of Social Sciences at Loughborough University, we are blessed with an admirable and congenial bunch of friends and colleagues. For their encouragement and good fellowship, we would like to thank Fred Attenborough, David Buckingham, David Deacon, John Downey, Graham Murdock, Sabina Mihelj, James Stanyer, Georgina Turner, Dominic Wring and Liesbet van Zoonen. Most of the book was written between summer 2010 and summer 2011, and during this time we also embarked on a three-year programme of research investigating media and remembering in everyday life. We would like to thank the Leverhume Trust for funding this project (F/00 261/AC) and Nicola Allett, who joined us as a Research Associate on the project, for helping with the organisation and administration of the research. We appreciate her patience during those times when we were preoccupied with planning or writing one or other chapter in the book. The media and memory research is not drawn on here, but it certainly informed some of our thinking as we developed our ideas for what follows. John Sutton of Macquarie University read the whole manuscript for us with scrupulous care and attention, and offered a number of valuable comments and suggestions. We have acted on many of these and the book has been improved as a result; so thank you, John – we very much appreciate your critical engagement with what we have written. Catherine Mitchell and Felicity Plester at Palgrave Macmillan have been helpful and constructive throughout the whole time we have been working on the book. Most of all, we would like to thank Steve and Karen, our respective partners, for their forbearance and support, especially when we have been clattering away for hours on our keyboards. We are truly grateful to you both for your abundant presence in our lives.

Emily Keightley and Michael Pickering

An Outline of What Lies Ahead

Memory studies is an intellectually vibrant, yet still emergent field. Many disciplines meet there, but hardly as yet converge. Effective interdisciplinary synthesis will no doubt take some time to develop, and will be the work of divers hands. While we hope to make some contribution to this, our aim in what lies ahead is relatively modest. It is directed at certain critical issues in the recent study of memory which have so far been largely ignored, and at certain aspects of current thinking and practice which we believe should be reconsidered. The main area of neglect which we deal with, and address throughout the book, is the relationship between memory and imagination. Imagination and imaginative engagement are of vital importance in acts and processes of remembering. In focusing on both particular and divergent past scenes and scenarios, they help us integrate memories into a relatively coherent pattern of meaning that informs our sense of a life as we have lived it. They enable us to establish continuities and shifts in the trajectories of our experience over time, and creatively transform memory into a resource for thinking about the transactions between past, present and future. Yet in seeking to explore the significance of imagination for memory, we have to a great extent found memory studies deficient. Their relationship is one from which the field has so far shied away. The focus has been almost exclusively on memory, with little if any attention paid to imagination.

We find this rather curious because, in what are everyday occurrences and activities, using and relating to the imagination is commonplace. We read a novel and imaginatively interact with the characters and the narrative action; we listen to a piece of music and certain scenes or feelings are imaginatively generated; we watch particular films or television programmes and subsequently use them as imaginative resources.

1

In these examples imagination and memory act in concert, both at the time we are immersed in music or fictional narrative and subsequently, as what is given to us through our imaginative engagements with them becomes interwoven with our own social and historical experience. 'Imagination' here is given positive valence, but of course the term has various meanings and applications, which include those where aspersions are cast upon the veracity of a statement, as for example when what has been said is dismissed on the grounds that 'you're merely imagining it'. Even more negatively, the term may be used as if it were synonymous with wild fantasy, where doubts are levelled, sometimes with a kind of brass-tacks bullishness, at someone's ability to recognise the demands and pressures of 'the real world', as in the accusation that 'you're living in cloud-cuckoo land'. The realm of the imagination is then utterly divorced from the realm of necessity or truth. So while our cultural and aesthetic experiences involving the imagination are many and varied, and the role of imagination in them is regarded as legitimate or appropriate, once used in a negative or pejorative sense the values of imagination for processes of recollection are inevitably called into question.

This is where the problems start, with the sundering of memory and imagination from each other. Memory is then confined to empirical tests of veracity, and imagination regarded as necessarily suspect in its relation to memory's adherence to some 'real world' of the past. It is this hard-and-fast situation, where memory and imagination are rendered antagonistic by being separated from each other, that we want to challenge. In doing so, we take an immediate cue from various academic disciplines where imagination may be constrained by certain procedures of method or criteria of analysis, but is not rejected out of hand. When we refer to the sociological imagination or the historical imagination, this involves our capacity to move from one perspective to another, to alternate between individual and collective forms of experience, to bring large-scale, impersonal and local or intimate aspects of social and historical life into relationship with each other. Such moves are regarded as important components of sociological and historical interpretation and analysis, so is it really the case that memory studies is rejecting imagination out of hand? We cannot believe this is the case. It is, as we have suggested, more a matter of neglect, of it having been overlooked. But it is a serious omission, and one we need to redress.

The relationship between memory and imagination has not been entirely ignored in memory studies, but only by a small margin. Barbara Misztal, for example, does address the relationship in her book on theories of social remembering, but devotes only five pages to it.[1] There she cites various literary, philosophical and historiographical examples which illustrate the impossibility of splitting memory and imagination off from each other. This is useful, but limited. We need to go beyond selective quotations from a few celebrated figures, and beyond remarks which say little that is new or challenging in relation to conventional thinking. How memory and imagination relate to each other needs to be given concerted attention and considered afresh. The need is made stronger by the paucity or sketchiness of reference to this question being representative of a broader pattern in which the relationship is played down or skirted around, regardless of whether it is individual or collective memory that is being discussed. Memory is commonly seen as a constructive or reconstructive process, but when we look to see where imagination contributes to this process, we find a large and unacknowledged gap. The intention of this book is to fill that gap, and try to think anew about how the relationship between memory and imagination may be said to operate. Before we begin this task, we need to tackle another obscured relationship in memory studies.

This involves the vital partnership between experience and memory. It is only by first attending to experience and memory that we can start to rethink the relationship of imagination and memory. Experience is an important analytical category for memory studies because it is central to the relations of past, present and future that are germane to the whole field. The common distinction between experience as process (lived experience) and experience as product (assimilated experience – the knowledge crystallised out of previous experience) correlates with the equally common distinction between the process of remembering and memory as the product resulting from that activity. Experience provides the basis for thinking backwards and looking forwards, as it links up with memory and remembering in any given present, but how this linkage occurs is something that needs to be examined at the outset.

So experience is where we begin. The first chapter of the book discusses the dynamic relation between immediate and congealed experience on the one hand and remembering and memory on the other. In exploring this relation our approach to the remembering subject is cast in terms of our successive versions of self-identity as these are constructed over the course of time. We contextualise this in modern and late-modern times since it is characteristic of such times that we have come to believe the self to be continually transformable. This belief is itself predicated on acceptance of a self as able to be reconfigured. In modern times, we do not see ourselves as determined by our place in a social or cosmic order; the modern subject is regarded as self-defining and self-realising. This is of course a contestable definition of the subject, and one that would need to be advanced with considerable qualification. In striving to avoid both oversocialising and undersocialising the remembering subject, we ground memory in experience since in our conception of it, experience as lived and interpreted is necessarily registered in the interspace between selfhood and social order. It is also through experience that we negotiate processes of change and patterns of continuity. In their mutual comprehension, the meanings we impart to experience through the ways in which we recollect it are neither determined from their outset nor constant over time. While unfolding in time, experience acts back on that process of development across time, and memory is key to this transactional movement. It is in such movement that we can first identify its creative potential.

Another reason for starting with an exploration of the relationship between experience and memory is that both are viewed as personal and social, situated and mediated, proximate and distant. Seeing how these dimensions are interactive is an important aspect of our project to rethink the relations between individual and collective memory, which we discuss in the middle of the book. In order to prepare the ground for this discussion, we spend the first half of the book developing the argument that our ability to turn experience as process into experience as product depends upon a mutually generative tension between memory and imagination. In much thinking about memory it is set up in strict opposition to imagination. Addressing this problem is the purpose of the second chapter in the book. For some the problem may seem somewhat chimerical if they do not see any hard-and-fast distinction between them as forms of knowledge, or regard them as having twinned roles in artistic creation. This kind of association has, for example, been a common feature of literary studies or art history with, among other things, imagination being accepted as significant for the aesthetic form in which memory is represented.[2] But in wider public discourse the opposition is clearly, if not starkly apparent, and this has been replicated in contemporary memory studies, unwittingly or not, with a marked tendency to separate memory and imagination and, when imagination is exceptionally taken into consideration, to attend to their differences over and above their potential interaction. In order to see how this has come about, we chart the changing historical relationship between memory and imagination and consider the particular epistemological shifts which have been involved in order to assess what has been lost in their separation.

We also assess the various positions that have been taken in thinking about the relationship between memory and imagination. Increasingly, it is the sense of their mutual antagonism that prevails. In memory studies, the conceptual aggrandisement of memory has occurred in inverse proportion to analytical engagement with the role of imagination in acts and processes of remembering, while in contemporary critical discourse, imagination seems to be viewed with sceptical excess, as for example is evident in the weight of negative connotations acquired by the word 'imagined', which has become all-too-easily used as if it is only equivalent to whatever is regarded as fabricated, illusionary and ideologically tainted. Our own position is that memory and imagination are closely akin, though significantly distinct, and can only be considered as suspect or not in relation to the context in which their relationship becomes manifest. On the one hand this means that memory is a vital resource for imagining, and imagining is a vital process in making coherent sense of the past and connecting it to the present and future. The remembering subject is faced with far more vacant spaces than spaces filled with available memories, yet it is out of what remains or can be recollected at will that we construct the story of ourselves and our lives. Such a narrative is not built purely and simply out of memory. Life stories are constructed just as much out of how we imagine our memories as fitting together in retrospect. On the other hand of course, distortion, exaggeration, falsification, even outright invention may exist and these may derive from the imagination as well as from various ideological forms and frames. What we imagine may not necessarily be rooted in any verifiable memory, but the possibility of this does not in itself deny the positive role which imagination plays in the narrative development of a life-story or the reconstruction of past experiences. Our memories are not imaginary, but they are acted upon imaginatively.

Some of the problems in thinking about 'memory' may seem to stem from the term itself, for it is has an imperial scope and so embraces a vast territory that includes areas designated by the legend – 'here be dragons' of forgetting.[3] That is why for many it makes sense to distinguish between forms and processes of remembering across a broad spectrum from cases of bodily remembering, where memory is felt as intense physical sensation, through *mémoire involontaire* with its joltingly evocative madeleine moments, to intentional memory as part of an effort to build up detailed and connected maps of meaning across entire lives or communities. We see the value in these typologies and draw on them in what follows; we also found them helpful in making certain distinctions and qualifications as we initially sketched out what we wanted to say. But we have not engaged with them directly and substantively in this book because our primary interest is with intentional acts and processes of remembering as these operate in concert with imagination and imaginative engagement. Here again the value of memory has become rather inflated in its conceptual currency. We can illustrate this with reference to certain acts and occurrences in our memory which seem to have a dramatic presence, where we may say, because of this quality, that they are as real as when they happened. This is only true of their representation, for it can only be as representation that they exist in our memories, and over time they need to be imaginatively connected together if they are to contribute to the longer-term maps of meaning to which we are referring. Two considerations follow. Firstly, when we remember them we do not experience them in the same way as we would if they were to magically recombine in front of us and be materially as they were when first formed. They do not belong to experience in that way. While this may become a source of pathos or regret, it also provides us with a critical perspective on the interrelations of memory and imagination. What we remember and imagine are akin in the sense that we may describe them as vivid, faithful or lifelike, whereas we do not use these terms to describe what we experience within any particular present as we live it. We use these terms to distinguish between, say, a face and the portrayal of a face, or a face and the memory of a face. This is not to diminish the likeness or the memory in favour of the actual face, for memories and imaginings are both important in creating a credible likeness. They enable us to seem to perceive what is not there, and so make the absent present, or at least they do this when they *are* taken to be vivid, faithful or lifelike, yet what is absent can only appear present through its reconstruction in and across time. It has no other presence even though its cross-temporal reference may seem stacked with resonance. Secondly, while memories and imaginings are distinct from one another, when we make memories become vivid once again through the way we engage with them across time, or when they have a definite value for us as past experience that helps sustain us in a changed present, they attain a clear imaginative edge or form a distinct line of temporal connection which we have traced in our imagination, so helping to make past and present in some way cohere and have continuity across time.

It is because of such considerations that our central concern in the book is with remembering as a creative process. This is what is denied when memory and imagination are cast asunder. The transformative potential of memory is attenuated and the role of remembering is limited to repetition of the past rather than being seen as central to the creative production of meaning about the past, present and future in their various interrelations. While this argument is balanced with attention to the ethical dangers of postmodern relativism and of subsuming memory into fiction (in its pejorative sense), we give priority to the argument itself because it was via thinking about what is lost in the separation of memory and imagination that we were led to write this book in the first place. That is why our central focus in what follows is on rethinking their relationship so as to account for the mutually productive ways in which they interact. How they interact may depend upon what is being recollected, in what way, and why, but as already noted, in memory the past is not directly transmitted to us in pristine form; it comes back to us only in fragments out of which we puzzle together their connections and distinctions, patterns and configurations. Memory is mobile and formative, not merely repetitive; it is this which gives memory its creative potential, but the potential is only realised through the productive tension that arises between memory and imagination. Through this tension imagination reactivates memory and memory stimulates the imagination. The creative quality of these interactions has a cross-temporal resonance, with memory necessary in thinking of the future, and imagination necessary in thinking of the past. It is in order to understand better what this involves that we develop the concept of the mnemonic imagination.

This can be roughly characterised as an active synthesis of remembering and imagining which is essential to our understandings of the relationship between past, present and future. It is through the mnemonic imagination that our engagements with the past move through a series of interactive dualities: the constitution of selfhood and the commission of social action; the interplay between experience and expectation, memory and possibility; the relations between lived first-hand experience and mediated or inherited second-hand experience. Exploring the movement between these dualities is crucial if a more fine-grained comprehension of the ways in which past, present and future experience are brought to bear on one another in processes of remembering is to be developed, and the full extent of the creativity that this involves is to be recognised. It is because past, present and future co-exist in patterns of continuity and discontinuity within the experiential manifold, with the mnemonic imagination as the dynamic in which these patterns are reconstructed and negotiated, that what has been taken over from the past is continually being revised in order to accommodate an open and continually unfolding future. This has become a commonplace of modernity, with its future-oriented temporality generating a need not only for new experiences but also for the recurrent reassessment of past experiences. If memory is the medium of that reassessment, imagination is what animates the material on which it draws. Through the productive tension between them, the mnemonic imagination facilitates the transformation of experience as process into experience as product. This is the core of the mnemonic imagination, and through it as well experience is brought into a state of creative interaction with expectation and movements beyond it. The interaction may, for example, cause us to revise our expectations while our understanding of the past may be revised by our expectations having been exceeded. There are various possibilities that may ensue as a result of the interaction, and collectively they show how the mnemonic imagination is vital in providing us with a framework for comprehending past and future and so enabling action in the present.

In the first half of the book we are primarily concerned with establishing how the mnemonic imagination is vital for the processes of individual recollection and the assimilation of experience in the ways so far outlined. It is perhaps because we are attracted to the phenomena of memory as sociologists that we are sensitive, in this section of the book, to the dangers of adopting a sociologically hidebound approach. The main consequence of this is that, while we endeavour to see these phenomena primarily through social frames, we also try not to lose sight of the fact that, first and foremost, it is individual subjects who do remembering, and for whom memories are reanimated in a changed present. That is why we begin the book by dwelling on the ways in which individuals use their mnemonic imagination in helping to bring past, present and future into some cross-temporal pattern so as to sustain a sense of self-identity across the different periods of their lives. Across time we change, and since memory provides a complex set of links back into the past, much of our analytical focus is initially on how, in our particular life-trajectories, there are certain constituent features which define us in recollection even as we change, and help us relate our successive selves to each other in terms of who we were, are and might become. In such processes the creative work required is accomplished by the mnemonic imagination, and as such it is across time a key component of identity formation and maintenance. While it seems to us important that we give this careful consideration, that cannot of course be the whole story, and so after the first two chapters we step out from this initial analytical focus to show the relevance of the concept of mnemonic imagination to extra-individual phenomena as these are manifest in broader configurations of memory within societies.

This shift in our primary focus of attention is signalled particularly in Chapter 2 where we attend in detail to the relations between individual and collective memory. The greatest danger in thinking about these relations is setting them up as neatly separable domains of mnemonic action. This is quite false because no form of remembering is either individual or collective in any singular or unified sense. We may still lack adequate ways of handling the vital betweenness that arises across individual and collective memory, regardless of whether we are working towards a sociological conception of this or one oriented more to a cultural psychology of remembering, but this is no excuse for an all-too-convenient division of labour between, say, cognitive psychologists studying individual memory and critical sociologists devoting themselves to the study of collective memory. All too often these two dimensions of memory have been considered separately and the dynamic nature of their relationship has been neglected. In early psychological and some philosophical accounts, social aspects of remembering were ignored in deference to memory as an individual faculty. In contrast, more recent sociological accounts of collective cultural memory have obscured the role of the individual as an agent in the processes and practices of collective remembering. Along with the dangers of approaching memory either in an individualist or socially determinist manner, we emphasise the pitfall of reifying collective memory and speaking as if a social group or community remembers in the same way as an individual. This can be avoided by focusing conceptually on the relations between personal and popular memory, and the interplay between situated and mediated experience. Sociologically, this is the only way memory makes any sense at all. The key to these relations and this interplay is the mnemonic imagination. The mnemonic imagination facilitates the transactional movement necessary for their coexistence, and when necessary helps realign personal and popular memory through its interanimation of these two dimensions of identity and experience.

In taking up the common-sense distinction between lived, first-hand experience and vicarious, second-hand experience, we try to show how they act in co-relation even if they clash with or contradict each other. The kinds of second-hand experience primarily or in the first instance associated with media consumption which are most commonly identified and referred to are spatial in orientation and synchronic in occurrence. It is these which loom large when second-hand experience is being discussed. We use the opportunity of studying memory and remembering to offset this by attending to second-hand experience which is primarily temporal in orientation and diachronic in occurrence, for it is such experience which is by contrast relatively neglected. Overcoming this neglect is vital in seeking to bring personal and popular memory back into view of one another. We conceive of these complementary dimensions of remembering as informing senses of continuity and duration, change and reorientation in people's social and self-identities, and offer mnemonic imagination as a concept which allows us to develop a clearer understanding of how we continuously rove back and forth between these dimensions of our remembered experience. It is in this movement that mnemonic imagination contributes to the creation of social and cultural identities that are both durable and flexible over time. The interaction between personal and popular memory is thus reconceived as a dialogic and creative process in which mnemonic imagination negotiates and integrates individual and social elements of experience.

At this point we should add a caveat. In exploring the creativity of memory, our considerations of the potency of certain memories as well as the capacity of our imaginative powers have, at times, inclined us towards a way of writing of them that we would not finally espouse. This involves personifying memory and imagination, and speaking of them as if they are autonomous agents. It is a common enough tendency, and the examples we could cite are legion, but it is of course always people who remember and imagine, and in whom and for whom the mnemonic imagination gains operational force as they apply it to their thinking of past, present and future and the ways in which they interrelate. We indulge this occasional tendency in how we have written about the mnemonic imagination only for the sake of convenience, thus saving readers from elaborate reams of qualification and tiresome disqualifiers. We hope that by highlighting the distinction between remembering as experiential process and memory as experiential product that we shall, in the first half of the book, sufficiently disabuse readers of any confusion arising from this short-cut choice of phrasing.

From Chapter 3 onwards we try to keep individual and collective remembering in more or less constant view of each other. With this in mind, the remaining chapters of the book are designed to emphasise the value of the concept of the mnemonic imagination by showing in a more concrete way what happens when it is in active operation, and what is involved when such operation is thwarted by acts or representations that close down its access to the past, or when it is blighted by certain experiences that do not become available for its creative engagement. In two of these chapters we look at different forms of nostalgia. We argue that this distinctive modality of memory cannot simply be equated with an uncritical escapism and bland consolation in the past, along with a concomitant loss of faith in the future. It cannot be reduced to a singular or absolute definition. Nostalgia is certainly a response to the experience of loss endemic in modernity and late-modernity, and it can certainly be trivial or become trivialised, but in its modern temporalised manifestations it is various and so not necessarily confined to a search for ontological security in the past. It can just as possibly be a response to the desire for creative engagement with difference, or a sign of social critique and aspiration. It is because of this variation, accommodating progressive, even utopian impulses as well as regressive stances and melancholic attitudes, that we attempt to reclaim nostalgia from its indiscriminate detractors. As Andrea Rítívoí has claimed, nostalgia prompts certain important questions regarding the function of remembering, and raises 'distinctions between escapist fantasy and the imagination as repository of ideals, considerations of identity as a self-sufficient entity or as a culture- and context-bound entity'. She notes that 'nostalgia encourages one to differentiate and to contrast, and as such, it functions as a potent interpretative stance, a tool of comparison and analysis'.[4] This is very much as we approach it, focusing on it not simply because of the past/present contrasts upon which it is based, but more importantly developing it as an opportunity for demonstrating the diverse ways in which we respond to social and cultural change in modernity and late-modernity. Of course, nostalgia cannot be properly reclaimed and rehabilitated unless we also develop a critical account of the ways in which it is exploited and misused. We produce such an account in Chapter 5 where we introduce the concept of retrotyping as a way of showing how regressive forms of nostalgia are able to forestall or block the workings of the mnemonic imagination, and permit only 'escapist fantasy'. Our discussion of retrotyping is linked with a critical interrogation of the thesis of cultural amnesia, and of Pierre Nora's historical claims concerning *lieux de mémoire*.

Retrotyping is one particular way in which, usually for consumerist purposes, the past is rendered in such a way that the mnemonic imagination is denied active presence, and connections to present and future are stymied. In the last chapter of the book we attend to a quite different obstruction of the mnemonic imagination. This abides in the consequences of traumatic experience for the process of remembering, and for the ability of the mnemonic imagination to creatively energise the temporal tenses in our narrative understanding of past experience, so bringing the past to active account in the present for the sake of the future. In our discussion of these difficulties, we argue against the ways in which the term 'trauma' is so often used in a profligate and cavalier manner.

This can be just as exploitative as retrotyping, though in a completely different register. By distinguishing between trauma and painful pasts, we are able to present various examples and cases which show where the mnemonic imagination is able to facilitate the process of assimilating difficult experiences, and where it is unable to do so. The point of this is to show that the mnemonic imagination is not an entirely free agent, able to go where it will and operate without constraint.

In elaborating the concept of mnemonic imagination, throughout the book as a whole, we are attempting to develop a sociological aesthetics of remembering. We argue that such an aesthetics needs to operate with a critical awareness of the asymmetrical social relations in collective remembering and the ideological structures of national commemoration and mediated memory of the past, but not be confined to it. The explanatory power of such an aesthetics has to embrace the creative dimensions of remembering, and this for us is the primary value of the concept of mnemonic imagination. It is not, however, an exclusive value, for aesthetic considerations always imply ethical ones, especially when we focus on processes of remembering in common, across the relations between first-hand lived experience and second-hand mediated experience. The creative dimensions of remembering entail an ethics of memory in that they have to negotiate the suffering of other people in the past. How can we respond to such suffering, how should it be collectively engaged with, what may be validly taken from it and in what ways can such suffering be considered as an active component of popular memory? These are the kinds of questions we pose. The ethical demands made on us by the past sufferings of others can be responded to or ignored, but we argue that when we try to empathise with the memories of another's pain or distress, of the unjust or intolerable occurrences of which they have been the victim, the mnemonic imagination is that synthesising force which retroactively brings our own experiential horizon into contact with what we were hitherto unconscionably in ignorance of. The mnemonic imagination is the means by which, in our responses to the past, we are able to exceed our own limits in the present and engage in reciprocal communication between self and other. The potential of this for popular memory is that it can then become the site of dialogue between ourselves, and both immediate and distant others across time. Such dialogue is vital to being an active witness of painful pasts.

We began this introduction by referring to memory studies as an interdisciplinary field. If at present it seems to be characterised more by its multidisciplinarity, we believe that its promise lies primarily in the ways in which it will be able to arrive at fruitful interdisciplinary points of synthesis around some of the issues that are central to it as a field. Our book is intended in its own small way to help move us in this direction. While we attempt to foster our own interdisciplinarity as much as possible in what follows, our approach is inevitably steered in various ways by our own disciplinary backgrounds in sociology, cultural history and media studies. Likewise, in writing about the relationship between memory and imagination, we inevitably bring our own set of research interests and intellectual preoccupations to the table. These concern the ways in which processes of individual and collective memory relate to questions of communication, representation, creative practice and historical hermeneutics. We nevertheless consider such questions to be sufficiently broad for us to encompass the main factors involved in the uses and abuses of the past, and in the ways the past may be drawn upon as a resource in individual recollection and cultural production. The mnemonic imagination is central to the manner in which the past attains or regains significance for the present and future, and makes of remembering a creative process. In what lies ahead, we hope to establish fully all that this involves, and show why the concept of the mnemonic imagination helps us overcome certain major areas of neglect in thinking about the phenomena of memory that are integral to our everyday lives.

1
Memory and Experience

The remembering subject

During the final period of his life, Michel de Montaigne produced a series of essays which have become famous for their shrewd insight, practical wisdom and digressive, conversational style. They covered a wide range of topics, but their key underlying topic was Montaigne himself. In writing them, what he was studying most of all was his own self, his own formation and development as an individual subject: 'I am myself the matter of my book'. His reading and thinking were assessed against his own experience, but never egocentrically, never as a means of burnishing his own opinions or stoking his pride. As he reflected on his experiences and the contingent, unpredictable ways in which he understood himself through them, he drew on past events and his own memory, defective though he felt it to be, at one point citing Terence: I am full of cracks and leaking everywhere.[1] 'On Experience', the last essay of the third volume of the essays, begins with the acknowledgement that experience and the memory by which it is recalled are both finite and fragmentary, and this has to be the basis for how we proceed, with the mind always stretching out and trying to exceed its capacities. Montaigne took his experiences as the source of his self-understanding, but found no abiding stability there: as a subject he had changed through time and his self had no fixed centre; it could only be portrayed as it seemed, and as he saw it, at any particular moment. At the start of his essay 'On Repentance', he sketches an account of this mutability of his experiencing self, which he characterised as in a process of continual becoming, constituted over time as a succession of selves developed at different stages in his life, and with varying manifestations in the specific, temporally defined circumstances he had found himself in:

> The world is but a perpetual see-saw. Everything goes incessantly up and down ... Constancy itself is nothing but a more sluggish movement. I cannot fix my subject. He is always restless, and reels with a natural intoxication. I catch him here, as he is at the moment when I turn my attention to him. I do not portray his being; I portray his passage; not a passage from one age to another ... but from day to day, from minute to minute. I must suit my story to the hour, for soon I may change, not only by chance but also by intention. It is a record of various and variable occurrences, an account of thoughts that are unsettled and, as chance will have it, at times contradictory, either because I am then another self, or because I approach my subject under different circumstances and with other considerations ... Could my mind find a firm footing, I should not be making essays, but coming to conclusions; it is, however, always in its apprenticeship and on trial.[2]

We begin with this self-reflexive account because it provides a key coordinate for how we approach the remembering subject in what follows. From a contemporary perspective, it appears as a remarkably prescient account, anticipating a modernist, pluralised version of the self in which the individual cannot be conceived as given, unitary or built around an essential core but is instead, across the span of a lifetime, marked by a variety of different roles, dispositions, projects and fields of occupation which never add up to one complete, cohesive and coherent whole. This does not mean that we cannot and do not strive for a sense of coherent meaning in our own life-narrative, but rather that this striving for meaning necessitates an active process of reconstruction in which any conception of what links our successive selves across time is partly dependent on the past and partly upon 'different circumstances' and 'other considerations' to those which may have preoccupied us during previous stages of our lives. The story must suit the hour, but the hours perish and are laid to account. The considered, mature account then matters more than the expedient tale told in the passing hour, and this presses upon us the task of forming an assessment, based upon what we have judiciously taken from experience, of the fluctuating range of influence and significance in our changing sense of individuality, seeing our experience as occurring at specific moments while being continually redrafted across time as 'a record of various and variable occurrences'. It means coming to terms with the unsettled nature of this self-produced account on the part of the remembering subject. Amidst the limits, ambivalences and contradictions of our experience, we can absorb from Montaigne a sense of the need to live, at least in some measure, with uncertainty and doubt. Since there is no 'firm footing' for the mind, the remembering subject faces an unstable and shifting terrain of accumulated experience on which to make 'assays' and is himself always in movement, according to both intention and chance – 'I am then another self'. The remembering self is inconstant, and so prone to error and divagation, but in Montaigne's case this is turned to positive account, for there is a commendable sense of modesty and lack of dogma alongside a sceptical intellect and an awareness of the fallibility of his own judgement.

We need immediately to complement this conception of the remembering subject with a different point of emphasis. It is one we have already mentioned in talking of the need to create a sense of coherent meaning in our life-narrative. We may lack any firm footing in attempting this, and find difficulties in locating and locking onto a sense of ourselves at particular times in the past, but most of us manage to achieve certain consistencies of attitude and aptitude, certain ways of seeing and doing, across the continual redrafting of our remembered autobiographical script. Certain lines of evaluation and criteria of assessment, even though subject to revision, also become central to the quality of narrative patterning that we construct out of the experience we assimilate. The redrafting of memories of our past experience is always in process, always a cumulative assemblage of what was recalled at different stages of our lives by successive versions of the person whose memory was thereby revised, but it is nevertheless around these relative consistencies, and what we try to hold onto in our ongoing revaluations of experience, that our sense of ourselves across the particular times in our lives hangs together and perdures. This is an important qualification to what we want to take from Montaigne. It constitutes the second major coordinate in the way we approach the remembering subject.

It is in line with this that we should avoid exaggerating the shifts and turns involved in our temporally successive selves – whether for the sake of literary effect, because we are romantically inclined to celebrate continual self-development, or in order to foster the conceit of those who, as assured individual subjects, write of the subject as multiply divided and fragmented.[3] While it is always possible that changes in our sense and realisation of self may be dramatic and radical, taking us at times into desperate situations, more frequently such changes are slower and gradual, becoming intertwined with various underlying continuities, from week to week and year to year. There may be greater alteration between changes in self-identity the longer the period between them, but there are also connections consciously made across time and without these the remembering subject would not be able to weave together a relatively coherent narrative, or have any conception of how temporal passage itself consists of varying rhythms of movement alongside the maintenance of experiential pattern and linkage. Even where radical change occurs, as for instance in character or in values, such change has to be accounted for in the narrative terms of transformation from an 'earlier' to a 'later' self. Accounting for selfhood in the way Montaigne outlines somewhat paradoxically involves a certain consistency of view in its ability to conceive not only of contingency and succession but also of the subject himself experiencing the variation of experience from one time to another and establishing certain relationships between the different elements of the variation. If we were utterly subsumed by the vagaries of experience, we would fail to see any duration and structure in our temporally extended experiences, or be unable to feel and articulate how the memory of a particular experience has acquired resonance in the process of understanding our growing up and self-formation.

Our ability to do this does not derive from, and so become expressive of, any absolute or wholly original version of the self, but we do nevertheless all have some sense that while our memories are shared and to a great extent intersubjectively constituted, there is something special about those we call our own, something that they impart which is qualitatively vital to our sense of ourselves, and of significant meaning in our lives. This of course only applies to conscious recall through which certain past experiences are recapitulated and reassessed in any particular set of present circumstances. As such, remembering involves a complex, mutually shaping mixture of what is private to oneself and what is shared with others. Aspects of inner experience – personal secrets, undisclosed preoccupations, intimate feelings – are not split off from the social world of encounter and relations with others in which remembering is a mundane occurrence, but defined and given identity as a consequence of situated forms of social interaction, belonging and communicative exchange. As with subjectivity more generally, the subjectivity of the person remembering is associated with cognitive, performative and cultural elements of symbolic activity, and involves the coexistence of coercion and freedom, inheritance and critique:

> It is actually more than coexistence: it is a relationship of interconnection between the symbolic structure which is handed down

through different forms of socialisation (family, primary groups, peer-groups) and the capacity for self-reflection and consciousness. If we do not save these two dimensions of subjectivity, we end up with a foreshortening of our perspective, interpreting for instance class-consciousness merely as a cultural phenomenon, or conversely reducing it to a disembodied concept, without any relationship with the actual contents of the thoughts and feelings of daily life.[4]

In line with this dynamic sense of interconnection, we conceive of the remembering subject as someone who is operative within the social relations sustained in the practices of everyday life, yet capable of thinking critically about herself and her situation, able to assess different experiences and understand how different investments have been made in them, or how personal involvement affected the perception of them at the time they occurred. She is never founded in any form of pure, natural, ontocentric experience to which a social integument is subsequently added; she is involved in experience that is social through and through, yet at the same time this is given an individualised imprint such that she regards certain of her experiences as personal, sometimes intensely so, and remembers them as such. At the many points where experience and memory integrally cross-refer, they are shared with others and socially defined by their contexts of occurrence and use, and also have the quality of 'being mine', of being conceived as indispensable to an embodied self-identity and how we think of ourselves as individual persons.

The public and personal aspects of memory imply different evaluations of the meanings associated with them. These qualitatively distinct assessments are important even though what is shared and what is taken as private are in many respects interwoven. So if we see individuality as always, without exception, socially and historically conditioned, we do not approach the subject who remembers as resulting wholly from an interiorisation of pre-given norms and values, established codes of conduct and institutionalised forms of behaviour. That would amount to a sociological conception of the remembering subject from which any dynamic psychology has departed, along with the agentive capabilities to which we have referred. It would simply be the reverse of those forms of psychology from which all aspects of the social have apparently been evacuated in favour of what seems entirely internal to the subject.

It is in order to steer between these two pitfalls that we are adopting experience as a category of analysis. The term 'experience' has various different manifestations, and historically has been used to address and validate many different ideas, so any attempt to give it a singular or absolute definitional sense would fail to recognise its multiple applications and varied developments across a number of different fields. While accepting this and the various implications they entail, there are definite analytical benefits to be derived from considering experience alongside memory. The first of these is that experience can be conceived as traversing the space between individual subject and social institutions. It is through this contingent, often uneasy, yet unavoidable movement that experience becomes the interspace within which we negotiate our self-identity and our social identity, and the ways in which these do, or do not, match up to each other. Needless to say, this interspace is one that is always temporally configured, for within it the play between the remembering subject, the experience remembered and the social forces that intervene in this relation is continually changing.

At any particular juncture in our lives, experience is in part directed and shaped by our own agency, and in part by conditions and pressures outside our individual control or command. It is always manifest in a dialectical process moving between possibility and limit, aspiration and constraint. As a result we all experience events or longer-term processes of change in individual ways, but we do not individually arrange or superintend all the experiences we have. Some of them may come unexpectedly around the nearest corner and knock us sideways. In spite of this we are responsible for our own lives and the quality of narrative pattern and distinction they attain. Experience is never exclusively personal or public, interiorised or outwardly facing, self-directed or the blind product of social forces. It crosses between these mutually informing categories and in that movement is formed the synthesis of self-definition and definition by others that we call the self.[5] This is only one way of conceiving of experience, but it is an important one, for in refusing any definite location for the individual subject it can help us avoid both social determinism and psychological essentialism.

Selfhood should neither be oversocialised nor undersocialised precisely because of this traversal movement of experience, so that personal and social experience are seen as two currents within the same confluence, and so only relatively distinct.[6] This includes the distinction between internal and external orientations of selfhood, with these coexisting along a single axis according to which a person is known both to herself and to significant others. Selfhood is then the reflexive sense of who we are as individuals, defined in relation to other people who are both like and unlike us in a whole range of ways. This reflexive sense draws upon remembered experience. It has always to follow after immediate lived experience for it requires at least some degree of temporal distance if it is to be realised. It cannot be instantaneous, precisely because 'I cannot turn round quick enough to catch myself'.[7] Remembering is therefore always retrospectively part of our temporally unfolding experience, and so occurs at definite points of time within the intermediate space between individual subject and institutional orders. It is then manifest as an active process of arranging the past into a relatively coherent narrative of personhood situated in particular sets of social relations. The narrative pattern only appears as we look back and are able to gain some perspective on what has previously transpired, for events *become* meaningful rather than being instantly meaningful at the moment of their occurrence. It is as a result of such a pattern that we can then recognise experience and what is made of it as characterising the individual subject and conditioning what, and maybe how, she or he remembers. Remembering is, in this respect, the experience of experiences, but only in that changing patchwork sense of which Montaigne spoke so eloquently.

The main implication of memory conceived as a changing patchwork is that the subject remembered by the remembering subject alters and shifts from one period of his life to another, along with the meanings and values of autobiographical memories in their more varied and complete ensemble. Consequently, the remembering subject is different from the self in whom a memory was formed, while that memory itself has no fixed form, however precise and vivid it may seem at any specific moment of recollection. Even the most vivid memory may change in its meaning for you at different junctures of your life. The remembering subject is also different again from the self that is subsequently remembered in association with any particular memory. It is because of these continual shifts and alterations over time that memory is always in apprenticeship to experience, and the past subject to a continually provisional process of reconstruction. As Mead once put it, our 'reconstructions of the past vary in their extensiveness, but they never contemplate the finality of their findings'.[8]

In a continually mobile pattern, some memories endure, some have only a midterm span and others attain no secure or sedimented position at all. The changes may in some ways be small or even imperceptible, but nothing remains wholly static and no bedrock of memory exists as some permanent and enduring ontological base for what is either mutable or ephemeral to pass over it. For these and other reasons, there can be no single, unitary self to which remembering relates: just as self-conception and self-understanding always relate in various ways to place and historical period, so also within the span of a single lifetime are they inseparable from where we are and what we do during specific periods of our lives. Yet it is despite, or rather, because of these variations that we necessarily attempt to construct some semblance of relatedness, if not cohesion, in how we remember ourselves across different periods of our lives and across the variations of our experience – necessarily because without this any conception of selfhood would be, if not impossible, then certainly on shaky ground. If we cannot attain such relatedness over time, in stories of the self or development of the self, we may feel that the value of our experience and how we stand by it is somehow under threat.

This leads to a second benefit in taking experience as an analytical category for thinking about memory, for what is selected and absorbed from it constitutes the unavoidable autobiographical material from which life-stories are achieved in the temporally defined construction of personal identity. Théodule Ribot, in the late nineteenth century, was insistent on this connection: 'our self at each moment – this present perpetually renewed – is in large part nourished by memory ... our present state is associated with other states that, rejected and localised in the past, constitute our person as it appears at each instant'. In sum, self-identity 'rests entirely on memory'.[9] While at times these cross-temporal associations may be defined primarily in terms of our own individual pattern of life-experience, there is of course throughout a dynamic interplay between individual and collective experience and the memories that move between these categories, sometimes in relations of symmetry and integration, at others in relations of conflict and contradiction. Examples of both are evident in the memories of old Australian soldiers and how these corresponded with the Anzac legend. For some this masculinist legend afforded a positive affirmation of their experience and helped them compose a past they could live with quite comfortably, while for others it jarred markedly with what they had experienced and remembered, 'stories of pain or fear' which forced them into 'alienation or silence'. 'It was not until the Anzac legend was tempered by the war in Vietnam, a much more controversial military engagement', that their memories 'could be publicly articulated and recorded'.[10]

Looking at experience as the source material for autobiographical memory leads to the question of how memory works in recounting experience and so narrating the self. One way of answering this would be to say that the individual subject acts not only as an authorial self, continually scripting the story of a particular life, but also as a sort of editor-in-chief of the memories made to matter and cohere in the preferred version of who we think we are. The remembering self is then principally 'an editorial self that consciously or unconsciously selects the memories that wrap us around with the sense of our dignity, our erotic power, our nonchalance, our good will towards mankind, all those pleasures that our self-consideration craves'.[11] Its tongue-in-cheek irony aside, this has a limited conceptual value. Its value is that while self-esteem may tread a tightrope between vanity and humiliation, it is impossible to live without some measure of it, and we draw selectively on the memories that best furnish it. The editorial self then protects a needed sense of the integrity of self-identity. Its limit, which is already hinted in the ironic tone of its formulation, is that integrity is not simply to do with how well our self-conception hangs together or how the various aspects of our identities support and endorse each other. Drawing on Ricoeur's discussion, two rather more significant features of personal identity in the temporal extension of experience, both of which presuppose memory and a validation of the remembering subject, are character and keeping one's word. Character refers to those relatively durable features of a person – dispositions, values, habits, traits – by which a person is identified, re-identified and, over time, assessed, judged, and remembered, while keeping one's word refers to the ability to remain faithful to promises or commitments, and be trustworthy and reliable despite the vagaries of experience and the relentless passing of time.[12] Integrity also involves such features as these and requires individuals to hold true to them in their memory, despite the lack of any firm retrospective footing. In a life as it is lived, some measure of self-constancy, even if this is itself in sluggish movement, acts in concert with a continually unfolding plot and its temporally defined rhythms of development and change.

The individual subject is thus a product of experience in the dual senses of having to respond to social forces, norms, conventions and institutions, and of being able to accept responsibility for self-initiated actions, take certain critical steps and make potentially innovative moves. In both senses experience changes us, on the one hand because we cannot control certain experiences that lead to change, such as becoming involuntarily unemployed, being unjustly persecuted or suffering a physically debilitating accident, and on the other because we can change what we experience, whether this is a consequence of an abusive partner or a poor meal at a local restaurant. Experience as it occurs and is manifest in both directions also affects what we remember but in complicated, sometimes unpredictable ways, partly at least because ongoing experience is a changeable admixture of what is familiar and unexpected, with both having repercussions for what gets brought up in processes of remembering:

The good navigator does not go by the rule book; and she is prepared to deal with what she has not seen before. But she knows, too, how to use what she has seen; she does not pretend that she has never been on a boat before. Experience is concrete and not exhaustively summarizable in a system of rules. Unlike mathematical wisdom it cannot be adequately encompassed in a treatise. But it does offer guidance, and it does urge on us the recognition of repeated as well as unique features.[13]

In offering guidance, at times directly, at others haphazardly, experience can be assimilated and drawn on in a myriad of ways. These include how we consider or treat certain memories and acts of remembering. Experience is, for example, implicated in our considered assessments of whose memory we may trust and whose not, what constitutes reliable remembered evidence of a past event or when it may be appropriate to broach people's memories of certain events in the past and act upon them in the present. Such assessments may involve attempting to bring into some kind of alignment and reconciliation different, and perhaps conflicting versions in the sometimes subtly and sometimes glaringly disparate accounts of events among those who have participated in them and who share certain memories about them. This is just one example of the ways in which experience involves negotiating between the social in our constitution of selfhood and selfhood in our social constitution. Experience is, as we have suggested, the interspace where this negotiation occurs.

Quite what is involved in this negotiation and in both discovering and constructing a sense of pattern and structure in our experience across time is the concern of this chapter. Its production is the work of the remembering subject, but what is being worked with is difficult to describe, not least because experience makes the remembering subject just as much as it makes the remembered self. How experience is threaded through our successive selves relates to its third benefit as a category of analysis for memory studies. In a preliminary way we can realise this benefit by viewing the category from the complementary perspectives of experience as change and experience as continuity.

Experience as it is recollected and reassessed is both temporally continuous and temporally specific, and as any particular mode or modality

of experience develops into a definite social form in which we participate, it is continually subject to change, transformation and succession.
This is especially so in the modern period, with its accelerating pace
and motion seeming the only constant. Experience under conditions of
modernity has been increasingly felt to be provisional and mutable, and
this appears to place a premium on our own present and our ongoing
self-development as we adapt to ever-shifting currents and movements.
The past not only piles up behind us but also varies in its meaning
and significance as experience is subject to relentless disruption, loss
and renewal. This creates a problem for the remembering subject as to
what constitutes experience as the object of memory when subsequent
experience has changed so much how previous experience is conceived,
interpreted and understood. Relative distinctions may be made between
an experience as it was felt and apprehended in the past and how it has
been reflected upon since, but its meaning then cannot be said to run
clear through to its meaning now without posing an unerring and static
self as the guarantor of such continuity. This is one of the problems we
all negotiate in thinking about our own memories and how we relate
to them in a relentlessly successive series of present moments. The
remembering subject is always in a process of becoming and so always
in some way changing.

If one of the consequences of this, especially in modernity and late
modernity, is that the experience we relate to in memory shifts in meaning over time, we nevertheless continue to distinguish between past
experience and the experience of remembering in our lives as they are
lived in any specific present. This distinction is central to experience
as a temporal relation. Even though its meanings and how these are
evaluated may change, there is a certain continuity extending from past
experience into the remembering experience. This continuity is central
to experience as a broad resource upon which we can reliably draw in
the present as we assess the continuous change of the passing of time,
for change can only be assessed as such when understood in relation
to what is at least relatively continuous. Without some conception of
continuity against which it can be assessed, change would be a largely
vacuous concept. This means that there is a duality of structure inherent
in experience which is characterised by its continual unfolding in time
while also acting back on that continuing development across time. The
significance of this is that while experience has a backward and forward
quality to it within any particular situation in time, in apprehending
the relationship between the past and present meanings of an experience, it is through memory that we impart a transactional movement

to the duality. This is one aspect of the creativity of memory which we shall explore in the book. The movement which is then realised in the transaction ensures that both these dimensions of experience over time are kept in play, operating with mutual reference to each other in our sense of a life being lived. Remembering as an active process of ongoing reconstruction and rearrangement is what gives meaning and significance to experience in the continuing and dynamic interrelationship of its lived and learned dimensions. We need now to look at this in greater detail.

Remembered experience

The point of conceiving of the remembering subject as we have is twofold. Firstly, it breaks with the notion of any direct or unmediated continuity between experience and memory. Continuities in experience are reconstructed over time in the context of the changes which the passage of time has brought, with memory itself changing in its interconnected patterns of meaning, significance and value. Secondly, it is in relation to such changing patterns that we strive imaginatively to re-engage with past experience and carry it forward as a relatively coherent narrative. Much of our mundane day-to-day experience is forgotten, yet we attempt to collect together the fragments left in the wake of what is lost and reassemble them so that they tell some sort of credible and self-enhancing story. Without that, lived experience would be mere flux and we would have little sense of a temporally extended personal and social identity upon which we and others closest to us can in some way rely. What we recall of an earlier experience is rarely, if ever, that experience as a whole, and this requires us to build imaginatively on what we recollect and make connections across time, always with the imperative need of the present shaping what we bring back, and bring together, at any particular stage in time.

One of the most common ways of conceiving of experience as a temporal relation is through the distinction between assimilated experience as we have so far sketched it, referring to the knowledge that is crystallised out of previous experience, and experience that is lived in any particular, contingent moment. Lived experience refers to a subject's immersion in the flow of action and interaction with others, and to our immediate observation of and feelings about the various encounters and situations we find ourselves in, from hour to hour, day to day, week to week. While we are so immersed, the meanings of events, encounters and episodes may be relatively inchoate, not yet realised in any developed manner that can be firmly carried ahead into the unfolding future, across the changing years of our lives. This is what we meant in saying that what happens to us becomes meaningful over time as we develop and gain a more durable sense of its significance. It is through this sort of process that we are able to distinguish between lived experience and what subsequently ensues when a particular experience or set of experiences is delineated in memory and certain associations and values are attached or reassigned to them by the remembering subject. The meanings of experience and the definite values derived from them are more fully constructed and considered than they were at the time any particular experience occurred. As experience has been worked up in memory and reflected upon, at different stages in our lives, it then develops a cumulative quality as layer upon changing layer of experience in our memory acquires an increasing sense of their aggregated significance across the different times in our lives. In that sense, for better or worse, we understand ourselves in the present because of the past.

It is against experience in this assimilated sense that further change and development, gain and loss, continuity and disruption, can be assessed and absorbed. We can of course say that both of these dimensions of experience are lived in the sense that they involve encounter with who we are and what we do within the present, and that both involve assimilation insofar as they cover what has been moved through, and learned from, in a vast array of possibilities and consequences, at any particular time in a life being lived. Although immediate experience may not be immediately understood, it is always understood in the light of previous experience, especially in relation to what is familiar, routine, ordinary. Immediate and mediated dimensions of experience remain in play with each other and it is the sense of their interplay which characterises their temporal relation. The qualities and values of both generic forms and specific modalities of experience are articulated, weighed and arranged, in the contingent and always provisional art of practical understanding, only on the basis of the transactional relationship between them. The basis of this relationship occurs on the field of memory as it becomes temporally constituted.

The distinction made by adjectival addition between these dimensions of experience is accomplished in German by the two distinct terms *Erlebnis* and *Erfahrung*, where the former refers to immediate experience in the moment it is lived, and the latter to the point where experience is evaluated and the process through which we learn from accumulated experience in our biographical journey. The contrast is between a moment in time and movement across time, with the movement involving the cumulative quality of crystallised knowledge. The quality may be cumulative, but as we have noted from Montaigne, the knowledge is far from certain, and may at times be incomplete or contradictory, so what we take from the past when we remember remains unsure in status and ambivalent in meaning. Inasmuch as anything tangible and unequivocal is crystallised, it is still utterly at variance with a specific extended sense of *Erfahrung* that makes it equivalent to the methodical analysis and replicable scientific verification of experience that constituted the basis of the 'quest for certainty', John Dewey's felicitous term for the philosophical tradition that ran from Francis Bacon to René Descartes.[14] That quest and that sense of experience are inapplicable to the remembering subject, for in remembering there are no unwavering rules of observation, enquiry and proof that can be relied upon and followed. As Montaigne made abundantly clear, to remember is always to be reminded of uncertainty. This can be dealt with by trying to narrow experience down to a particular dimension or focus, as in the semantic derivation of experiment from experience and the establishment of experimental method as the basis of scientific observation and enquiry. That may seem to rid empirical procedure and knowledge of uncertainty, but it does so at the expense of Montaigne's heterogeneous, embodied and concrete sense of temporally extended experience.

Memory is always selective but it nevertheless embraces all kinds of encounter and all kinds of experience. That is why we must relate remembering to both of these broad forms of experience, *Erlebnis* and *Erfahrung*, for when experience is only seen as *Erfahrung*, as for example happened in its eighteenth-century reduction to the question of cognition, over time the pendulum always swings back towards the lived, phenomenological qualities of *Erlebnis*, as it did in the late eighteenth/early nineteenth century with the Romantic stress on the value of affective involvement in and self-cultivation through experience (*Bildung*), with Friedrich Schleiermacher's theological emphasis on religious faith as a subjective, intuitive experience, and with the theoretical emergence and elevation of aesthetic experience. In all of these examples experience was revalued and compared favourably in its revalued senses with the empiricist and Kantian epistemological conceptions of experience.[15] With *Bildung*, lived experience provides the raw material from which a mature appraisal and understanding is ultimately achieved – the mediated experience that is *Erfahrung* in its biographical sense.[16] The *Bildungsroman* itself is the first new literary genre of Western modernity, and it develops at this time in response to the emergence of the modern conception of the individual subject, centred around the problem of self-formation and the relationship of self and social structure, with a particular focus on the negotiation or struggle between the project of individuation and the demands of social institutions and conventions. The concern is with 'protecting and reconstructing the narrative of self-identity in the face of massive intensional and extensional changes which modernity sets into being'.[17] In modernity, the individual can no longer rely so implicitly and assuredly on an exemplary past or a guaranteed future, and so has to draw primarily on his or her own fund of accumulated experience.

This new sense of the value of experience for what we make of the world and what we have learned from living in it, implying growth and an expansion of scope for the remembering subject, has remained a key semantic feature of the term 'experience' ever since. In a sort of experiment with one's self, 'the episode becomes an experience if the individual manages to give it a meaning that expands and strengthens his personality'. The process of assimilation from episode to experience also requires the avoidance of two errors: on the one hand, not falling prey to the excess of restlessness suggested by Montaigne, where a subject is always reeling 'with a natural intoxication' and so cannot settle decisively on the meaning of an experience or extract from experience 'all the potential meaning it contains'; and on the other, not being able to move away sufficiently from the intensity that produces 'an excess of meaning' and binds us 'too thoroughly and too quickly'.[18]

In a conservative tradition stretching back to Edmund Burke, these errors have often been identified as characteristic of radical intellectuals and thus used by way of contrast in legitimating the prudential lessons from the past that are claimed as the bountiful yield of experience. An example is Alexis de Tocqueville's negative judgement on the *philosophes* of the French Enlightenment that 'they lacked the experience which might have tempered their enthusiasms'.[19] That use of the term contrasts strongly with unassimilated experience, which may be sensuously rich but hasn't yet become either piquant in memory or absorbed as practical wisdom: 'But I could say for a moment only what it was in her words that conveyed such peace and tranquility; I had the experience of it merely, not the understanding'.[20]

This qualitative sense of lived experience is nevertheless at times rendered as equal in value to understanding, and perhaps of even greater value, especially when understanding is reductively conceived as equivalent to rational deduction or explanation. There is an important theoretical line in this respect, connecting Dilthey's use of *Erlebnis* (ambiguous and wavering though this could be) with Dewey's sense of lived experience leading to, and culminating in, an intensely focused moment of fulfilment. If time could be punctuated like a sentence, *an* experience of this kind would signify as an exclamation mark amid the more general, unremarkable, transient prose of everyday life. Such a mark would proclaim the condensation of meaning and import that is involved, giving the moment both felt immediacy after a gradual process of build-up towards it, and forwards-bearing symbolic value across a life as it subsequently unfolds. *An* experience exceeds the meanings that are retrospectively invested in it. It remains a potent source of memory and is often returned to, even after long assimilation. As Gadamer put it, one is never finished with *an* experience: 'it cannot be exhausted in what can be said of it or grasped as its meaning'; 'its meaning remains fused with the whole movement of life and constantly accompanies it'.[21]

Experience of this kind carries significance backwards and forwards in our remembering because of the dynamic tension which continues between what was lived and what this has yielded. It is in this respect an exception or qualification to experience becoming meaningful after the event, since it may seem to acquire unto itself considerable meaning at the moment of its occurrence. Yet why it is memorable and why it is significant continues to be interpretatively mobile, in a creative process that involves each successive expression and retelling of it mediating the next. This is in itself indicative of its mnemonic salience. It seems to generate a self-reflexive process and encourage us to think of connections across time with similar moments, similar episodes in our lives. Wordsworth referred to them as 'spots of time' which are remembered and evaluated as experiential landmarks in a life trajectory, key features by which we track our self-development and from which we continually reorient ourselves in our onwards movement through time:

> There are in our existence spots of time,
> Which with distinct pre-eminence retain
> A vivifying virtue, whence, depress'd
> By false opinion and contentious thought,
> Or aught of heavier or more deadly weight
> In trivial occupations, and the round
> Of ordinary intercourse, our minds
> Are nourished and invisibly repair'd,
> A virtue by which pleasure is enhanced
> That penetrates, enables us to mount
> When high, more high, and lifts us up when fallen.[22]

The enduring quality of a standout experience in our lives is given emphasis in the expression that it has become etched in our memory. This commonplace reference to a durable form of representation – engraving onto copper or steel – catches the sense of self-evident certainty and definiteness that comes with *an* experience, and because it carries that sense we link it with similar moments that appear in their specific ways to represent a pivotal point in our lives, having marked consequences across time, in backward as well as forward directions. The contrast is always with experience that is pedestrian, methodically acquired, overly moulded by social convention or habitual behaviour, that does not lead to the feeling of some definitive conclusion or new start.[23] These two manifestations of experience are then understood as radically different, though in order to be understood as such they require each other, and so are considered in recollection as mundane stages in our lives and key points of transition between them. The latter are usually remembered more clearly because of their association with what was unforeseen or unfamiliar, with what is 'not seamlessly integrated within prevalent discursive schemes, routinised practices or expectations' and so with what 'disruptively stands out from and perturbs current horizons of signification'.[24] What is habitual, rehearsed or set out clearly in advance may not later become subject to conscious recall, unlike unexpected occurrences or subverted expectations: 'This leads him to an interesting observation ... whatever was willed, intentional, ostentatious, planned in his erotic life lost value, while adventures which happened unexpectedly, which did not announce themselves as something extraordinary, became in memory invaluable.'[25]

For what are then obvious reasons, events leading to disruption and change are more likely to be etched in the memory than those which are integral to established practice, but experiences of this kind may alter such practice before they become reintegrated in a more general and settled pattern. Their significance in recollection has to be considered in terms of both their disruptive effect and the eventual resumption of the more settled pattern, for memory is as much a dialectic of continuity and discontinuity as is *Erlebnis* in its reworking of what is unexpected or new into the pattern that has been interrupted.[26] Experience as process leads temporally to its points of climax, crisis or conflict, which may involve encounters with the new and unexpected or between opposed values or interests. These are then subsequently congealed in memory as the product of experience. Remembering is an active process of drawing on that product within a changed temporal situation, and is an element of lived experience in the present. Through its dialectic of continuity and discontinuity, moving across its back-ward- and forward-looking dimensions, experience links up memory as product with remembering as process.

This interlinkage is of critical importance because, as we have already pointed out, in modern societies individuals have increasingly had to draw on the resources resulting from their own experience in making an identity for themselves. Our experience is both derived from what happens to us directly, in situated occurrences and encounters, and from what we take from a broad range of cultural materials outside of local, everyday life, including those of the media and Internet as well as more traditional cultural forms like the novel, dramatic play or religious text. Daniel Bell was quite right in identifying, as one of the key characteristics of modernity, the premium put upon experience as the source from which we make ourselves: 'For us experience, rather than tradition, authority, revealed utterance, or even reason, has become the source of understanding and identity. Experience is the great source of self-consciousness, the confrontation of self with diverse others'.[27] But to this we need to add the explicit recognition that modernity and late modernity involve an increasingly broad and complex intersecting of situated and mediated experiences which may either enrich or erode our coherent sense of self or, indeed, alternate between the two such consequences. Experience as a fund of resources for self-identity may involve us in contradictory meanings and conflicting discourses, as well as in what is unexpected, uncertain and new.[28] All this makes the process of self-formation and development more and more of a hazardous enterprise, despite the criteria of relevance and priority that we use to filter the wide-ranging experiences available to us. Yet it remains the case that experience of whatever mode or dimension is still the key available resource by which and through which this process is impelled, and when we draw on and work with what we take from experience, it also remains the case that it is its storyable features we develop and bring to the fore. Narrative helps us select from, structure and coordinate our experience into temporal coherence and so give shape to our aspiring, onwardly developing selves. In acting as our own biographers, patterning our experience through narrative is central to the experience of remembering. We need now to stand back a little and see what this involves.

The experience of remembering

In parallel to the distinction between lived experience and what this yields in terms of assimilated experience, so in the relationship between experience and memory we distinguish between the experience that is being remembered and the experience of remembering. Experience as it is remembered corresponds to memory as the product resulting from the process of remembering, while the experience of remembering is always in some sense part of the flow of immediate experience in the present. We need to give greater consideration to these interrelationships in order to see more clearly what they offer for the experience of remembering in any particular temporal interval. We use the word interval here because an experienced present is not one which starts and finishes in the snap of an instant. Phenomenologically, we live through and apprehend an event – a conversation, an incident in the street, a film we watch at the cinema – as a sequenced ensemble, with its own particular durational unfolding and its own particular temporal direction within this unfolding. In this way we distinguish between 'before' and 'after' within an event, but not as separate stages. In experience, they are felt and apprehended through their interconnectedness. The athlete runs, and we witness the race. The musician plays a chord, and as this is combined with other chords, in a dynamically interconnected movement, we hear the tune as a whole, a coherent succession of sonic elements that we apprehend as a melody. We cite these analogies in order to illustrate the rhythmic flow running through and running together the various components of an experienced present. It is this tempo which helps impart to an experienced present its substance and quality. Lived experience in this sense is not represented, for it is only when it becomes identifiable as a past, as no longer lived in that immediate flow and tempo, that it can it then be represented within a succeeding present. Memory as a product of past experience is a representation in this sense, whereas remembering is an experienced process lived within a particular moment. If we then turn to ask what this representation entails, we can best approach the question via what is perceived as emergent or new.

The experience of something as emergent or new creates a sense of departure from what went before. There is a disruption to the continuity that has previously been established, for what is seen to be emergent or new 'is always found to follow from the past, but before it appears it does not, by definition, follow from the past' and for that very reason it attains its initial identification.[29] The way this is experienced as lived process and then subsequently assimilated as the product of experience is through interpreting why it was new, why it emerged, why it was different to what went before. The result is not only the re-establishment of continuity but also the construction of a newly conceived past in order to account for what departed from and broke with it. That is why 'a past never was in the form in which it appears as a past. Its reality is in its interpretation of the present'.[30] As Emerson put it, in his essay on memory, what was 'an isolated, unrelated belief or conjecture, our late experience instructs us how to place in just connection with other views which confirm and expand it'. He added: 'If new impressions sometimes efface old ones, yet we steadily gain insight' and with 'every new insight ... we come into new possession of the past'.[31] This process is integral to the creativity of memory, for it is through the ongoing participation in acts of interpretation and reinterpretation of what went before that we actively gain in experience. Any gain in experience involves a repossession of the past.

The past does not exist as a road along which we can travel back, exploring again the steps we once took or the events along the road we once experienced, checking here and there for enduring landmarks or an unchanged topography. This is not a useful metaphor because there is no direct or unhindered flow of traffic in the dynamic inter-play between memory as the product of experience and remembering as a process of experiencing. What constitutes such traffic changes its character and significance according to the presence it needs to attain within the present. That is why the past is always being remade. Mead once put this well in saying

> If we could bring back the present that has elapsed in the reality which belonged to it, it would not serve us. It would be that present and would lack just that character which we demand of the past, that is, that construction of the conditioning nature of now present passage which enables us to interpret what is arising in the future that belongs to this present. When one recalls his boyhood days he cannot get into them as he then was, without their relationship to what he has become; and if he could, that is if he could reproduce the experience as it then took place, he could not use it, for this would involve his not being in the present within which that use must take place. A string of presents conceivably existing as presents would never constitute a past.[32]

The experience of remembering therefore hinges around not only the temporal passage from the past to the present time in which the remembering occurs, but also the temporal distinction between lived experience in its present-centredness and assimilated experience in its orientation within any particular present time to what is being remembered from the past. In this manner, memory is a vital component in making sense of past experience but with past experience only being usable for this task because of its continued reinterpretation and continued repossession in successive present durations. It is this which makes experience meaningful in the long term, in a cumulative yet shifting pattern which involves shaping particular experiences into stories, and at various stages in one's life, reassessing the significance of those stories for a temporally extended self. In this way experience is made and remade *as* memory in a developing process circumscribed only by the limits of human finitude.

The mediation of remembered experience by narrative has been widely recognised in philosophy, sociology and cultural theory as well as the psychology of memory.[33] Turning experience into stories of one kind or another is central to making sense of what happens to us, and to helping us remember particular incidents and episodes in our lives, especially as we grow older and our experience becomes progressively schematised. We do not of course organise our memories solely through written narrative. Compiling a photograph album or associating certain events or periods in our lives through recorded music are also conventional to remembering, yet these familiar sound- and image-based examples of remembering personal experience are often, if not always, accompanied by narrative, by the stories we tell in direct relation to them. In an oft-cited article, Stephen Crites argues that narrative is inherently the formal quality of experience as it is understood across time. Here again, as remembered experience is mediated by narrative, we hear or read a sequenced ensemble of words and sentences, with its own temporal unfolding, but it is the narrative which structures the experience being remembered, told and heard: 'Experience can derive a specific sense of its own temporal course in a coherent world only by being informed by a qualifying structure that gives temporal contours to its own form'.[34]

In his discussion of the narrative quality of experience, Crites claims that without memory, 'experience would have no coherence at all'. There are two ways in which this is the case. From the first perspective, 'memory has its own order' which is manifest as the order of succession: 'the order in which the images of actual experience through time have been impressed upon the memory'. Here memory is the product of experience, but in the remembering process, 'the recall is not total, the chronicle is not without lacunae … it is for great stretches quite fragmentary'.[35] The fragmentary character of memory obviously compromises to some extent the order of succession inherent within it, and makes the remembering subject, as Montaigne well knew, an interrupted subject. If this is the case, then how is it that our conception of memory in relation to our life-narrative does not share these features of fragmentation and interruption? To ask this is not to suggest that sequencing and order do not exist in our memory, for clearly we rely on these features in even the most routine forms of mundane remembering, and without them no one would be a reliable witness to anything. This takes us to the second way in which memory brings coherence to experience, and it requires a further distinction between routine remembering and the actively concerted process of recollection, for our consultation of memory in trying to trace where we left our watch or our spectacles or our rail ticket is not an act of recollection in the sense we are referring to, but more to do with routine remembering stepped up a notch or two. Actively concerted recollection occurs when storytelling builds creatively on the order of sequence inherent in memory, despite its lacunae and points of disjunction, for in storytelling 'the story is never simply the tedious and unilluminating recital of the chronicle of memory itself'.[36] It is only through the act of recollection that experience becomes illuminated.

The illumination consists of bringing together at different times in our lives the past, present and future in the dynamic relation of their different modalities. Narrative is the form in which the relation between these distinct modalities is conjoined, whether this consists of significant personal stories or stories with a broader cultural resonance. As we have seen, it is not as though this relation is realised in any smooth, unbroken move from one incident to another, for what is often impressed most upon the memory is what is unexpected, that which subverts expectation or thwarts anticipation, or what yields the sense of a definite conclusion or fresh start. Yet just as the anticipated future is indeterminate, so the remembered past is determinate, 'a chronicle that I can radically reinterpret but cannot reverse or displace: what is done cannot be undone.' The tensed modalities of experience across time coexist in a state of tension within the present because of the narrative form applied to them. It is narrative which supplies a degree of continuity across the discontinuities between past, present and future, and the narrative that is implicit in the possibility of experience 'must be such that it can absorb both the chronicle of memory and the scenario of anticipation, absorb them within a richer narrative form without effacing the difference between the determinacy of the one and the indeterminacy of the other'.[37] It is in this way that the act of recollection through narrative illuminates our experience.

The narrative forms that become the framework for understanding and illuminating experience do not of course remain fixed across time; they are flexible and changeable, varying not only according to whom we are addressing, but also according to the distance between the chronicle of memory and the act of recollection. Yet without the various narratives that we tell and combine together as a life-narrative, we would not be able to develop and hold to a sense of temporal continuity across the distinctions between past, present and future. Our actions across time would not be intelligible and we ourselves would not be accountable without the psychological continuity that is presupposed by the concept of personal identity. That sense of continuity derives from the way narrative is emplotted, as for example in relation to a pattern of personal growth and development, so informing our self-identity by providing an itinerary for our life-journey or an explanation for its diversions. Devising a plot transforms many incidents into one story, synthesises heterogeneous components into an overall composition, and brings together the abbreviated sequencing and order of isolated memories within the integrated temporal framework supplied by the life-narrative. 'In this sense, composing a story is, from a temporal point of view, drawing a configuration out of a succession.'[38] Emplotment is thus a link-making means for putting experience into temporal concordance once we have, in more circumscribed ways, realised the quality of narrative inherent in certain specific experiences:

> One of the most basic principles of plot construction [in autobiographical memory] is that the remembered I traces a continuous spatio-temporal route through all the narratives of memory, a route continuous with the present and future location of the remembering subject. It may be that there are interruptions in what one remembers, but these can never be taken to imply violation of the principle. This principle imposes a kind of unity on all the narratives; there has to be a coherent story to be told about my movements which will fit with the contents of all my various memories.[39]

Of course, how firm our grasp of this principle might be at any particular juncture in our lives would depend on a range of factors and so across our lives be variable, but without a more or less continuous or at least periodically resumed effort after attaining a measure of narrative coherence among the heterogeneous elements of our experience over time, we would gradually descend into a muddle of dissociations and broken lines between the remembered and the remembering I, as well as become less accountable to others and in danger of losing credibility in their eyes. We should also add that what is taken from experience does not necessarily remain durable across time – its significance is often provisional – and we should always remember from Montaigne that there is, on the one hand, no unassailable ground for the authenticity of some particular experience in which either personal or collective identity is deeply invested, and that on the other the meanings given to any experience remain uncertain and unstable. The I who recollects continually reinterprets and reappraises the remembered I (or 'me') through its spatio-temporal route, using 'me' as the text to be reassessed. In doing so, the remembering subject nevertheless imparts a degree of unity to the text through the way it is emplotted, in a selective process that links events to other events but does not recount all earlier events because 'there is no narrative which can tell *everything*'. 'What is told is selected because it is understood as having a meaningful place within the narrative', and is then '*given* meaning through its very inclusion in the narrative'. It is because of processes of emplotment that 'prior events seem inevitably to lead to later ones, and the end of the story is understood as the culmination and actualisation of prior events'.[40] These are not effects deriving from the incipient order of memory, but from the active process of recollection as mediated through the narrative structure given to experience as it is told and put into social circulation. In the perpetual see-saw that is the world, the remembering subject, at least temporarily, then overcomes the interrupted subject by bringing a narrative coherence to what may otherwise be disjointed events, isolated in time, bereft of any continuity of meaning, whose relationship to each other remains unseen because untold. Emplotment is, as Ricoeur has put it, the 'creative centre of narrative'.[41] In this sense it is central to the dialogic space which exists between memory and imagination, and it is to this space that we shall now turn.

Temporal transactions

In the previous section we hoped to have made clear that in acts of remembering we do not return to the past and bring experience from it wholesale into the present. Recollecting the past cannot be understood as simply reliving it. In recollection, the past is re-collected in its surviving fragments and remnants; these are collected together again in thinking back to the past and as a result of this process are rearranged, reinterpreted and recontextualised in a series of changing present times. The story of our lives changes as we change, across this unfolding series. At any point within it we face backwards towards past experience which has helped make us who we are, and forwards towards future experience which will help make us who we shall become. Memories which contain traces or distillations of past experience have of course contributed to the formation of a certain character and temperament, along with a definite set of dispositions which influence how we respond to what happens to us in the present. These dispositions help shape what we make of the past and how we regard it. What happens in the present may also change in some way the dispositions which help to characterise someone as a person, so the trafficking between past and future is always moving in both directions, albeit at variable rates. This is manifest in the present across the enormously broad and motley range that constitutes human experience.

We now need to add to this the vital question as to how previous experience is reactivated in the present, as part of this trafficking between past and future. The trafficking involves two twinned processes: remembering, of course, but also imagining. This may occasion some surprise. In common-sense parlance, we rarely use the verbs 'to remember' and 'to imagine' interchangeably. To do so would seem contradictory and confusing. To say in a court of law that you imagined seeing the accused enter your neighbour's house through an open downstairs window would immediately invalidate the account, relegating it to the domain of fiction or fantasy. The claim to an experiential truth would be rejected and the case thrown out. In contrast, saying under oath that you remember seeing this event is to make a claim to the empirical value of witnessing and to demand an appropriate recognition of your experience. The distinction between saying that something is remembered or something is imagined seems indivisibly connected to the semantic distinctions between lived experience (equivalent to truth) and make-believe (equivalent to falsehood), so much so that remembering and imagining seem as if they are a dichotomous pair in their own right, much like 'is' and 'is not'. In this popular (and indeed forensic) use, only memory seems to have a verifiable relationship to truth, staked on the claim that 'I was there' or 'this happened to me'. The embodied experience in a specific time and place seems to be transparently accessed through memory and invested with a unique ontological status, distinct from imagination.

In contrast, to imagine seems to break the link with experience. The meaning of imagined accounts is not indexed by a sense of faithfulness to life as it is lived, but to an altogether different evaluative frame. This frame has little concern for empirical proof, but instead is concerned with possibility and potential, with semantic plurality rather than a definitive singular truth. When we say 'I remember' we are making a claim about the truth of our experience, but to say 'I imagine' seems to involve making a claim to meaning that extends beyond the reality of our experience, to a realm that is lodged not in the experienced past, but projected out towards a putative alternative to the present or forward to a yet-to-be-experienced future.

These distinctions between memory and imagination are as routinely made as the distinction between fact and fiction, but as with that pairing, their long-term relationship across the years and decades of our lives is much more complex than their opposed binary usage would suggest. There are mutualities and interactions between them, and in thinking about memory it is important we attend to them. Denying or disregarding them encourages us to consider remembering as an archaeological faculty simply concerned with accessing the past by digging through sedimented experience, as if each past layer has been set down and left undisturbed during successive periods. We cannot talk of memories simply as accretions of past experience because experience does not become inert once it is past. The active process of remembering as an experience in the present which is situated, performed and socially contextualised must also be accounted for. To fully conceive of the dynamic relations between experience as process and experience as product, it is necessary to move beyond a notion of memory as an excavation of past experience and its reinstitution in the present. It is because the past does not remain static and unchanging once it has become configured as the past that the archaeological metaphor is inappropriate. Certain images and ideas may over time seem to be relatively stable, but more broadly over the course of a life being lived the past is subject to a continual interchange of remembering and forgetting, with what seemed vivid at one time slowly fading and falling away, and at another time what has been obscured coming to attain a newfound importance, for what may be any of a vast array of reasons. The meanings of specific events and episodes in the past and how we value them become modified and revised in a complex arrangement with how we are changing, and what it is within the present that we require from the past, for the remembered past is not static: 'You think that just because it's already happened, the past is finished and unchangeable? Oh no, the past is cloaked in multicoloured taffeta and every time we look at it we see a different hue'.[42]

Equally unhelpful in considering the relationship of experience and memory is the storehouse metaphor. Locke provides an early use of this:

> The other way of retention is the power to revive again in our minds those ideas which, after imprinting, have disappeared, or have been

as it were laid aside out of sight. And thus we do, when we conceive heat or light, yellow or sweet, – the object being removed. This is memory, which is as it were the storehouse of our ideas. For, the narrow mind of man not being capable of having many ideas under view and consideration at once, it was necessary to have a repository, to lay up those ideas which, at another time, it might have use of.[43]

The storehouse notion fosters an understanding of memory as simply the imprints of experience, available for straightforward retrieval in the present as if items of experience exist discretely in the memory and can be located like catalogued books on a library shelf, or a page in the index of a book. Metaphors of imprinting, engraving, copying and indexing remain persistent, as do notions of 'some static, permanent, distinct storage form that experiences leave'.[44] It is, for example, only recently (since the mid-1990s) that cognitive psychologists have moved away from 'localist' accounts of memory traces towards a constructive and distributed conception of the process of remembering.[45] Other unfortunate associations of memory as a repository can also follow. Whether directly or indirectly, the storehouse metaphor allows memory to be loaded with positivist notions of accuracy and veracity, so encouraging and endorsing its separation from the imagination as a more wilful and less reliable faculty which interferes with the proper process of knowledge acquisition through what we see or hear and stack away for subsequent retrieval. Imagination is locked firmly outside the storehouse, and with all doors and windows barred; it must roam as it will and as it supposed to do, without restraint. Imagination as a wild, undisciplined creature may have a certain Romantic appeal, but it is misleading in that it distracts from the myriad ways in which imagination acts more mundanely, more regularly and continuously in our everyday lives, and does not work in isolation from other modes of thinking and feeling.

In preparing the way for our fuller discussion of the relationship of memory and imagination in the next chapter, we want finally to run through a third common conception of it which we shall eschew and hope to move beyond in the book as a whole. We have already raised this in pointing to the truth-claim associated with the act of remembering, a claim refused to the act of imagining because this is associated with the suppositional quality that is the consequence of it being confined to projections into what has not been or is yet to be experienced. Maintaining a rigid boundary between remembering and imagining in this way assigns them solely to a particular tense: memory to the past, imagination to the future, with neither allowed to move from their allotted locations. There are various manifestations of this temporal polarisation, and even where distinctions between them are less marked, their differential temporal allocation remains clear.

We can see this, for example, with another seventeenth-century English philosopher, Thomas Hobbes, who considered imagination and memory differing 'only in this, that memory supposeth time past and imagination does not'.[46] This may seem to support the idea of rigid boundaries between them, but Hobbes's conception of the distinction between them can be understood in at least two ways. On the one hand, in clearly relating them to alternative temporal referents, it may seem to help pave the way towards their modern separation, allowing them to be mapped onto the conceptual opposites of fantasy and rationality, progress and tradition. On the other hand, it sees memory and imagination as closely aligned, having only one major differentiating feature which may nevertheless not alter certain similarities in the forms they take. Hobbes does not provide for us an early-modern exemplar from which modern misconceptions can be rectified, particularly as both memory and imagination were for him based upon the 'decaying sense' derived from perception, which was assigned a higher position in the hierarchy of human faculties.[47] We nevertheless find suggestive his emphasis on 'differing only in this', the temporal associations and orientations that are in question. It is this which seems to us worthy of much fuller exploration as it takes us beyond the memory/imagination divide and instead regards distinctions between them as fluid, changing over time, and by no means necessarily antagonistic. In this respect we are taking a certain cue from Hobbes since, although we obviously understand remembering as central to distinct formations of experience, we do not see it as separate from other cognitive or affective modalities of consciousness. We see it instead as operating most of all in conjunction with imagining, as for example in the ways it finds expression and meaning in narrative, provides a dynamic sense of temporality, and flows vitally into the constitution of self-identity.

The significance of this conjunction is central to our discussion in the book as a whole. We examine the relationship between memory and imagination as a key strand in our thesis that remembering is a creative process. Memory is not mechanically reproductive, the means by which the past passively repeats itself in our minds. Our alternative conception of memory requires an account that attends specifically to the ways in which the past is reactivated, reinterpreted and represented – given definite form as a depiction but also *re*-presented – in the present. Accepting such an account means that we should cease denying the presence of imagination in processes of recollection and attend instead to the dialogue between them. It is the centrality of imagination to the interconnection of experience as product and as process, to the exchanges between the temporal tenses, and to the relationship between personal and collective engagement with the past, that has made their conventional separation so inhibiting. In charting the relationship between memory and imagination, and seeking to re-establish the ways in which they mutually inform each other through their temporal transactions, we shall identify not simply their differences but also their points of interconnection in the processing, synthesising and assimilation of experience.

2
The Mnemonic Imagination

Reconciling memory and imagination

We have spoken so far of certain pitfalls associated with thinking about the relationship between memory and imagination, and suggested that we want to see this relationship in terms of an interstitial space between past and future in which cross-temporal transactions are made. It is through such transactions that lived experience in the present becomes transformed into assimilated experience in a changed present. The remembering subject engages imaginatively with what is retained from the past and, moving across time, continuously rearranges the hotchpotch of experience into relatively coherent narrative structures, the varied elements of what is carried forward being given meaning by becoming emplotted into a discernible sequential pattern. It is that pattern which is central to the definition of who we are and how we have changed.

Mnemonic phenomena are of course far more complicated than that, with for example repeated experiences becoming telescoped over time into a single generic memory of them, calendar events and seasons, days at work and evenings with friends merging together across time, and the once-regular experience of someone now no longer in contact with you being condensed into a few assorted moments or characteristic features. It may seem also, as we look back over a long sweep of years, that all we are left with is 'islands in a confused and layered landscape, like the random protrusions after a heavy snowfall, the telegraph pole and the hump of farm machinery and buried wall'.[1] This is in some ways an appropriate metaphorical image for the impression we may develop of a blurred stretch of remembered time, one whose component parts have become indistinct and blended into one another, but such impressions may change; snow melts, definite shapes re-emerge, and the landscape becomes clearer in detail once again. In view of this, we need to be careful, not only about generalising but also about offering up statements that admit no qualification, because we can easily go further and say, with John Banville, that we 'imagine that we remember things as they were, while in fact all we carry into the future are fragments which reconstruct a wholly illusory past'. Banville goes on: 'The first death we witness will always be a murmur of voices down a corridor and a clock falling silent in the darkened room, the end of love is forever two cigarettes in a saucer and a white door closing'.[2] Such images are of course easily recognisable cinematic clichés, but this does not mean they cannot be effective. As with the potency of cheap music, they may provoke imaginative engagements with what memory carries beyond their stock associations. This is to recognise their emotional power, and their audience value, but we cannot doubt that aesthetic staleness eventually calls for imaginative renewal. Banville clearly recognises the power of imaginative engagement. He sees imagining as crucial for what we make of past experience, but as he gives with one hand, he takes away with the other. Imagination usurps memory and in this action confirms the unfortunate split between them. If Banville's examples of visual or auditory mnemonic associations are figuratively tired and without symbolic power, this is precisely because memory and imagination have become separated from each other. It is not because what we remember is wholly illusory. We cannot remember things exactly as they were, but this does not mean we cannot reconstruct things in ways we believe are at least reasonably faithful to the meanings carried by the fragments that remain with us, or think back imaginatively to past events and situations, exploring what happened in the light of how we have changed, along with the world around us.

In some ways it is understandable that there is a reluctance to challenge the alienation of memory and imagination from each other. There are, for example, cases where we confuse what we imagine with what we remember, or what we remember with what we imagine, just as there are others where we are not sure if we have seen someone in the past few weeks, or heard a particular song on the radio, or if we have imagined seeing this person or hearing that song. We know how memory can play tricks, and how imagination can be fertile. Such cases may involve us in difficulties about what we know or create obstacles to what we want to find out. But here's the rub. The source of our consternation in these moments of difficulty or confusion lies in the close resemblance between remembering and imagining. In such cases, as we acknowledged in the previous chapter, it can be extremely important that we make every effort to distinguish the one from the other, but the resemblance between remembering and imagining should not be construed solely as a problem we need to overcome. That is what has happened as a result of the rigid separation of memory and imagination and the decontextualised dissociation of remembered-images and imagined-images. These wrong steps have led to the entrenched belief that memory is an independent faculty, beavering away on its own and having no association with faculties cognate to it, as imagination is said to have. This may allow us to concede that we draw on our memory when we imagine, but it prevents us, sometimes quite emphatically, from thinking of how we draw on our imaginations when we remember.

Most of the time of course we do not confront the resemblance between remembering and imagining as a problem. We know that imagination can exceed memory because, in the main, memory is reliant on experience, whether this is first-hand or second-hand, whereas imagination is not. You may imagine you are Miles Davis playing trumpet on 'So What', or Joni Mitchell singing 'River', but you cannot remember doing so. This is nevertheless a fallible distinction. Memory can be unreliable and imagination can be persuasive. The grounds can shift; the balance between them can alter. So the distinction between memory and imagination remains crucial, but one that does not benefit at all from being extended as a once-and-for-all separation. For example, the distinction is not only important to us in the temporal extension of conceptions of ourselves; it is also vital in a more day-to-day manner if we are to be considered reliable or honest or clear-headed, and if we are to consider ourselves so. Remembering going to the bank to settle a debt and imagining doing so are not interchangeable. Asserting that they are would obviously be foolish, but we need not be afraid of folly in arguing that the difficulties we have at times in distinguishing between remembering and imagining cannot be resolved by attempting to draw an absolute line between them.

It is central to our argument that there is no such line, but memory and imagination in themselves do not have one fixed mode or form. How they operate in relation to each other depends on what kind of remembering and imagining are involved, for there are various kinds of both processes and the imagination does not have the same bearing on all kinds of remembering. Two of the most notable and talked about are those forms of imagining and remembering which are voluntary and involuntary. With involuntary memories, for example, those which reappear unbidden or are reawoken by some unintended act, vivid scenes may seem to be brought forth in our minds and even seem revelatory in what they appear to show. These can then form the nucleus of important passages of autobiographical recollection or literary fiction in which the involuntary memory spreads out laterally in casting light across broad landscapes of the past. Long before Proust, the Baptist minister John Foster, in his essay 'On a Man's Writing Memoirs of Himself', recognised the value of such memories in recovering the past:

> In some occasional states of the mind, we can look back much more clearly, and much further, than at other times. I would advise to seize on those short intervals of illumination which sometimes occur without our knowing the cause, and in which the genuine aspect of some remote event, or long-forgotten image is recovered with extreme distinctness in spontaneous glimpses of thought, such as no efforts could have commanded.[3]

If we seize on them and imaginatively rework them, these short intervals of illumination may cast light forwards and backwards from the event they mark, and allow us to begin linking together other elements whose relation to them had not hitherto been apparent. But memory is not only about spontaneous glimpses and those moments when past faces, events and settings shoot up against all expectation. Such acts of remembering, regardless of the imaginative uses to which they are subsequently put, are quite different to remembering as active reconstruction. It is in remembering of this kind that the imagination is crucial. In order to see why this is so and why the imagination then comes into such close orbit around the realm of memory, we need to situate their relationship in the context of the passage of time as we sketched it in the previous chapter.

There we saw that lived experience of the present is temporally extendable. It does not consist of isolated instants that are apprehended and remembered as discrete elements in the passing of time. As Husserl put it, lived experiences 'spread out in such a way that there is never an isolated punctual phase'.[4] Husserl conceived of the present as a point instantaneously overcome in one direction by every new experience flowing continuously backward in retentional phases, and overcome in the other by flowing continuously forward into new experience in protentional phases. These phases in combination begin the constitution of temporal duration, and within this we can distinguish the recent past and the imminent future as components of the experienced present. While accepting this, we do seem to reconnect with certain special moments, and so savour them: 'It is a strange thing, after all, to be able to return to a moment, when it can hardly have any reality at all, even in its passing. A moment is such a slight thing ... that its abiding is a most gracious reprieve'.[5] This both supports and qualifies Husserl's conception of the present, and shows again that there are different forms of remembering. So, inter alia, we need to differentiate between recall as a process of bringing back isolated events from the past, and recollection as a distinct process which develops ordered sequences and meaningful connections across time, between different events and episodes in the past. We have described this as an actively concerted process that creatively builds on the incipient order of sequence and connection in memory but is quite different from merely reciting the chronicle of memory itself. Recollection is therefore distinct from recall in that it involves imaginatively working on the past in order to vicariously relive certain experiences in the present. It does not work in this way on what has been recently experienced, which belongs to retentional phases, for these are more the domain of recall or what we called routine remembering. Much of what enters into these phases is subsequently lost from consciousness, so we can recall what we did yesterday in quite considerable detail, but much of this detail passes away as time itself passes and new yesterdays enter the frame. In this respect we need to make a further temporal distinction.

The detail accompanying our memory of recent time belongs to the ephemeral past, and as noted, soon becomes confined to whatever seems to us most significant or to whatever we are not able to forget because of how we have experienced it, or how it has left a marked impression on our minds. In such ways, certain details of the ephemeral past survive in our longer-term memory, but memory in this sense of it relates to what we shall call the enduring past. It is to the enduring past that recollection relates. Certainly, in our memory of the enduring past particular events, experiences and episodes may have become condensed, fragmented, and disjointed, but it is then the task of recollection in its actively concerted modality to reassemble, reorder and reconfigure these memories in such a way that they contribute to and become a meaningful part of the discernible narrative pattern moving across time that we referred to earlier.

It should be clear by now that in conceptualising recollection in this manner we are moving sharply away from conceiving of memory as composed of images which are regarded as copies of their originating experiences. We do not call such copies to mind when we remember. This is not to say that memory does not partly consist of images; clearly it does, and some are very vivid. But why is it that certain scenes in our memories of them are described as vivid, which is a quality chiefly apparent to our vision, when we do not describe them in that way at the time we experience them? It is because we are still to some extent living in the shadow of a tradition of seeing remembering as if it is akin to seeing. That tradition may have become part of common-sense thinking, as for example is readily apparent in the prevalence of the colloquial reference to the mind's eye whenever remembering is being discussed, but it is only relevant to one dimension of experience: that of experience as product. Imagist conceptualisations of both memory and imagination attend only to the relation of the product of these faculties, not to their modes of operation as processes. The inability to conceive of their complex operation as processes is a result of their remaining fixed on the reproductive role which is demanded if memory-images are to be understood as empirical transcriptions and straightforward imitations of experience.

Ryle directly contests this. He proposes that neither imagination nor memory involve either weak or strong experiences because when you imagine or remember hearing a sound, there is no auditory sensation at all. Nothing is heard, at either a high or low volume, however intense our remembering or imagining. As Ryle puts it, 'an imagined shriek is not ear splitting, nor yet is it a soothing murmur, and an imagined shriek is neither louder nor fainter than a heard murmur. It neither drowns it nor is it drowned by it'.[6] Ryle argues that this is true also of memory: remembering is rather to have learned or come to know, rather than to actually see, an image. What is evident then, is that the concept of the image (and memory-image) as weaker or stronger representations of reality fails to account for the relationship between memory and imagination, firstly because they cannot be properly distinguished, and secondly because imagist approaches fail to account for how the experience of these faculties differs in any meaningful sense from an original sensory experience.[7]

If we turn instead to a concern with the operation of memory and imagination as processual faculties, we encounter again the division between their temporal orientations as the major way of characterising their differences. Mary Warnock seems initially to be helpful here in moving beyond the imagist concern for memory-as-product by characterising the temporal specificity of memory as standing in contrast to imagination as a constituent feature of the embodied experience of remembering. By addressing memory as an embodied experience in its own right, she suggests that, as with pain, we feel its location in experiencing it, and in experiencing it we necessarily interpret its pastness.[8] Undeniably, this allows the consideration of remembering as a process, as something that exists in and through time, but positing an essential affective property to all remembering does not account for the precise way in which memory connects us to experience, and how past experiences become invested cross-temporally with meaning in the present. It is unclear where this property of pastness resides and how it comes to be invested in experience, while imaginings of alternative pasts and alternative futures do not. It also fails to account for the instances in which we are unsure of whether an event is remembered or imagined, where the sensation of pastness is no guarantee of an experiential connection with the past in and of itself. So while Warnock carries forward Ryle's emphasis on remembering and imagination as processes, the precise nature of their difference remains somewhat vague.

Here we might ask if Sartre, in his essay on the imagination, is helpful in offering the distinction between imagination and memory as one which is less concerned with the temporal 'feeling' of memory than with a distinction between the real and the unreal. Sartre claims that in the act of imagining any given thing, '*I present them to myself*, in themselves. But at that moment that ceases to conceive them as continuous present in order to grasp them in themselves, I grasp them as *absent*.' In contrast, if 'I recall an incident of my past life, I do not imagine it, I *recall* it. That is, I do not posit it as *given-in-its-absence* but as *given-now-as-in-the-past*.'[9] This explanation also suffers from an inherent vagueness in its attempt to distinguish between memory and imagination. The distinction it posits is too easy because it pays no attention to people, situations, or buildings half-remembered, and the 'odd certainty that just out of reach' exists 'a way of explaining all these inconsistencies – the ache of love gone and opportunities missed, the contradictory landscapes and disconnected places'.[10] It ignores the poignant sense of loss – the quality of being given back *only* in its absence – when we are struck by our memories of a dead parent, a lost friend, a rare book we failed to purchase in an auction, and when, in relation to such memories, we imagine how in our pasts we could have taken a different path or behaved in a different way, and so ended up in an alternative, more desirable place.[11] The distinction is in any case commonplace, simply reproducing the assumption that memory is constrained by reality and imagination is not. This is an assumption that Warnock accepts, suggesting that although we can confuse the imagined 'nothingness' with the 'retired reality' of memory they are, in fact, quite different.[12] Any overlap between the faculties is then cast as an aberration. This, as we hope to show, is also too easy.

To see such overlap as aberrant means that we remain at an impasse. It simply confirms the separation of memory and imagination, this time not as image-based products, but instead as processes that are divergent in their orientation to both time and experience.

We have reached the point where we can conclude that dealing with memory exclusively in relation to images, and exclusively in terms deriving from visual perception, results in a delimited and distorted conception. Memory does not consist solely of pictures. It may consist instead of what we retain in the longer term of important conversations, popular tunes, intense feelings, evocative aromas or shock news bulletins on the radio. More importantly, whatever material it yields is not necessarily a more or less analogous image of some past experience; it is not identical to that experience, but instead involves a creative regeneration of past experience in such a way that its meanings in relation to what is past make sense and have significance for us in the present. It in this sense that Ian Hacking rejects memory as unlike a video record and instead suggests that 'the best analogy to remembering is storytelling. The metaphor for memory is narrative'.[13] As we noted in the previous chapter, in recollection the past is not possessed, but repossessed, and this requires the interpretative activity necessary for us to have any sense of the distinctive qualities and textures, and definite limits and possibilities, of particular times and experiences in the past. In itself this derives from multiple acts of recollection in the past, for in our thinking of the past we are the continually changing result of processes of remembering over time, and for this reason among others memories cannot be considered as if they are like unchanging archaeological exhibits, laid out for display on a museum table. 'Past events do not lie brightly, overtly before our gaze, but are instead swaddled in a thick tissue of prior recalls and prior recallers, each adding colours and shadows to the original.'[14]

We also need to move beyond the modernist association of memory with the past, and imagination with the future, and think instead about the necessity of memory for thinking of the future, and of imagination for thinking about the past. These are steps we shall follow throughout the book, and in doing so we shall not be running memory and imagination indiscriminately into each other. The distinctions we make between them are what make them not only compatible, but also necessary for each other in establishing and maintaining over time the quality of discernible pattern – order, sequence and structure – in our lives as we live them. If, as Montaigne pointed out, drawing on memory is a perilous act, the question that has always to be asked, from various different perspectives, is how it is possible to create this pattern and know that it has meaning for us in any given present. In actively concerted recollection, memory is neither a psychological faculty acting independently of other faculties nor an activity sufficient unto itself and the resources it alone can garner. Crucially, it acts in productive tension with processes of imagining in bringing certain memories into meaningful presence within the present. In Dilthey's explanation of this, while 'every memory image is made up of acquired constituents, the momentary state of consciousness determines which of these constituents are employed in the formation of the image', to which he added, quite crucially: 'the same image can no more return than the same leaf can grow back on a tree the following spring'.[15] No memory can return to the present unmodified or always in exactly the same temporal sequence, for 'just as there is no imagining which does not depend on memory, so there is no recollection which does not already contain within itself one aspect of the imagination'. Recollection is therefore 'at the same time metamorphosis', a formative rather than merely a reproductive process.[16] Across the disjunctions of time, forgetting and unreflected-upon participation in habitual routine, the imagination in this productive tension with memory weaves together the complex pattern of our past. Through imagination we develop a sense of the temporal relations between different experiences, different episodes and different stages in our lives. Without this sense of temporal interconnectedness, ranging across the recollected past and the contingent present of the remembering subject, lived lives are unliveable.

Our position therefore is that only an illusory sense of the past is constructed when imagination is irrevocably set off against memory. As we shall argue throughout the book, imagination is vital in reactivating memory, and memory is vital in stimulating imagination. Any characterisation of the imagination as a way of thinking unconcerned with referents in the world, and of memory as oriented only to an experienced reality, confines and constricts the ways in which we can think about our relationships with different temporal spheres. What is at stake is the ability to reconcile both continuity and creativity in relation to experience. We can see examples of this ability when fictions of the future are couched in the imagery of the past or draw on past experience, and when memories act as a fertilising ingredient of fantasy. Experience that has long since been enacted, can, via remembering, be interwoven with playful imaginings of what might have been or what is still to come.

The ways in which past experience can be a resource for imagination cannot be recognised while at the same time denying the sociality of

imagining. The transactional value of these instances in the present cannot be adequately grasped where a rigid separation of imagination as an
individual orientation to the unreal and memory as a straightforward
recall of the past is instituted or maintained. The conceptualisation of
memory in the entrenched terms of truth, falsity and the 'real' fixes the
temporal orientation of communication of, and about, the past. It is
restricted only to determining what has been, rather than connecting
with and being constitutive of what might have been, or what might
come to be. When imaginative involvement is denied to our engagements with memory, the past can no longer be conceived as a resource
for potential transformation, inspiration or change. To tie remembering
exclusively to once-lived experience is to radically underestimate the
ways in which we think in and of the past in the present and the constitutive role this has for the remembering subject in orienting a sense
of self within particular social and cultural frameworks.

Mobility of remembering

In seeking to extend our thinking about the relationship of memory
and imagination we turn now, perhaps counter-intuitively, to the story
of Funes by Jorge Luis Borges. We do so because it provides an instruc-
tive example of their drastic separation. Borges's narrator tells of the
young Ireneo Funes who, after being injured in a riding accident, was
able to recall every minutiae of his experience.

> He told me that before the rainy afternoon when the blue roan had
> bucked him off, he had been what every man was – blind, deaf,
> befuddled, and virtually devoid of memory ... He had lived, he said,
> for nineteen years as though in a dream: he looked without seeing,
> heard without listening, forgot everything, or virtually everything.
> When he fell he'd been knocked unconscious; when he came to
> again, the present was so rich, so clear, that it was almost unbearable,
> as were his oldest and even his most trivial memories. It was shortly
> afterward that he learned he was crippled; of that he hardly took
> any notice. He reasoned (or felt) it was a small price to pay. Now his
> perception and his memory were perfect.[17]

Funes was 'able to reconstruct every dream, every daydream he had ever
had'.[18] While the narrator marvels at Funes's prodigious memory, he
also begins to recognise the terrible futility of total memory. Its consequences are many, and they are all debilitating. A memory determined

solely by past experience is far from being an aid to understanding the meaning of the past; it is antithetical to it. The past is rendered useless by its immutability. William James gave clear recognition of this in the late nineteenth century:

> If we remembered everything, we should on most occasions be as ill off as if we remembered nothing. It would take as long for us to recall a space of time as it took the original time to elapse, and we should never get ahead with our thinking. All recollected times undergo ... foreshortening; and this foreshortening is due to the omission of an enormous number of the facts which filled them.[19]

Funes is unable to foreshorten his recollections; he suffers from static recall in an absolute sense. For him, there is no possibility of distinction between past experiences in order to form evaluative judgements relevant to a later time. The past is not available for selective use in the present; the possibility of narrative form is precluded. Generalisation beyond the particular into the realm of expectation and possibility is rendered impossible. The overarching consequence of Funes's total memory is the inability to synthesise past and present in order to create new meanings, potentialities and aspirations. While revelling in the richness and clarity with which he can bring back the past 'as it was', down to the finest of details, Funes is robbed of the space for creating fresh funds of significance. Such space is crowded out of the present by the infinite presence of the past. For Funes, the past is not a creative resource; it has become a prison cell of never-ending perception. In gaining a memory with perfect fidelity he has lost the capacity to forget and so use the past to generate temporal knowledge about the world. Experience as process has squeezed out the possibility of generating experience as product. The consequences of a past event can never be explored or learned from as he is unable to isolate events from the continuous flow of experience, apply general frameworks of understanding and interpretation, or make sense of the world by moving between the particularities of experience and the commonalities and universals of social life. At the same time continuity between past and present cannot be perceived because minute changes in people, institutions and objects disrupt any sense of similitude through time. In this sense, far from being perfect, Funes's memory is completely redundant, since it has disabled the capacity of the primary mnemonic form of narrative. This lost capacity is an imaginative one.

To assess the precise nature of this loss we turn to what might seem a rather unlikely source: the twentieth-century experimental psychologist

Frederick Bartlett. His work has at times been disregarded as asocial and individualistic in current research on memory in sociology and cultural studies, but this is misleading and overlooks much that is of value within it.[20] Bartlett developed an understanding of memory as more than a descriptive recapitulation of past experience. He was opposed to dualistic conceptions of individuals and the social settings in which they act.[21] Indeed, he argued that social organisation 'gives a persistent framework into which all detailed recall must fit, and it very powerfully influences both the manner and the matter of recall'.[22] By identifying remembering as a complex process of mediating between the temporal tenses and moving towards a synthesis of personal experience and non-experiential social knowledge, Bartlett provides a route into thinking about imagination as the interlinking faculty allowing traffic between perceptual experience and socially situated meaning in the processes of remembering. For us his work repays critical attention because it defies certain common-sense notions of how memory works and in doing so is helpful in rethinking the relation between memory and imagination. In particular, Bartlett decisively turned against the sense of something fixed and permanent once it is set down as memory, so that what is subsequently remembered is identically brought forth as if it were an unchanging object laid out for display, always remaining the same whenever we come back to view it, regardless of the time, occasion or context for doing so. This understanding of remembering continues to circulate in popular currency and is precisely the kind of 'perfect' memory displayed by Funes. For Bartlett, particular memories do not stay temporally fixed as permanent records of experience, being retrieved through remembrance 'exactly as they were when first stored away'.[23] As his experiments on remembering demonstrated, memory is selective: it simplifies and condenses, deviates and distorts, elaborates and embellishes.

Unlike the deformed memory of Funes, mobile remembering for the most part rides on the back of forgetting and is able to travel between past and present because of this, but at the same time the process of remembering operates according to particular cultural expectations, frames of meaning and ways of conceiving the world. It is organised through definite sets of memory schemata, but these are not fixed and unchanging. They are themselves in process, 'constantly developing, affected by every bit of incoming sensational experience of a given kind', and acting in concert with each other.[24] Bartlett was insistent on this quality of mutability and revisability. In proposing his concept of memory schemata, Bartlett placed on the table what was for him an important caveat. He pointed out that the term 'schema' is unfortunate in relation to the process of remembering, suggesting an arrangement of some kind that is at once persistent and fragmentary, 'too definite and too sketchy'.[25] It fails to convey the activeness of what is involved, the ways in which memory schemata are 'carried along with us, complete, though developing, from moment to moment'.[26] His preferred term was 'organised setting', but he retained the term 'schema' so long as it was understood as signifying the active organisation of past experiences in 'the ongoing dynamic adaptation between people and their physical and social environments'.[27] Memory schemata are necessary in everyday practical life if we are to avoid wasting 'a vast amount of time going over and over again various chronological series' precisely in the manner of Funes. This doesn't happen because in the process of remembering 'we are being determined by events out of their precise order in a chronological series, and we are free from over-determination by the immediately preceding event'.[28] For Bartlett, 'in a world of constantly changing environment, literal recall is extraordinarily unimportant'.[29] There are times when accuracy of recall may be important, but generally what is of overriding significance for us are our 'main preoccupations' – 'that is, settling current matters at hand as they emerge in communicative action'.[30] Remembering is 'far more decisively an affair of construction rather than one of mere reproduction', with common features of what is involved including 'condensation, elaboration and invention' along with 'the mingling of materials' belonging initially or at other times on other occasions to different schemata.[31]

So the constituent materials of various schemata are not permanently assigned. When circumstances arouse a particular memory orientation, according to Bartlett, this becomes organised through a definite schematic organisation, but how a memory schema relates to constituent materials, how it is organised and how it operates, changes over time, as does its relation to other schemata. It is in such transformations that imagination is crucial. What Bartlett describes as the 'capacity to turn round' on one's own schemata means that they can be reshuffled and reorganised. The 'constructive character of remembering' makes it a matter of dynamic adaptation in which different, interacting schemata provide the active organised settings through which past events or experiences are reconstructed.[32] While what is called to mind anchors such reconstruction, there is always a creative element in the way we use memories and put them into narrative form. This leads Bartlett to conclude

> Remembering is not the re-excitation of innumerable fixed, lifeless and fragmentary traces. It is an imaginative reconstruction, or

construction, built out of the relation of our attitude towards a whole active mass of organised past reactions or experience, and to a little outstanding detail which commonly appears in image or in language form. It is thus hardly ever really exact, even in the most rudimentary cases of rote recapitulation, and it is not at all important that it should be so.[33]

In a recent overview of theories of remembering, Barbara Misztal pits Bartlett's memory schemata against imagination.[34] This seriously misinterprets him. As this citation from him makes clear, it is the active and flexible schemata of memory themselves which bring 'remembering into line with imagining', and establish them as 'an expression of the same activities'.[35] In approaching memory as constructive, Bartlett differentiated it from constructive imagination only as a matter of degree, for 'all manner of changes in detail constantly occur in instances which every normal person would admit to be genuine instances of remembering'.[36] Quite what would fall outside this reference to normality is unclear, but the significant point is that changes of direction and sequential order, complexity of structure and thematic significance are regularly attendant on the process of remembering. 'There is seldom a simple, direct transmission from a single past experience through discretely stored inner items to a clearly defined moment of recall, for each memory is many memories'.[37] What remains in memory, which is significantly less than what is continually being forgotten, changes and goes on changing over the ongoing course of our lives, with what we remember being drawn upon at different times and in different circumstances, with different emotional valences and different measurings of their significance. It is this that allows us to move between experience as process and experience as product.

As we have already shown, remembering and imagining are not synonymous, but in various ways they do exist in mutual relation to each other, and are different only 'in the range of material over which they move and the precise manner of their control'. Constructive imagination is relatively freer in operation, less predetermined by its initial orientation and able to move over a broader range than memory itself, with a greater capacity for determining its points of emphasis. Memory and imagination are nevertheless mutually reliant and always inform each other's activities. Memory is not a single or unitary faculty 'containing all its peculiarities and all their explanations within itself'.[38] On the contrary. Memory and imagination are linked by the active schemata that provide frames of meaning, application and coherence.

It is these socially organised frames which constitute 'the basis for the imaginative reconstruction called memory'.[39]

Bartlett conceived of remembering as an ongoing dynamic process in which traces of the past 'live within our interests and with them they change'.[40] Two features of this need emphasising. First, what he called our 'efforts after meaning' always connect with some setting or schema against which what is remembered is evaluated and, where required, argued for in its social value as an account of past experience.[41] Second, as well as wielding socially acquired skills in the appropriate cultural conventions of remembering in everyday life, the process of remembering is an imaginative reconstruction which enables us to turn around on our schemata, reshuffle their constituent elements and reorientate ourselves to what we draw from past experience. John Shotter puts this well: 'Everyday practical remembering is not just a matter of self-consciously remembering facts, but of sometimes "re-feeling" certain events, sometimes of being able to reorder by reshaping such feelings to imagine either new relations between well-known things, or completely new worlds.'[42] Past experiences are creatively recalled and imaginatively reconceived for their bearings on our present and future lives. It is of this capacity that Ireneo Funes has been robbed.

The story of Funes makes clear how much is at stake if imagination and memory are separated in any hard-and-fast manner. In what follows we intend to show how the imagination allows a synthesis of processual experience with social schema in the continual formation of experience as product. We explore how the new meanings which we grasp from our passage through time – some of which endure and contribute significantly to the constitution of our identity, and some of which are fleeting and insignificantly absorbed into the story of a life – are generated in the conjoined action of memory and imagination. We shall explore the temporal implications of this dual action and demonstrate how a more nuanced account of our temporal experience emerges from it. The major consequence is that it reveals as limited and inadequate the conventional triad of the *has-been*, the *now* and the *not-yet*, and allows us to take into account other temporal experiences such as the *might-have-been* or the *may-be-again*. This moves us beyond a unitary positioning of ourselves as oriented to the past or the future at any given moment, into a simultaneous habitation of these various temporal domains which together inform the process of making sense of our experience. It is in this multidimensional action that memory and imagination are locked together as a distinctively mnemonic imagination.

Imaginative synthesis

Bartlett provided a first step in reconceiving the relationship between memory and imagination.[43] He showed that in order to be meaningful, memory involves active reconstruction rather than straightforward repetition. The direct implication of this is that remembering processes are creative as well as iterative. Bartlett's conception of remembering as involving creative practice takes us to a point where we can talk with some confidence about the constructedness of memory, but this in itself is hardly revelatory. Talking thus may also encourage the reduction of our analytical attention to manipulated memory, as if this is all that constructedness entails. It is commonplace in sociological and cultural studies of memory to talk of the porosity of the boundaries between memory and history and the ideological codes and conventions upon which their construction depends.[44] Questions remain as to the nature of this bringing the past to bear on our present and futures and how it is possible for memory and imagination to operate in conjunction to generate temporal meaning. Paul Frosh has suggested that 'memory needs to be theorised in relation to the imagination in ways that move beyond denigrating its illusionary character and ideological motivation'.[45] For us this requires engaging directly with the experience of imagining creatively, and exploring the ways in which it is constitutive of our senses of temporality. The first issue that requires attention is how imagination can be involved in remembering when the defining feature of remembering is taken as a sense of fidelity to the past. For Bartlett, the flexibility and mutability of memory clearly lies in the mediation between the personal and social demands of the present on the one hand, and experiential and social knowledge of the past on the other. New mnemonic meanings are generated but also limited by the social and cultural contexts in which they are generated, but imagination operates beyond this. It involves a range of specific actions and operations which allow us to generate various new kinds of meanings, including those transformative accounts of the past that challenge and resist institutionalised versions of historical events or processes, and provide the basis for social action in the present. The distinction we are drawing here is between an analysis of the constructedness of memory and an assessment of its creativity. In doing so, we wish to move beyond charting the ideological construction of memory in order to combine this with an exploration of the transformative potential of the past in the present.

In exploring exactly how imagination operates as part of the remembering process and the kinds of meanings it can generate, it is helpful to turn to Kant's reflections on the imagination. Kant distinguishes between the reproductive and the productive imagination: the former is associated with the reproduction of an absent thing in a manner which we would recognise as remembering; the latter is associated with the production of new meaning. As the process by which experience is presented in the form appropriate to our a priori categories of understanding, imagination involves a dual action of reproducing experiences in the present, and organising them into meaningful combinations. Imagination furnishes our conscious engagement with the world with coherence. However, Kant maintained a separation between the productive powers of imagination and its reproductive capacity to make present something that once was, in its absence. For Kant, the power of imagination 'is either *inventive* (productive) or merely *recollective* (reproductive)'.[46] While not a straightforwardly dichotomous pairing, this distinction problematises the relationship between intersensory, embodied experience and reflections upon it which generate new understandings of the world. The reproductive imagination is clearly associated with remembering and the productive imagination with atemporality and that which has never been. Such a distinction would seem to deny the possibility of remembering as a process anchored in past experience being conceived as generative of qualitatively new meaning, and would hold reproduction apart from the action of creativity. Kant goes even further than this. As Edward Casey has noted, he explicitly rejects a conception of the productive imagination as creative:

> But the productive power of imagination is nevertheless not exactly creative, for it is not capable of producing a sense representation that was never given to our faculty of sense; one can always furnish evidence of the material of its ideas ... It must get the material for its images from the senses.[47]

This would appear not only to refute the possibility that past experience can be involved in the invention of new meaning, but also that even where the imagination is at its most productive, its reliance on experience means that it cannot be considered as creative. It is our contention that we can reconceive Kant's notion of productive imagination to show that it is in fact a central part of remembering and that this is a creative process.

When we tell others stories concerning our own experience, we are ourselves in the midst of the story and not apart from it; the telling and the told act backwards and forwards on the teller in a reciprocal and continually changing relation. In 'communicating experience we creatively transform it, bringing into synthesis what otherwise would remain diffuse and dispersed and in that synthesis, posing a new set of possibilities'.[48] In this sense 'recombinations and rearticulations of ideas and practices must also be seen as relevant ways whereby innovation comes about in social life'.[49] Through the passage of time the remembering subject is not handling unchanging objects of memory but rather adapting those objects in an ongoing process of trying to understand how the past has led to the present. This may involve the effort of coming to terms with things one wishes had not been said or actions that had not been taken, 'yet on the whole, the past is what has led to the present, and only "now" is one able to change this course, and project oneself into the future. In the process of appropriating the future, through one's actions, the nature of the past is constantly reinterpreted'.[50] This is the productive imagination at work, not in the realm of that which has never been but in that of what has been which remains necessary in our efforts to shape the future. Here Kant's concept of synthesis becomes singularly apt. By synthesis, Kant refers to 'the act of putting different representations together, and of comprehending their manifoldness in one item of knowledge' which is the 'mere result of the faculty of imagination'.[51] It is the action of synthesis, performed by the productive imagination, which allows experience to be combined and rearranged in innovative ways that make genuinely new meaning possible, whether this is expressed as a painting, a poem, or an orally conveyed autobiographical story. For Kant nevertheless, this 'is a blind but indispensable function of the soul' and so the imagination remains at the level of an intermediary function which is directed and determined by supervening categories of understanding.[52] In this conceptualisation of imaginative synthesis there is no sense of directionality or of the orientation of the imagination to the external world. Although Kant provides a framework for understanding how we can synthesise disparate perceptions into a meaningful unity, it is the work of Merleau Ponty and, later, of Paul Ricoeur that gives the fullest expression to the directed operation of imaginative synthesis in acts of remembering lived experience.

In his work on the relationship between imagination and art, Merleau Ponty claims that 'imagination is not opposed to our everyday lived experience. Even the most ordinary instance of perception relies on imagination'.[53] Unlike Kant, who draws a firm distinction between the knowable and fantasy, Merleau Ponty does not oppose the real and the unreal, experience and imagination. Instead he sees them as interconnected and interdependent in the present. By repositioning the real and unreal in a dialectical relationship, Merleau-Ponty declares the 'primary function of imagination to be a dialogue between inside and outside, between the being that is in the world and the world that being is in'.[54] Imagination is the faculty that allows us to move between personal experience and social meaning. Without it we would not be able to connect the perceptual and the symbolic; there would be no dialogue between the introspective and the intersubjective. The relationship between experience and imagination also needs to be seen in a temporal dimension, opening up the possibility of reconciling imagination both with present perception, and with past experience through the remembering process. The interplay between imagination and experience does not only implicate the immediate present, and the synthetic action of imagination does not merely act on our present perceptions. We can imagine future possibilities and alternative pasts, which by their very nature must at the same time index an experienced past. We appear then to be both imagining experiences that we might have had or may come to have, while at the same time remembering the experiences that we did have. This is nicely illustrated by Alice's conversation with the Queen in Lewis Carroll's *Through the Looking Glass*:

'Living backwards!' Alice repeated in great astonishment. 'I never heard of such a thing!'
'– but there's one great advantage in it, that one's memory works both ways.'
'I'm sure mine only works one way', Alice remarked. 'I can't remember things before they happen.'
'It's a poor sort of memory that only works backwards,' the Queen remarked.[55]

When we consider Bartlett's conceptualisation of remembering, we see that remembering involves both the reproduction of past experience, reorganised into new forms, such as revised autobiographical stories, and at the same time, the production of qualitatively new meaning in the present. We may think of a social event that we have attended, reproducing it in the present. But at the same time we may fantasise about conversations we have held, not just reproducing them but also exploring alternative responses we could have made to questions, or supposing how the evening might have proceeded had we chosen an alternative seat at the dining table. This may be short-term or long-term. It may take place soon after an event as we run through it in our minds:

> Left alone, in his room, lying on a spring mattress that gave unexpectedly whenever he moved an arm or a leg, Levin did not fall asleep for a long while. Not one of the talks with Sviazhsky, though he has said a great deal that was clever, has interested Levin; but the conclusion of the irascible landowner required consideration. Levin found himself recalling every word he had said and in imagination amending his own replies.[56]

Such amending or adding to what we remember in imagination can just as vividly extend back over considerable periods of time:

> I still wake up at night, thinking, *That's* what I should have said! or *That's* what he meant! remembering conversations I had with people years ago, some of them long gone from the world, past any thought of my putting things right with them.[57]

These reworked memories involve not just imagining a past experience as it was, but imagining a past experience as it could have been. The reproductive and productive imagination operating in concert in remembering acts allow us not simply to 'revisit' the past but more significantly connect it in new ways to the present and future, in the realm of possibility as well as the mode of experience. In bringing imagination and experience into dialectical alignment, Merleau Ponty situates imagination likewise in a symbolically constitutive role. Imagination is what makes our experience meaningful and allows us to turn it into experience as product. The retrospective action of the imagination mediates then between the horizons of experience and expectation in acts of remembering. It enables us to relate our experiences to the realm of possibility. The synthetic function of the imagination allows a 'grasping together' of temporal tenses. Far from being disconnected from remembered realities, imagination provides us with the capacity to connect and use these as the basis for action in the present. The imagination operates in a range of ways, and these can be grand or low-key in their consequences, but here we are identifying a particular set of operations constitutive of experience over and within time. These operations in their overall combination define what we shall call the mnemonic imagination.

The concept of the mnemonic imagination provides us with a way of thinking about the relationship between understandings of the past, our actions in the present and our ambitions for the future. In doing so, we can posit the mnemonic imagination as generating the action which allows continuity with the past to be achieved while also allowing for the accumulation of new experience, and the sense that it will contribute to a story that is still unfolding. It makes possible the grasping together of the past, present and future in ways that create new meaning. This is vital for the construction of our narrative identity where the story of who we are involves the interweaving of who we have been, who we could have been, and who we may become. What emerges from this synthesis is a renewed sense of self and a renewed way of being in the world. It establishes a position from which we can act intentionally.

This imaginative grasping together of experience in its interacting temporal dimensions is conceptualised further by Ricoeur. He demonstrates how this operates in communicative practice by tracing the capacity of the imagination to generate new meaning in his account of the occurrence of semantic innovation in narrative. For Ricoeur the semantic innovation which occurs in the narrative process of emplotment 'can be carried back to the productive imagination, and, more precisely, to the schematism that is its signifying matrix'.[58] This is ineluctably a temporal process. The schematisms of the productive imagination synthesise the temporally disparate elements of plot: cause and effect, motivations and resolutions, the biographical before and after. In doing so new ways of understanding the world in the present, upon which action can be predicated, are generated from these pre-existing semantic features.[59] Ricoeur is clear this is not a purely literary phenomenon.[60] Personal identity is inevitably narrative identity insofar as disparate elements of experience are drawn together by the productive imagination into a unified plot which has a temporal span. In this way the mnemonic imagination helps us construct our sense of narrative self by grasping together the disparate elements of experience in our lives into a knowable whole which exists in and through time. Without the mnemonic imagination, selfhood would be inhibited and we would not be able to generalise, extrapolate or work at the level of the symbolic. As for Funes, history as well as memory would be reduced to the interminable flow of unorganised perception recalled, but not recollected. In short, narrative in all its forms would be impossible, our criteria for judgement would be disabled, social action would be hobbled, and relations between self and other would collapse in undifferentiated repetition.

It is the operation of the mnemonic imagination, which always involves imagination in its productive mode, that allows the creative synthesis of experience in the present. Where does this leave memory itself? Is what we remember of past experience merely the plaything of our imaginative powers? It is again Ricoeur who suggests an answer:

> To memory is tied an ambition, a claim – that of being faithful to the past … If we can reproach memory with being unreliable, it is precisely because it is our one and only resource for signifying the past-character of what we declare we remember. No-one would dream of addressing the same reproach to imagination, inasmuch as it has as its paradigm the unreal, the fictional, the possible, and other nonpositional features.[61]

Remembering is a process identified by its ambition or claim of being faithful to the past in a search for truth; truth not only of factual evidence, but also truth of the self and truth about one's place-in-the-world and agency within it. Where imagination is the mode by which experience is creatively synthesised in the present, remembering is the synthesis of experience which involves the attribution of 'having been' and its application to 'moving towards'. It is in this synthesis that the significance of the past is revealed to us and to others with whom we interact in our everyday lives. As Sue Campbell has suggested, there is a good deal more to 'good remembering than that our memory declarations are true', for such remembering is in many cases a quite 'complex epistemological/ ethical achievement', and it is because of this that neither 'reproductive fidelity nor the truth of declarative memory seems adequate to how successful remembering often tries to capture the significance of the past'.[62] Our faithfulness to the past in remembering is vital, yet not sufficient for understanding the value of memory in the present. We need to account for memory as a transformative force in the present, showing how it becomes usable and how it is involved specifically in social, political and ethical action. We can remember honestly, being as attentive as we can to how the past was, and as responsive as we can to what others remember, but we can also remember imaginatively, allowing 'the capacity of our experience of the past to shift and evolve in ways that track the changing significance of the past to our present needs and knowledge'.[63] By bringing together imagination as a synthetic faculty capable of creating new meaning and new significance in the present, and memory as a set of resources capable of maintaining a faithfulness to the past, we can begin to see how we might understand past experience as funding a capacity for action in the present, and how this might be oriented to the future and to our horizons of expectation. As Ricouer notes, 'the possibility of historical experience in general lies in our ability to remain open to the effects of history ... We are affected by the effects of history, however, only to the extent that we are able to increase our capacity to be affected in this way. The imagination is the secret of this competence'.[64]

The secret is best revealed in the identification of memory that does not involve the imagination. Bergson calls memory that doesn't involve the synthetic-representational 'pure memory'.[65] In this form memory is pure sensation, embodied and manifested in the feeling of 'being back there then'. This intense affective experience pierces us in the manner of Barthes's *punctum* and moves us beyond the reach of conventional discursive frameworks of remembering and beyond the reworked representation of the past to ourselves or to others.[66] The smell of an old school classroom, an unsolicited song favoured by a long-gone lover, an uncanny likeness in a face can disrupt the present, dissolve the distance between the remembered and remembering self and connect us intimately to our own experienced past. In contrast to memories that are intersubjectively constituted and reactivated, as for example with memories of a family holiday, one of the definitive features of this kind of memory is its incommunicability, our inability to represent this experience of remembering in the schema of understanding to ourselves, and beyond this, to others. The absence of imagination renders this mode of memory 'pure' in terms of its evocation of past experience as intensely personal and individuated, but at the same time it renders it limited as a basis for social action in the present since it cannot be shared, represented or communicated – or at least not easily – according to our shared schema of understanding. The sensation of 'pure memory', characterised by the unexpected evocation of the past, contrasts with intentional object-oriented recall (although subsequently it can itself become the object of intentional recall).[67] For both Ricoeur and Bergson this involves an effortful engagement with the past, characterised by the act of searching, but activated by imagination. This 'effort of recall consists in converting a schematic idea, whose elements interpenetrate, into an imagined idea, the parts of which are juxtaposed'.[68] It is this effort which turns mere recall into the actively concerted recollection we outlined in Chapter 1.

What this polarity reveals is that it is imagination which permits memory to be constructed and reconstructed in the present; and more than this, through its synthetic representational capacity, it is imagination which allows the past to persist actively in the present. Imagination is not only the means by which we are able to apprehend and possess the past for ourselves. It is also the means by which the past is made communicable and therefore available for scrutiny, negotiation and contestation in social life. It is imagination that enables us to meaningfully connect the objects, actions and experiences of the past with those of the present and future. This dynamic interaction of the temporal tenses is a creative process. For example, in a discussion of artistic creativity, Malcolm Bowie traces the ways in which 'the memory of an earlier artwork' can be 'the trigger that sets a new artwork going'. The 'new work is not a gloss, an exposition or a commentary but the reinvention of an experience, with all its risks and hazards left in place'.[69] When imagination is not in play, these interconnections become impossible and the past becomes hermetically sealed off from the present and future. It is impoverished as a call to action.

On the other side of the process of creative remembering, memory does not figure simply as the poor relation of imagination. In such remembering, at both an individual and social level, imagining possible futures and alternative presents is anchored by the referential action of memory. José Maurício Domingues argues that 'social memory provides the patterns for the structuring of the social "imaginary", that is, the hermeneutic-cognitive dimension of social life, for the development of social relations'.[70] Although we might not agree with the ordering of the social memory and the social imaginary here, what Domingues demonstrates is that without some connection to a remembered past, social relations lose their referential moorings. Where imagination has free reign it is difficult to insist on any frameworks for judgement or grounds for critique as there are no referents against which imaginings can be judged. What makes one imagined future any better than another? When anchored by faithfulness to the past, not any future will do. Imagined futures can only be judged in relation to the past; they can only be evaluatively weighed, measured and critiqued in terms of how the wrongs of the past might be righted in them, or how the historically marginalised might be recognised through them. The mnemonic imagination holds these two realms of temporalised social action in productive tension, and in doing so affords us the capacity to move between the horizons of experience and expectation.

Experience and expectation

We all move between these horizons, for the simple reason that there is 'no history which could be constructed independently of the experience and expectations of active human agents'.[71] In thinking conceptually about the different temporal modalities they involve, we shall draw

initially on Reinhart Koselleck's use of them as analytical categories for
investigating the relations between past, present and future across as
well as within particular periods, and through these relations the qualities of lived historical time 'where different spaces of experience overlap
and perspectives of the future intersect, inclusive of all the conflicts
with which they are invested'.[72] Their shared temporal dimension is
the present, with experience being the 'present past, whose events have
been incorporated and can be remembered', and expectation the future
present: 'it directs itself to the not-yet, to the nonexperienced, to that
which is to be revealed. Hope and fear, wishes and desires, cares and
rational analysis, receptive display and curiosity: all enter into expectation and constitute it'.[73] As such, experience and expectation are
metahistorical concepts in the same way as time and space, yet while
they are everywhere interconnected as conditions for possible histories,
such histories are always definite and specific and their application as
concepts has to relate to histories in their particularities as well as their
pluralities. Their dual function as historical and metahistorical concepts
makes it possible to say that 'every human being and every human
community has a space of experience out of which one acts, in which
past things are present or can be remembered', but also that 'one always
acts with reference to specific horizons of expectation'.[74] The space of
experience is always historically specific and as such informs the various
experiences that occur within it. It is comprised of the past gathered and
available within a given present, but this changes as a result of the passing of time and the incorporation of new experiences along with the
reassemblage of those already incorporated. In a parallel range expectation can vary from the strongest hope to common likelihood, and may
of course be thwarted by surprise and what has not been expected or
anticipated, so leading to new and possibly unfamiliar experiences. The
gain in experience then 'exceeds the limitation of the possible future
presupposed by previous experience'.[75]

Koselleck uses the metaphorical figure of the horizon to demarcate
the reach of expectation into the future, and the concept of space
to mark the limits of the accumulated past in experience within any
given present, but as one of us has argued before, the four analytical
coordinates of horizon and space, experience and expectation, can be
more productively applied if they are regarded as interchangeable, with
experience also seen as having its horizon and expectation existing
within a specific space that is partly chosen, partly designated. We can
then move to such uses of 'horizon of experience' as a finite limit or
a limitation which has been exceeded, or as a general background of

intelligibility in everyday life, and 'space of expectation' as the socially and historically specific location in which future figurations are drafted and acted upon, in a fuller range which moves beyond expectation into the realm of possibility:

> If to expect is to foresee, it is the familiar which is expected. Possibilities are not expected to the extent that they diverge from the familiar, from the normal recurrent patterns of everyday life. Unless they are strong, they are beyond expectation. Possibilities are more to do with aspiration than expectation. Where expectations are almost guaranteed their fulfilment, possibilities are, as it were, expectations without guarantees.[76]

Reconceived in this way, experience as horizon can be considered as involving both structures of continuity in the present and articulations of change in the future. Expectation then becomes aligned more with structures of continuity in accommodating itself to the horizons of existing social relations and practices in everyday life, while possibility is aligned more with articulations of change in aspiring to horizons beyond what is institutionally established, where relations and practices might operate otherwise. In such ways as these they can then be seen together as providing a framework for talking about lived historical time organised around the principles of proximity and distance, with the distant past and the distant future setting the limits of what we can remember and what may seem possible to us in our place and period, our current space.

It is because experience is always a space of traversal movement between the individual subject and social institutions operating within it, and constructing meaning across it, that it requires both memory and imagination; the former for bringing the past into the present and the latter for the kind of creative reworking proposed by Bartlett involving the organising and schematising of past experience (in a fluid, flexible and plural sense). In facilitating cross-temporal interanimation, the mnemonic imagination provides us with the capacity to turn around and 're-feel' such experience. The metaphorical extension of horizon from the field of vision to temporalities and temporal orientations refines our understanding of how past and future co-exist in any given present. Expectation and experience not only coexist as temporal projections in the here and now, but also feed into and affect each other, as for instance when lived experience, being reality-drenched, 'binds together fulfilled or missed possibilities' which enter into it and act back on it: 'This is the temporal structure of experience and without retroactive expectation it cannot be accumulated.'[77] Although events of the past cannot be changed, 'the experiences which are based upon them can change over time' and 'new hopes or disappointments, or new expectations, enter them with retrospective effect'. At the same time the 'penetration of the horizon of expectation is creative of new experience' and the historical perspective that we develop 'is formed and transformed by the confrontation of horizons occurring in our present engagement with the past'.[78] Horizons of experience and expectation change according to the space of the present from which we view them, but they have always to be seen as a conceptual double, working in transaction with each other. Koselleck's dictum drills this home: 'No expectation without experience; no experience without expectation.'[79] It is then the tension between experience and expectation which, 'in ever-changing patterns, brings about new resolutions and through this generates historical time'.[80] To put this at its simplest, we can have no engagement with the past without an engagement with the future, and no engagement with the future without an engagement with the past. Temporal meaning is generated out of the differing degrees of their interpenetration. Here again we can see the value of the concept we have introduced, for the mnemonic imagination is the mechanism through which experience and expectation are brought into a state of productive interaction. It is in this respect a condition of historical consciousness.

Anders Schinkel provides support for our general line of argument here in his critical appraisal of Koselleck's two historical categories. For him as for us, the interpenetration of experience and expectation have not been fully conceptualised in Koselleck's work, and as a result it is not altogether clear how distinct his conceptual couplet is from the historical binaries of classical sociology. We shall return to this shortly, because for now we want to emphasise that expectation always has a clear basis in experience, for it is imaginative projection from the space of experience that produces the horizon of expectation, while breaks or ruptures with established configurations of experience define the horizon of the possible. This provides us with another illustration of experience and expectation necessarily informing and influencing each other even though their relationship remains contingent. Another example of this is the sense that for the majority of the time there is a definite extent to what we experience, where we mainly experience what we are able, or what we expect to experience. Schinkel illustrates this with the case of a medieval Christian frame of reference. This had 'no room for "progress" in the modern sense, which means that nothing would or could be recognised as such'. For this reason 'the space of experience is also the space within which experiences may occur; it sets the limits of possible experience'.[81] Expectation of an onward drive for development and a rapid pace of change was not part of the medieval mindset.

Schinkel insists, as we do, that while the content of experiences and expectations may change, the categories themselves cannot be disconnected. They are always in greater or lesser degree co-determining. In those cases of lesser degree, when strong tendencies towards their separation prevail, pathological consequences ensue: we become prisoners of the past or martyrs to the future. For most of the time what changes is their relation. It is central to Koselleck's uses of these twinned categories that they can help explain the altered conception of historical time that was ushered in during the onset of modernity, or what he calls *Sattelzeit* (saddle time, the period of transition during the late eighteenth and early nineteenth centuries). The relevance of the two categories in this respect is that they are intended as conceptual tools for thinking about structures of continuity and forces of change in the historical process. If their relation necessarily changes when their content changes, this depends on what it is which forms the connection between them. This is where Schinkel identifies imagination as the missing category in Koselleck's conceptualisation of historical time. It is imagination which enables us to move between experience and expectation. Imagination for Schinkel is a mediating function which is necessary in order to

> have expectations at all – to be able to distinguish the future from the past, and to have some sense of what this future might be and to have an attitude toward it. This imagination can be stronger or weaker, and it can be more or less creative.[82]

The nature of the changing relationship between experience and expectation and the meanings generated from their interpenetration in the present depends on imagination since it is this which connects them to one another. We agree entirely with this, but Schinkel remains rather vague about how imagination moves between experience and expectation. As we have already suggested, in drawing on Kant's notion of synthesis we can see more clearly how this might be enacted. Synthesis is the process involved in bringing together disparate elements of experience to form new understandings, and in doing so it refers us to our own expectations and to prefigurings of other experience in the realm of possibility. This could be something as simple as examining our past achievements and failures in considering whether it might be possible for us to do something new such as write a book, sail around the world, or care for an ageing parent. The new meaning generated from this synthesis is the conclusion that we might come to, which is grounded in our own experience but indexes an expectation of our future or possibilities that might be open to us. We imagine the way our life might be in the future, but we do so with reference to how it has been in the past. Imagination provides us with a way of connecting experience with the realm of possibility, and so exceeding normative expectations. In doing so it synthesises continuity and change in our temporal experience of the present, and helps us turn our faces to the future.

Schinkel's insertion of imagination as a middle category between experience and expectation is useful in various ways. It can, for example, help explain why, when expectations are of necessity based in experience, they may diverge between people with similar experiences because of how their imagination has mediated the relation between them. So it is surprising, to say the least, that in acknowledging past experience as crucial to expectation, temporal projection into the future, and our engagement with the realm of possibility, Schinkel makes no mention of memory as a faculty that allows us to refer to this past at all. Indeed, while it is the case that imagination is the category missing from Koselleck's analysis of temporal relations, remembering is the missing category in Schinkel's. Schinkel's attempt to refine the analytical value of Koselleck's couplet by introducing the category of imagination is compromised by his failure to see how it is crucially allied with memory and processes of remembering. This is another reason why we have introduced the concept of the mnemonic imagination.

The significance of this can be illustrated by reference to the dual movement that is attendant on processes of backward referral. This allows us to evaluate and measure our expectations against our experience and provides us with criteria for their judgement, but over the course of time referring our expectations back to the past changes our interpretation of and orientation to memories of previous experience and the relations forged between them in our understanding of the past. That in turn may lead to the revision of our expectations. This is the mnemonic imagination at work. It is the action of the mnemonic imagination that allows past experience to be schematised and organised in meaningful ways, which then provide the basis for imaginatively projecting oneself into the future. It always works in both directions. Imaginative projections of expectations and possibilities come to inform the ways in which the past is remembered and organised into meaningful narratives. If for instance we think that it may be possible for us to meet up with a long lost friend, this possibility might direct us to selectively remember the past that we shared with them and in doing so narratively reconstruct our previous experience of them. This may then lead us to project particular expectations of this meeting into the future. We may then choose to meet them or not, or to present ourselves to them in a particular way.

All these points should have made clear that it is not sufficient to say that imagination projects us into the future and towards horizons of expectation and possibility, while memory returns us conservatively into the experienced past and some fixed settlement of memory. Imagination and remembering do not work independently in separate temporal dimensions, and again the concept of mnemonic imagination is designed to show this. It is in their combined action as mnemonic imagination that we can synthesise experience and expectation as a framework for action in the present. Bringing the horizons of experience and expectation into view of one another enables us not only to act in the present but also to remember our past and form expectations in particular ways that are meaningful now and that can suggest or help form particular lines of social action in the future. This is true not only of our everyday lives in the social worlds we live in but can be applied to historiographical practice as well. Beverley Southgate, for example, has recently pointed to the need to connect analysis of the past to future possibilities and expectations, with the aspiration of providing a meaningful framework for critiquing the present and for establishing future-oriented action.[83] The mnemonic imagination is directly relevant to this need since it works to draw together elements of experience into a meaningful whole from which we can project possibilities and act in the present. At the same time this action of mnemonic imagination is dialectically related to our aspirations and the realm of possibilities, which then turn to help shape what we remember, influence the elements of the past we select, and inform how we make sense of these in experience as product. The mnemonic imagination generates movement between the horizons of experience, expectation and possibility. It brings the temporal tenses together and synthesises them productively in order to achieve new meaning in the present.

A major concern for Koselleck is the sharp divergence between experience and expectation which he argues has developed in modernity. For him modernity has denaturalised time and this has led to a marked increase in our awareness of the temporal gradations between 'then' and 'now', 'earlier and later'. The consequence of this is not only that our investment in the future increases in proportion to the decline in our connections with the past, with 'time as a scarce resource for mastering the problems that the future hurls at the present', but also that our faith in the space of our experience decreases as our faith in the horizon of expectation deepens.[84] The modern contrast between existential doubt and scientific truth is just one instance of this shift, but it is more generally apparent as a result of the ideology of progress and development in that what the future seems to offer becomes increasingly detached from what the past does have to offer.[85] The past no longer serves as a template for the future, and expectations can no longer be satisfactorily deduced from previous experience.[86] As we have already argued, it is because they act in concert with each other that experience and expectation cannot drift entirely apart; there must always be ways in which expectation is grounded in experience. What changes are their respective content and the nature of their relationship. This is to distinguish properly between the two as historical and metahistorical categories, whereas at times Koselleck allows too much slippage to occur between them and so 'despite his efforts to the contrary ... turns into an advocate of change and modernity'.[87] It is then that he buys too excessively into the classical sociological thesis of a dichotomous opposition between tradition and modernity. Adapting Schinkel's point, we can therefore say that what changes the relation between experience and expectation is what connects them. The mnemonic imagination in modern times generates new expectations (of progress and development) as a result of drawing upon a certain configuration of experience (continual disruption and a rapid pace of change), but it is also more active in the ways experience and expectation become wedded together as the range of possibility is radically expanded under the conditions of modernity. The example that Schinkel uses is vocation. In pre-modern times expectation differed little from experience so that, for instance, if my father was a farmer, then as I grew up it would be highly likely that becoming a farmer would be my expectation for the future. In modernity, our experience of cross-generational familial vocations is engaged with more imaginatively, with a broader range of work opportunities becoming available to us. The question which then arises is why and how we are able to move further beyond our experience and engage in more creative ways with a broader range of expectations and possibilities. And how is the mnemonic imagination involved in this shift?

We would suggest that it is the nature of experience that is synthesised by the mnemonic imagination and used as a basis for the projection of possibilities that provides the first clue. While pre-modern societies have been dominated by first-hand, lived, or embodied experience which can support a given range of possibilities and expectations, realised and activated through the imagination, modern social life is characterised by the prevalence of second-hand, vicarious or mediated experience. The radical expansion of communication networks, representational forms and their infinite reproducibility has broadened the scope of our experience so that it reaches beyond our sphere of embodied experience, and requires a much greater engagement with the anthropological other.[88] This should not be exaggerated. As one of us has previously noted, in attending to modernity's usurpation of place by space and local experience by much broader configurations, it is easy to forget 'how people have long travelled imaginatively to other times and places via biblical tales, folk songs and stories, or more recently via novels, verse and various theatrical entertainments. Staying at home and going places is not exclusive to the experience of television'.[89] It is, however, undoubtedly the case that under conditions of modernity the intermixture of situated and mediated experience expands in scale and diversity. Such conditions provide new opportunities for the interpenetration of the horizons of experience and expectation, and make the mnemonic imagination more active and creative, as the past can be brought into the present in a variety of new ways.

Of course, following from the critical perspectives on media and mass culture which emanated from the Frankfurt school, doubt has continually been cast on the potential of mediated modes of experience to provide genuine temporal and historical engagement in the present. For Adorno in particular, the cultural commodity marks the fixing or freezing of memory, so cancelling its active processual engagement with the past and reducing it to a object of consumption. Mediated experience as a resource for imaginative engagement with the past, projection of possibilities into the future and action in the present, has been most radically rejected in postmodernist accounts of contemporary popular culture as characterised by an endless parodic interplay of simulacra.[90] This is a hopeless thesis. As Kearney argues, 'the gravest error of anti-historical postmodernism is to neglect the hermeneutic task of imaginative recollection and anticipation'.[91] The concept of mnemonic imagination is intended as an attempt to develop a counter-path to such anti-historical inclinations. Although collective memory may be manipulated in various ways, and social amnesia wittingly or unwittingly encouraged, this is by no means the entire story of contemporary popular culture. Insistence that it is produces analytically skewed and intemperate accounts. A more moderate and nuanced conception of the possibilities for remembering and for a historical consciousness in late modernity is provided by

Andreas Huyssen. Although he constructs the agency of remembering subjects in contrast to 'a media world spinning a cocoon of timeless claustrophobia and nightmarish phantasms and simulations', he sees an increasing social preoccupation with the past, collective heritage and cultural memory as a healthy sign that people are contesting 'informational hyperspace' and 'expressing their need to live in extended structures of temporality'.[92] We would advocate going one step further than this. It is not simply that the intensive mnemonic activity characteristic of the late twentieth and early twenty-first centuries is resistant to the temporal collapse of the horizons of experience and expectation. It is also the case that the representational possibilities of late modernity offer new ways of deepening and extending the interpenetration of experience and expectation via the creative action of the mnemonic imagination.

Values of the concept

The concept of the mnemonic imagination provides a way of redressing the deleterious consequences of the analytical separation of memory and imagination. These include the tendency to regard memory as referring only to the past and imagination only to the future. The concept runs counter to this tendency, insisting instead on their continuous interpenetration. Imagination and memory neither operate in separate temporal arenas nor do they possess utterly distinct characteristics. Our use of the concept is not meant to suggest that they are one and the same underneath, but rather to say that in actively concerted recollection they mutually inform and aid each other. It is also intended to help free memory from its empiricist shackles. A memory is not a straightforward analogue of past experience and remembering is not the mere repetition of it at a different time. Nor, as the storehouse metaphor would have it, is memory simply an imprint of past experience, perfectly preserved and simply dusted off for reuse in the present. The concept of the mnemonic imagination moves away from seeing remembering in those terms. It encourages us to think of remembering as involving an active synthesis of past, present and future which results in the creative production of new ways of understanding the past, in a continual process during a life as it is lived, retrospectively considered, and retroactively assessed. It is only by conceiving of remembering as in part an imaginative act that the production of temporal meaning through this synthetic process can be understood.

The mnemonic imagination provides the conditions for transformative action in the present oriented towards an anticipated future. This allows us to turn our attention to the ways in which memory is far more than straightforward recall since it embraces the manner in which experience may be flexibly reinterpreted in the present and able to take on new meaning that is then opened up for critical examination. It does so without denying that memory has an undeniable connection to a specific and definite experienced past. The inputs of imagination into the process of remembering may well be directed towards getting closer to, or enhancing fidelity to, that experienced past. So the concept does not flirt with the seductive temptations of relativism. By conceiving of memory and imagination as operating in tandem rather than as hermetically sealed processes, it is meant to demonstrate how they keep a mutual check on one another. What is possible is anchored in the realm of what-has-been in a process of continually referring back, while past experience is continually reoriented and reinterpreted in looking ahead to the emergent realm of expectation, anticipating and directing what is to come.

As well as taking us beyond the boundaries of an experienced past and connecting memory to other temporal spheres, the concept of the mnemonic imagination is designed to overcome the limits of an individual-centred focus on remembering which excludes the crucial influence of social interaction and exchange. In energising the move from sympathy to empathy the concept turns us towards an engagement with the various pasts of others, relates us to their horizons of expectation and most importantly responds to them on the basis of this knowledge.[93] The claims that the victim of injustice makes on the perpetrator are in the order of recognition and empathy, of seeing another for who she is and imagining their frustration, anger and pain. In isolation, memory is directed towards the past, and in that process alone the question of what should be remembered is impossible to answer. The concept of mnemonic imagination allows us to see how individual experience and the pasts of others interconnect, how we all have individual memories but how at the same time all memory is indissolubly social, and we are all in the same historical mix whether we look backwards or forwards.

Remember again poor Funes, for whom there is no organising rationale, no social schemata for bringing into the present particular aspects of past experience, and no capacity for turning around on the temporal modalities and relational settings of remembering. In an essay on dreams, Robert Louis Stevenson wrote that while the past is gone, 'yet conceive us robbed of it, conceive of that little thread of memory that we trail behind us broken at the pocket's edge; and in what naked nullity should we be left!'[94] If this is one nightmare scenario, merely repeating your own personal experience, like Funes, is another of equal magnitude. The perspective-shifting possibilities provided by the mnemonic imagination allow us to deploy social schemata, recognise our obligations to others and in doing so make sense of our own past intersubjectively as well as engage temporally with other people's pasts. Although not part of many of our personal or familial pasts, we respond in the present to the demands placed on us to remember the pasts of others: those of the Holocaust victim, the martyr, the conqueror.

In allowing remembering to be released from the prison of individualism, and recognised as a process operating in the public as well as personal realm, the mnemonic imagination can be conceived of as opening up the possibility at a collective level of an ethical relationship between self and other. Ricoeur's concern is with the ongoing dynamics of this relationship, particularly the maintenance of continuity in the relations between self and other, but also the possibility of change between them. Shared understandings of the past and the collective identities associated with them coexist with that which disrupts them. This allows challenges to be posed to shared narratives and established categories of belonging, and introduces novelty in place of convention. In his lectures on ideology and utopia, Ricoeur explores how imagination provides continuity in the form of order, and produces change and innovation through its disruption of order. In synthesising disparate elements of experience, imagination allows the past to be brought into view of the present and future, and establishes continuities between them, while at the same time creating something new from this synthesis, breaking through or changing pre-existing conventions in a 'glance from nowhere'.[95] Ricoeur argues that ideology and utopia only work productively when in tension because once they become disconnected from one another 'they fall into extremes of political pathology: the one incarcerating us in the past, the other sacrificing us to the future'.[96] Imagination generates the action which holds these two domains in tension and in doing so lays down the path towards the recognition of commonality based on shared identity. At the same time, it gives warrant to flexibility in these relational frameworks by encouraging new sites of identification to be explored, and alternative visions of the future to inform action in the present. In this context, the other is not irretrievably disconnected from the everyday social world, determined by a reified difference. Instead, social relations are continually revised, reconceived and acted upon in the creative interplay between past and future in the present. So, with the mnemonic imagination, just as the action of imagination prevents the past being closed off and disconnected from the present and future, the temporal faithfulness of memory prevents imagination from being bracketed off from the real world of everyday social relations.[97]

By drawing memory and imagination together in one temporal cross-animated action, it becomes possible to see how actively concerted recollection might pose challenges to established norms of social conduct and order, and in doing so, to the criteria for judgement of what is remembered. The schemata through which past experience is made sense do not function only as a way of sustaining the social conventions and conditions of any particular present. Seeing memory and imagination as reciprocal and mutually constitutive in acts of recollection opens up to us the creative potential that imagination allows memory to attain when they reflexively interpolate or conjoin with one another. The concept of mnemonic imagination recognises the sociological aesthetics of memory as practice, and points to the ways in which memory is always mixed up with particular values and judgements about value associated with the relations between experience and expectation in any given present time.[98]

The mnemonic imagination extends our analysis beyond a presentist assessment of the constructedness of memory in order to show, firstly, how the grasping together of past, present and future is possible in temporal consciousness; and, secondly, how this grasping together permits the establishment of a narrative identity which endures through time. The grasping together of past, present and future by the dual action of memory and imagination is also what enables us to act intentionally as the past can be used to inspire and inform expectation and possibility and therefore motivate action in the present. At the same time the horizon of expectation within the space of the present may cause us to revise and reinterpret the meaning of the past. It is only by considering memory and imagination as part of the same activity within temporal consciousness that shifts in interpretation and the generation of new meaning can be fully accounted for.

Rather than being a concept that provides an analysis of the linear unfolding of time, the concept of mnemonic imagination encourages a radical rethinking of temporal experience. It would, for example, facilitate the analysis of experiences in which we sense the dilation and constriction of temporal spheres as we hear an old song or accidentally come across a photograph of a dead parent in a drawer. In assessing the creativity of memory our concern overlaps that of David Middleton and Steven Brown, who in their investigations of memory are concerned less with what happened in the past and more with exploring 'how we actualize alternative *trajectories of living*.[99] While Middleton and Brown attend specifically to the analytical value of imaginary futures that are built into the past and the specific role of imagination in 'gap-filling' and 'hesitating' in discursive interaction, we share in their wider assertion that 'memory matters not as the forensic links in the continuities of persons, groups, and places, but in the way we cut into the flow of experience'. They go on to suggest that 'forgetting is not frailties of memory but the return of experience to imaginative re-elaboration'.[100] We would go even further and suggest that all remembering that produces new meaning in the present involves this imaginative re-elaboration of experience. An exploration of this re-elaboration requires an analytical focus on how experience as product is re-experienced as process, and so reconstructed as reinterpreted product. This is then one point where the hermeneutics of remembering come into their own.

In providing a conceptual tool for pursuing a sociological aesthetics of temporal experience, we hope to exceed a purely phenomenological or purely aesthetic emphasis and incorporate an ethico-political dimension as well. The concept of the mnemonic imagination provides us with a route to understanding both the creative and reified dimensions of remembering. As already suggested, these dimensions are held in a mutually constitutive tension and it is the mnemonic imagination that enables the move between them. We shall see in a later chapter that when memory and imagination are hived off from one another and their active dialogic relationship closed down, opportunities for fixing the past and its relations to expectation for the purposes of ideological exploitation become possible. It is through the dynamic interconnection of memory and imagination as we have sketched it that we are able to enter into a discussion of the ethics of memory, and to develop criteria for its ethical evaluation based not simply on an indexical relationship to personal experience, but rather on its referential connection with the experience of the other, on the kind of action that it facilitates in the present and the kind of future towards which it provides a leading orientation.

At the same time as acknowledging the ways in which their relations can be reified, opening up the creative ways in which past, present and future are brought into view of one another brings us to our final point in justifying the need for developing the concept. The aesthetics of experience are not realised and practised in a historical vacuum. The mnemonic imagination not only opens up for scrutiny the metahistorical conditions for engaging with the past in the present, but also provides ways of assessing the temporally specific instances in which this occurs. As we noted in the previous section, experience and expectation are, as metahistorical concepts, the preconditions for possible histories. At the same time experience and expectation in any given instance refer to particular lives, particular experiences, particular futures. The space and horizon of experience are historically definite and concrete, constituted by continually accumulating experiences which are assessed and reassessed over the course of time, while the horizon and space of expectation are related to experience but able to transcend it, so reaching into the realm of possibility. The conditions for historical consciousness are laid down by our ability to move between and within these spaces and horizons. This is precisely what the concept of mnemonic imagination is designed to recognise. Our very notion of historical time is premised on the ability to re-imagine the past in relation to possible futures, and for the past to actively inform our hopes and fears, our dreams and forebodings. The concept is a precondition for thinking historically in this way because it bridges experience and expectation and allows them to be brought into view of one another. They are made meaningful through their dialogic relation and the concept is designed to demonstrate this. By showing how memory and imagination act in concert by operationalising particular pasts in the interests of ensuring specific futures and subjecting particular actions to scrutiny through the passage of time, history-making on both a small and large scale can be opened up for critique. The extent to which the past of others is brought into view in the present and seen to fertilise the space of expectation, and the extent to which the movement between the horizons of experience and expectation remains reciprocal even when constrained, are both grounds for evaluation of this kind. It is by positing the mnemonic imagination as the capacity to move between experience and expectation that we hope to contribute to the project of developing a sociological aesthetics of everyday life. The mnemonic imagination provides one of the necessary conditions for a historically situated cultural analysis. It is one which attends not only to the anthropological conditions of temporal consciousness but also intends, in any given case, a close examination of the socially and historically specific aesthetics of remembering.

3
Personal and Popular Memory

Already in the world

In the two previous chapters we have paid considerable attention to processes of remembering and their interaction with our imaginative capacities as these relate to the individual person. In doing so we hope to have made clear that although anyone's memories are in various ways specific to them, some are borrowed and adapted, many are shared and pooled, while together as a complex and changing ensemble they contribute as much to our social make-up as to our sense of selfhood. Added to this, how memories are organised, used and refashioned is dependent on the various social groups and environments in which people move during the course of their lives. In Edward Casey's words, memory 'is already in the world: it is in reminders and reminiscences, in acts of recognition and in the lived body, in places and in the company of others'.[1] There is always an interactive relationship between the ways in which memory helps sustain the development of our own individualities, the ways in which it is shaped by the cultural resources available to us, and the ways in which it is given point and purpose by the social conventions that order our way of life. Certain aspects of personal remembering clearly need to be considered in light of their particular distinctive features, but these do not hold independently of social and historical context, and in general memory and modes of remembering are structured and given form by the social frameworks of meaning and templates of evaluation that characterise particular groups, communities and networks. That is the perspective we have adopted, but at the same time the attention we have paid to personal remembering has been quite deliberate.

We explained at the outset of this book that we intended to establish the value of the concept of the mnemonic imagination initially in relation to individual recollection and the creative project of producing a reasonably sustained and coherent life-narrative for ourselves. It is important now, at this stage in our discussion, that we emphasise another reason for attending thus far primarily to personal remembering. It is to do with what seems to us a certain disequilibrium in memory studies where too often sight is lost of the individuals who engage in acts of remembering. Much of the work that has been done in memory studies over the past quarter century has focused on collective memory, with the objects of study being sites of public commemoration, social rituals of memorialisation, media representations of critical points of social change occurring within living memory, the difficult pathways of negotiation between remembering and forgiving as they become manifest in truth and reconciliation commissions and the like. This body of work has been of enormous value, especially where it involves confrontation with such catastrophic events and episodes as the Holocaust, apartheid, the two world wars, and acts of 'ethnic cleansing' (one of the dirtiest euphemisms in the language). The arenas of memory dealt with in such work obviously exceed the memories of any particular individuals, yet what is often evaded is how collective memory in its different manifestations empirically and conceptually relates to, affects and requires its instantiations within the formation and operation of personal remembering. This cannot be considered irrelevant or unimportant precisely because any overarching conception of memory in relation to social groups or formations in the majority of cases derives from individual memory, and while any study cannot remain there, neither can it escape that derivation.

Prescriptively we may note how imperative it is to attend to the manner in which remembering draws upon certain symbolic resources, finds expression in quite specific uses of language, and is in itself intrinsic to cultural processes of one kind or another. Culture as process is clearly impossible without a mnemonic dimension through which it can be carried forward, with the sense of moving forward only making sense in light of what is brought along into that movement. Any cultural artefact or product thus carries within it a memory of how it was made, or what was made of it in its continued uses and applications, in the temporally extended meanings and feelings invested in it. That would be one step, but we may then want to advance from this to think more broadly in terms of cultural memory, with cultures themselves operating in mnemonic terms. We would do so because it is clear that cultures manifest certain structures and configurations over time, and are inherited from the past in various ways even as they change. Such a move may lead to new insights or suggest new ways of looking in cultural analysis, but it would not alter the case that when we talk in terms of cultural memory we cannot thereby turn aside from personal remembering as if this had no bearing on our discussion. Although such remembering is always socially and historically realised, it remains central to how cultural transmission over time is engaged with and taken forward. This is where the imbalance so often originates. It is precisely because we want to consolidate the turn to memory as a social phenomenon that it seems to us vital not to underestimate or neglect the role of the individual as a remembering subject, or memory as critical to the ongoing construction and adaptation of personal identities over time. Attending to the individual in this respect does not undermine the social turn; on the contrary, such a turn is itself undermined when it fails to attend to memory as dialectically caught up in the processes through which we develop our individualities and become developed as social beings.

What is most fascinating about memory is that it intersects personal histories and social order, cognitive processes and cultural belonging. If we are to fly with this, the objective of memory studies must be to understand the complexities of memory's mutual involvement in self-consciousness and public representations. There are dangers of reductionism either way we look, whether towards the social group or formation, or towards the psychological or physiological aspects of memory. A socially determinist or mechanistic account would show the danger realised on one side, a mentalist or individualist account on the other. Both kinds of account would not only be analytically unsatisfactory but also represent a diminution of the interdisciplinary promise of memory studies.

In turning to extensions of memory beyond the individual and assessing the analytical value of broader-scale conceptions of memory, it is salutary to recall that, initially at least, such categories as collective or public memory involve a metaphorical application of the term. Overlooking this ducks the need to question the value as well as the purpose of such applications. What do they reveal and what do they conceal? Are they just suggestive figures of speech or do they have a conceptual validity in their own right, signalling an empirically different set of mnemonic phenomena beyond those associated with individual remembering? Since these are questions often brushed aside and conveniently left unexamined, it seems vital that we try to move towards some way of resolving the various difficulties that they raise. In doing so we reject any view of memory as autonomously produced by broad social configurations or far-reaching historical forces. This is quite different to acknowledging that such configurations and forces do indeed influence memory in certain determinate ways. Our point is that memory is not a discernible property of them. Memory does not exist in some sort of group mind or consciousness. Remembering is ordered and patterned by particular cultural practices, and these contribute to the social communication and exchange of memories, but at the same time there are aspects of remembering which can only be experienced on an individual basis, one example being 'that lengthening of perspective which memory imparts to objects'.[2] This temporally oriented perception is not something that could of itself arise within a social group, occurring as a form of collective realisation. It is not something that would be readily articulated at a group level since it is an experiential quality created in personal consciousness out of an intimate acquaintance with a specific inhabited environment encountered daily over the course of time. The example confirms that while we are socially constituted in what we say or do about the past, it is still primarily you and I as individual members of social groups who undertake the act of remembering specific occurrences or episodes in our lives. This invariably becomes clear, and at times starkly so, when your memory of an event or what someone said clashes with another person's memory of it. The ensuing conflict is between their memory and yours. Memories are not then shared, but contested. All of us have allies in remembering, when the memories of others vitally corroborate our own, but the times when our memories and the memories of others do not verify each other, when what happened and with what consequences are recalled in different ways and hotly debated, make clear that memory is always individually formed and socially manifested at one and the same time.

This crucial point having been made, it is because our interest in this chapter is more in the social than individuated dimension of memory that we need to broaden the scope of our discussion to include a more detailed consideration of the interactions of memory and imagination in relation to the varying social contexts in which they occur and the long waves of historical transformation by which the terms of their relationship are conditioned. That is why in preceding chapters we have gradually been moving towards our second focus of interest in discussing the mnemonic organisation of past experience in its communicative interaction with various changing environments, as well as in thinking about the historically varying relationship between experience and expectation and how the mnemonic imagination provides the key to their mediation. In this respect, our dual set of concerns in the study of memory and remembering obviously requires critical attention to the distinction between individual and collective memory. This is such a commonplace distinction in memory studies that it is often taken for granted, with insufficient discussion given to its analytical credentials, to the issues it carries in its wake and the problems it seems to entail. Can we, for example, satisfactorily characterise the relations between collective and individual memory as involving public memory objects and the mediatisation of public memory on the one hand, and private memory objects and the individualisation of collective memory objects on the other? It is questions such as these which need more fully addressing if we are to develop a better understanding of how various socialities mediate the relations between these forms of remembering, for certain issues seem to become blurred or continue without resolution when the focus shifts from memory and subjectivity to memory and social group or memory and nation. Instead of interaction between them, too often they lose sight of one another. It then seems as if they exist independently and have no apparent need of cross-reference.

In this chapter we want to consider in detail the relations between personal and popular memory, and we do so because it is only in terms of their relations that they make any conceptual sense. Conceiving of these relations as dichotomous inevitably leads to the reification of collective memory as an autonomous entity, and the assumption – even if it is only tacit – that a social collectivity possesses memory in an analogous manner to an individual. That is not and never could be the case. We shall argue that there is no big split between individual remembering and the transmission of memory at a broader societal level, as for example via museum exhibitions or such media of communication as television or the press, but we cannot directly apply how you, or I, remember our own past lives to the ways in which memory is transmitted within a whole social formation; there are quite different dynamics involved.[3] We have as yet insufficient grasp of the workings of memory transmission across the relations of mass (unitary) cultural production and localised (multiple) cultural reception, and in the face of that lack we need to ask in what senses we can legitimately conceive of public forms of remembering without falling prey to the seductive allure of catch-all categories. Such categories are descriptively grand but remain conceptually airy and elusive. In what ways can we talk about memory and remembering as collective? In what ways does the term 'collective memory' carry sociological weight and substance? In what senses is the meaning of the past widely shared and communally understood, and in what ways does memory extend beyond our lived experience or our immediate everyday relations as a broader social process? In order to begin addressing these questions we need to think about the kinds of experience involved in collective remembering and the kinds of engagement the mnemonic imagination makes with this extra-individual manifestation of past/present interlinkage.

First- and second-hand experience

One of the claims we have made for the mnemonic imagination is that it enables us to situate our personal relations with the past within a wider network of everyday social relations as these exist in the present and extend back over time. This is entirely compatible with a sociology of memory which explores particular traditions of remembering and the social rules they legitimate for recognising the past in the present. Despite this it remains unclear how we are able to remember in common or how the past we share with others is reconciled with the sense of self-identity through time to whose development the mnemonic imagination is central. We can begin to address these issues by pointing to the obvious differences between recollecting what we have personally experienced, and responding to recollections of other people's experiences that occurred in a particular period of the past through which we too have lived. They may be entangled, but we nevertheless compare and contrast our own autobiographical memory, derived from first-hand experience, with these broader patterns of experience which we have gained second-hand from the broad range of cultural and informational media available to us. This also is the work of the mnemonic imagination, but energised now not via the continuities and discontinuities between the 'then' of what is remembered of our own experience and the 'now' of the remembering subject, but via the similarities and dissimilarities between our own experience in the past and the past experiences of others as they have reconstructed them. Comparative mnemonic practices of this kind should not allow backdoor endorsement of the conception of memory as essentially an individual possession unaffected by others or by the social worlds in which we live. Instead, they are evidence of the intersubjectivity of remembering, and its mediation by the proximate environments in which we are embedded. It is from these environments that 'frames of meaning and understanding come to be applied' to an individual's own feelings and experiences, and 'individuals establish themselves as participating social members ... meaningfully connected to others'.[4]

It is of course empirically more complicated than this, at least in part because of the different forms of second-hand experience which we relate to and draw upon. We can for example distinguish between second-hand experience which is primarily situated and is, or seems to have become, integral to our own past experience, and second-hand experience which is primarily mediated and doesn't involve a direct personal stake in the remembering community within which it is recounted. The former is characterised by the family story, the intergenerational narrative, the intensive accounts of local experiences circulating in particular social groups and communities, the nodal anecdotes through which the fabled histories of friendships develop. The latter by contrast presents us with experience to which we have no direct or lived social connection. Viewing television coverage of natural disasters and wars, or watching a documentary reconstruction of the day-to-day realities of people in other societies, may draw us in on a wave of sympathy or help us appreciate how others live, but we do not have any immediate empirical relation to this kind of second-hand experience. We may still remember it as vividly as events in which we directly participated, which is one reason why these different categories of experience are heuristic and not in any way mutually exclusive. A family story may be communicated by the use of publicly circulated photographs and a mediated second-hand experience may come to involve social connections with those represented. Any experience is in any case mediated by the cultural forms of expression and discourse in which they are represented and made to make sense. A second immediate caveat to add is that these relatively distinct experiences are not intended to be construed as forming a hierarchical relationship of authenticity where lived social relations are privileged over mediated forms of experience. Such a relationship is often implicit in the ways these kinds of second-hand experience are distinguished, but in pointing to their differences we do not intend a value judgement of any kind.

The family story or intergenerational narrative are forms of shared experience that establish group markers in and across time. The experiences of which they tell are distinct from experiences of a more personal nature, but are just as closely assimilated into our life-narrative. The mnemonic imagination is as vital for this process of assimilation as it is for the connections we make across the different stages of autobiographical remembering. It is vital because it is through the mnemonic imagination that we navigate the areas actually or potentially held in common between personal and collective remembering. Socially inherited stories are a regularly encountered manifestation of collective memory and a crucial component of the extra-individual interlinkages mentioned earlier, but we need to go further than this and refer to shared and inherited remembering as so mundanely experienced that it is through the processes of pooling and transfer they entail that memories are not only rendered as being held in common but also by this condition tacitly inter-validated. These processes should remind us that there has never been a time in our lives when memory is reducible to first-hand experience. Memory always involves second-hand experience as well since no experience is met with our minds existing as a tabula rasa: the experience of experience is always a compound of both first- and second-hand forms. Our engagements with what are initially second-hand forms of experience are equally mundane. Adding to a point we made in the previous chapter, we are now so readily familiar with this via the cinema, television or the Internet that we can easily overlook the ways in which previous historical epochs have also commonly known such engagements even if they were of a quite different kind. Mnemonic transmission over time is historically continuous as well as being historically specific. Religious traditions and settled communities of place are just two examples involving the communication of memories of non-experienced events which, through oral narrative, embodied ritual and various other cultural practices, integrate second-hand experiences into the memories of individual subjects and make the rituals and practices themselves become part of first-hand experience.

The notion of second-hand memories has perhaps been most intensively considered in relation to the Holocaust and what have come to be known as second-generation survivors. Such memories relate to deeply troubling, at times traumatic experiences in whose shadow the next generation's members have grown up; these experiences become interwoven with their own and in some ways come to seem so like memory that they have been referred to as postmemory.[5] Although memory is crucially at stake, it is at times a profound sense of loss, rather than memories themselves, which has been most powerfully transmitted. This involves not only loss of the most awful extremity, but also the need somehow to stand witness to what was not personally witnessed: 'what we children received, with great directness, were the emotional *sequelae* of our elders' experiences, the acid-etched traces of what they had endured'.[6] A complex mix of such emotions as guilt, fear, shame, anxiety and panic as well as empathy and love are associated with the second generation's identification with their elders' experiences. For some, whose parents spoke of their experience and bore witness to their children, the stories they heard repeatedly down the years became internalised, so creating a longing 'to appropriate their narratives for our own lives': 'I always felt that my life had been inflected around an event I'd never experienced'.[7] Such responses in the longer term could exacerbate the emotional perils and trials attendant on the process of maturation and separation into a personally independent life. For others, a recurrent theme in their lives has been that memory was to a great extent forbidden, thwarted or restrictively filtered by their parents or guardians, who refused to talk of what happened during the unmentionable years, and hid family photos referring back to a pre-war Jewish past in cellars or the back of wardrobes, away from prying children's eyes. Their own need to remember and mourn and come to terms with dead brothers and sisters was ignored because the silence which swallowed up the past seemed to their parents to be 'proportionate to the horror that had annihilated members of their families, while they themselves had escaped'. Other responses to the past among second-generation survivors have involved the mental substitution of themselves for their lost siblings or, feeling exiled from the past which would have been the source of their identity, falling prey to a longing for what gave depth to life but had subsequently become drained of all legitimacy because it was as if the dead had carried off with them, within their disappearance, the very sense of remembering and forgetting.[8] Some tried to silence the silence by commemorating, celebrating, and immersing themselves in the cultural inheritance that the genocide seemed to have wiped away, so trying to find some access into the lost world that existed before they were born. This is a turn to second-hand experience of considerable desperation, but with the aid of the mnemonic imagination the move can become a fertile way of searching for meaning, for trying to make utter loss seem somehow meaningful, as one second-generation survivor explained:

> I've got a very old '78' that crackles so much it's now almost inaudible. It's a song in Yiddish sung by Sarah Gorby. I don't understand Yiddish, I don't know what the words mean, in fact I don't want to know. But whenever I listen to that song, I start crying. It's always at one particular point in the refrain, the tone of her voice becomes so sweet, so heartrending that I seem to sink back into the memory of some old cradle song, which no one ever sang to me – or that I've forgotten. And at that precise point, the same thought always occurs to me: did someone sing it inside the camp, did some woman try to comfort her child with that song as they were going into the gas chamber?[9]

Second-generation negotiation of this hazardous entanglement of memory and inheritance has involved a compulsion to rescue some meaning and significance from a past full of shadows and ghosts, a process that 'can be more frightening, more confusing, than struggling with solid realities', so that it is only gradually, if ever, that some form of symbolic recovery or imaginative assimilation is achieved.[10] Added to this is the continually shifting nature of attempted remembrance under these conditions, and the constant vacillation between the effort at empathy and the knowledge that what was involved in the first-hand experience of such horrendous suffering can only ever be approximated, and never imagined at first-hand. As Eva Hoffman has written, the second-generation inheritance of its forbidding history involves confronting 'such fundamental questions ... not only notionally or in the abstract but through close engagement, and in the smithy of the soul'.[11] Through the mnemonic imagination engaging with such questions, posed by the unappeased spectres and the enormity of loss, the haunting may end: 'The urge to rescue, to repair and salve, which many of us felt so painfully in our early transactions with wounded parents, can transform itself – if it is contained in sufficient frameworks of emotional safety – into the re-creative and reconstructive urge, into the desire for creativity and meaning'.[12] Ideally, as well, the grappling with all this may lead to a collective reconciliation of the past and its successions:

> As more writers of the second generation work through the meanings of living with the memory of the Holocaust, the community bonded by that memory grows to include all the empathetic witnesses as well. The direct connection between experience and remembrance is not severed; rather, it is redrawn to capture the complexity of effects of that experience beyond individual memories.[13]

Second-generation experience raises hard, vexing issues, and we shall have cause to return to them in more detail during our final chapter. For now, it is this ideal we wish to highlight, for it involves not only the transmission of suffering but also the preservation of its legacy. In this the Shoah, though not experienced in an embodied sense, becomes nevertheless the fundamental ground of remembrance, informing and orientating the imaginative synthesis of experience in the present by bringing the memories of the survivors, where they have been recorded, into the remembering practices and memories of the second generation. This is not to say that they are straightforwardly repeated (although key stories and narratives may indeed be recollected in this form) but that they structure the imaginative synthesis of experience in the remembering process to produce new, creative engagements with that past. New poetic forms, new modes of working through and new interpretations of the past may be produced in this process.

So even when it involves the almost unimaginable, second-hand experience can be negotiated by mnemonically imagining and confronting the past that haunts the present, creatively arriving at new understandings, stimulating alternative ways of representing or communicating the past in the present, facilitating cross-temporal reinterpretation or generating critique and action based upon it. In more general ways, the synthesising function of the mnemonic imagination allows disparate elements of both first- and second-hand experience to be reconciled into new semantic wholes, with other people's pasts being brought into view of our own experienced past and new meanings generated through their interaction. This is perhaps most obvious in what Rosenzweig and Thelen have called the mnemonic 'quest for identity' in which we look to the pasts of others, particularly family members or members of our community, to explain how we have come to be who we are, or more simply, to construct our personal lineage and the story of our forebears.[14] The boom in genealogical research in the late twentieth and early twenty-first centuries is testament to the historical specificity of this quest for narrative identity. Rather than living in *milieux de mémoire* where our connections with the past are unselfconsciously lived in everyday practice, our search for continuities with the past is said to have become increasingly self-conscious and externalised.[15] To the extent that this is the case, the role of the mnemonic imagination under these modern or late-modern conditions is expanded as we attempt to bring together and reconcile ever more disparate first- and second-hand experiences. Although challenging and open to the constant risk of failure, the creative possibilities that this provides are correspondingly enlarged.

Remembering beyond oneself

Far more than a vogue for family histories is implicated in all this. Public representations of the past are routinely considered to be the collective past; a corpus of textual forms extends a society's narrative of itself beyond the lifetime of its current members. This does not necessarily mean that their value as a resource for creative remembering is attenuated. They still remain open and available as resources for the mnemonic imagination in fostering relationships with those other pasts that they represent. Alison Landsberg has suggested that communication about the past or representation of it, either interpersonally or culturally, produces the possibility of the listener or viewer inhabiting and experimenting with alternative subject positions, and therefore empathising with the experience of others.[16] 'Prosthetic memory', her term for this kind of engagement with the pasts of others, enables one to 'take on memories of events through which one did not live, memories that, despite their mediated quality, have the capacity to transform one's subjectivity, politics, and ethical engagements'.[17] Accepting this does not of course obviate the need to ask how public representations of the past are generated, and how we actively share and validate their meanings with others. The major domain of prosthetic memory identified by Landsberg is that associated with modern communications media, but this becomes problematic as soon as we acknowledge forms of remembering in common which are divergent from or neglected by media representations of the past. In contrast, within the domain of lived social interaction and immediate relationships, the pasts of others in the social groups to which we belong are for the most part closely integrated with our personal understandings of the past. The shared practices through which these pasts are remembered become, in greater or lesser degree, part of our first-hand experience, particularly within the family, which plays a critical role in what Eviatar Zerubavel has called mnemonic socialisation.[18] This register of second-hand experience is always relatively distinct from those experiences represented in publicly circulating textual forms, especially where these relate to the pasts of those at a spatial as well as temporal distance from us. We may see such forms as constituting a public repository of popular memory which can be conceived as a community or society's representation of its own past to itself and to others, but in elaborating this distinction we have come to something of an impasse.

These two modes of second-hand experience seem to relate to quite distinct realms of social memory. On the one hand such experience provides formative material for the mnemonic quest for identity and enables us to interact with others over time in particular circumstances and settings; on the other, it involves us in much broader sets of public representations of the past which may relate to specific collectivities but then become seemingly independent of them, especially when generalised as some putative national aggregation of what they collectively entail. As an initial step towards reconciling these two modes, we conceive of social memory as an intermediate category coming between and having an interactive relation with both. In both cases it refers to the processes by which the past is constructed and understood, sustained and engaged with in the societies to which we belong. The knowledge of the past that is then produced extends in both cases beyond personal remembering even as such remembering is deeply informed by it, yet what memory means in the two cases is quite different.

It was established in previous chapters that mnemonically we make sense of our past individual experience within definite social schemata and frameworks of understanding. These, along with the linguistic and other forms of communication in which it is articulated, make our past experience intelligible and enable us to share its meanings and values in our everyday life. From this point there is then a considerable leap between talking of a socially formed sense of personal memory and talking of *the* collective memory of a society which is shared beyond our immediate network of social relationships. This is unwarranted because even if we are referring to some kind of engagement with collective identities represented as long-established, individuals and different social groups do not have an invariant relation in or across time to those identities, while the 'possibilities for and interest in invoking the past to found collective identities (of a national, regional, ethnic or other type) actually vary considerably in different contexts, and recall the conditions in which groups and individuals have (or have not) been able to choose from a number of action strategies to satisfy their needs'.[19] This is one way in which difficulties creep in, for if it is clear how personal remembering is shot through with the social relations of our past and present experience, how publicly constituted forms of the past enter into our personal understandings of past times or experiences is usually left unexplained.

More serious difficulties arise when collective memory is posed on the basis of this leap as an entity able to do remembering independently of any individual remembering subject. This is a specious proposition. It swings the pendulum from mentalism to the attribution of mental capacities to social groups, societies or nations. The swing seems in some ways like a peculiar throwback to an outmoded school of social psychology, carrying traces of Gustave Le Bon's notion of the crowd as a collective mind, which in turn formed one strand feeding into the development of mass society theory, but it is actually more directly derivative of Émile Durkheim's conception of *la conscience collective*, for Durkheim had a formative influence on Maurice Halbwachs, who is above any other the key progenitor of memory studies. The concept of collective memory, which has so preoccupied and vexed recent memory studies, stems directly from him. Rather like the theoretical presence of Adorno in cultural studies, though for very different reasons, Halbwachs's work is good to think with, or around. It is certainly important to pay tribute to him, along with Bartlett, for pioneering the shift of analytical focus from remembering confined to the individual psyche to remembering in the social contexts in which it is performed, and so challenging the exclusivity of focus in Bergson and Freud on remembering as a psychologically internal process.[20] But it is in this shift that certain problems emerge.

For Halbwachs, remembering is not and never could be simply an individual activity: 'no memory is possible outside frameworks used by people living in society to determine and retrieve their recollections'.[21] Memory is derived from the collective experience of a variety of social groups and collectivities – the family, the generation, the nation – and the articulation of memories in the present is collectively achieved, for remembering can only occur where a person situates herself or himself 'within the viewpoint of one or several groups and one or several currents of collective thought'.[22] In line with our argument in Chapter 2, if we conceive of both past personal experience and the present time of remembering as 'socially marked', we can see how Bartlett's schemata of organised memory, and Halbwachs's social frameworks of memory through which individual experience is remembered and made meaningful in the present, are more or less convergent.[23] These social frameworks are preconditions for recollection in providing us with the means for ordering, organising and imparting coherent patterns to our memories. As Ricoeur notes in his exposition of Halbwachs's conceptualisation of collective memory, 'the social framework ceases to be simply an objective notion and becomes a dimension inherent in the work of recollection'.[24] This makes remembering a social action which is conceived by Halbwachs as actively producing ourselves as social beings by connecting the remembered I in the social contexts of past experience to the socially situated remembering I in the present. It is in this connective process that 'we produce expanded versions of ourselves as social beings by bringing into view distinctions only visible by comparing our experience across two different social milieux'.[25] In this sense our personal remembering is collective as we cannot step outside the sociality of our experience, the complex nature of which is determined by the various social groups to which we belong. We always remember not as asocial individuals but as individual group members.[26]

David Middleton and Steven Brown have noted that Halbwachs characterises collective memory as shared frameworks of meaning involving categories, qualities and evaluative criteria. Members of social groups use these frameworks to organise their individual recollections, for these 'are systematically fashioned around these common elements which come to act as resources ... for making sense of the present'.[27] Again, language is one of the primary ways in which memory is localised in relational networks.[28]

> One cannot in fact think about the events of one's past without discoursing upon them. But to discourse upon something means to connect within a single system of ideas our opinions as well as those of our circle. It means to perceive in what happens to us a particular complication of facts concerning which social thought reminds us at every moment of the meaning and impact these facts have for it. In this way the framework of collective memory confines and binds our most intimate remembrances to each other.[29]

The example used by Middleton and Brown is the discursive act of naming a newborn sibling among the various members of a family. In doing that we situate 'our present utterance in a nexus of shared background understandings that delimit the place of our sibling in our kinship network'.[30] In this sense, although remembering is done by individual rememberers, it can only be articulated using the shared social resources of language and the semantic frameworks supplied by the groups to which one belongs.

This strand of Halbwachs's work seems to us to be consonant with the social mode of second-hand experience and with the synthesising role of the mnemonic imagination that we identified in the previous chapter. It demonstrates that sharing memory within groups means we are able to communicate about the past in ways that are recognisable and knowable to one another. It affirms how personal and interpersonal experience can be re-imagined and reinterpreted in new ways. The role of the mnemonic imagination is very similar, in this instance, to the one we elaborated in relation to Bartlett's social schemata. But with reference to Halbwachs's conceptualisation of the social nature of remembering, there is a more enlarged role for the mnemonic imagination as he explicitly states that we occupy a place not in one social group, but in many. As a result of this, remembering in modern societies involves a 'multiplicity and complexity of relations of all kinds'.[31] This seems indisputable, but it is here that the first problem emerges, for Halbwachs does not address how we are able to manoeuvre between these multiple frameworks of shared meaning through which our past experience is interpreted, or how we are able to reconcile the different sets of collective memory that they represent. They may well exist in tension or conflict with each other, yet invariably Halbwachs emphasised the 'unity of outlooks' between individuals and the ways in which collective frameworks of memory 'confine(s) and bind(s)' our individual memories to others.[32] This was entirely in step with his sociologically functionalist emphasis on memory as a means of uniting groups and maintaining solidarity between group members. It is because of such emphasis on 'community, consensus and cohesion' – which 'bears the stamp' of the period in which he was working, a period of European nation-building and of a search for national traditions which could legitimate nation-states – that Halbwachs tied the memories of individuals far too tightly to social groups and failed to see memory as a source of conflict and antagonism.[33]

Halbwachs does acknowledge that the individual remembering subject moves between groups and that this movement 'allows frameworks to communicate with and enrich one another' as the subject 'imports novel ideas' from other groups into new social contexts, but his conceptual framework for explaining how precisely this mnemonic exchange operates between groups is limited.[34] In his example drawn from Roman society in which a woman joins her husband's family on the occasion of their marriage, Halbwachs suggests that this requires her to synchronise those memories of her childhood that are renewed in her ongoing relationships with her family, with 'the ideas and traditions that have now been imposed on her by her present family'.[35] In contrast, in modern societies, where two individuals of equal social status begin a new family, they turn away from the past because 'if each of the spouses were to continue to wallow in former family memories, they could not think of them in common, since the spouses have different memories'. He goes on: 'To avoid conflict which cannot be adjudicated through norms accepted by both, they tacitly agree that the past is to be treated as if it were abolished when they cannot find in it any traditional element that could reinforce their union'.[36] For Halbwachs it is only when a couple have established their own familial framework of remembering that these older memories can be assimilated. In these two examples we see one social framework of remembering dominating another, or where competing frameworks are equal, the past turned away from altogether. We simply 'change memories along with our points of view … when we pass from one group to another'.[37] This is an unsatisfactory explanation. We do not simply pass from one group to another in this way; we simultaneously occupy multiple social positions. Yet where this is recognised by Halbwachs, he offers no mechanism by which the complex process of reconciling disparate social frameworks of meaning can be explained beyond suggesting that they are synchronised or combined.[38]

For us, the reconciliation of multiple social frameworks of remembering involves active negotiation and reflexive remembering. This is creative rather than simply reflective in that the individual remembering subject is required to trace new paths through networks of temporalised social meaning, rather than reproduce current mnemonic frameworks wholesale. We should not forget that sometimes movement between social groups is impossible, for there are groups which are defined less by the cultural traits and dispositions by which they are identified, and more by the symbolic boundaries through which they define themselves against categories of social, cultural or ethnic difference. You cannot readily participate in a collective memory from which you are categorically excluded, and against which you have been stereotypically constructed. Such obstacles are frequent, yet it is clear that modernity has greatly fostered inter-group mobility. It is there, in mediating and manoeuvring between multiple affiliations to different social groups and their respective modes of engagement with the past, that we find a further role for the mnemonic imagination. The concept allows the past to be conceived and reconceived in terms of proliferating and constantly changing social ties and forms of association, which instead of simply reflecting two or more social frameworks of meaning in parallel allows them to be actively synthesised to generate qualitatively new subject positions. In contemporary multicultural societies which are profoundly shaped by the experience of migration, national frameworks of meaning embedded in host communities have to be reconciled by individuals with the frameworks of meaning inherited from the social life of their homeland. This does not only actively constitute new identity categories, new social subjectivities and sites of belonging (however temporary they may be), but can also operate inwards, generating multi-perspectival narrative identities for individual subjects.

This may take us forward, but only to a certain point. Using the mnemonic imagination as a tool to develop Halbwachs's acknowledgement of plurality in social remembering into a dynamic process of mnemonic social creativity only allows us to account for the first kind of secondhand experience that we identified at the outset. The synthesis of multiple social frameworks doesn't account for public representational or mediated modes of second-hand experience. Halbwachs clearly notes public forms of memory that seem to transcend the lived contexts of social remembering as he distinguishes between 'a collective memory and social frameworks for memory'.[39] Although he positions groups as providing social resources for the recollection of experience, he also claims that

> Depending on circumstances and on its point in time, society repre-
> sents the past to itself in different ways: it modifies its conventions.
> As each of its members accepts these conventions, they inflect their
> recollections in the same direction in which collective memory
> evolves.[40]

This is the second major problem with Halbwachs's work which we want to highlight, for in this sense there is a collective memory which exists as a property of the social group or formation, distinct from the practices and processes of remembering personal experience using social frameworks of meaning. Here, the group is the mnemonic agent, imposing its conventions on the individual remembering subject and 'collective memory, in this sense, has a life of its own'.[41] As he claims, 'it is only natural that we consider the group itself as having the capacity to remember', and if this is so, then 'one may affirm that the memory of the group realises and manifests itself in individual memories'.[42] In his example of religious collective memory Halbwachs elaborates the nature of the memory which can be seen as the property of the Church. He emphasises its public and representational nature as it 'obeys the same laws as every collective memory: it does not preserve the past but reconstructs it with the aid of the material traces, rites, texts and traditions left behind by that past, and with the aid moreover of ... the present'.[43] James Wertsch considers this conceptualisation of collective memory to be a 'strong version' which rests on the assumption that it is legitimate to draw parallels between individual and collective remem-bering.[44] Here social frameworks of memory are not just regarded as 'socially generated templates for individual recollective activity, but as manifestations of a mnemonic capacity that was actually collective'.[45] It is here that Halbwachs crosses 'an invisible line, the line separating the thesis "no one ever remembers alone" from the thesis "we are not an authentic subject of the attribution of memories".[46] Crossing this line is a hazardous step that has subsequently beset our conceptual thinking about the memory/society relation.

Any attempt to move from a recognition of social groups as providing means and resources for recollecting personal experience and engaging creatively with the past, to a collective memory that exceeds the life of the individual who cognitively does remembering, poses insurmount-able problems of structural reification and determinism. In the latter form of remembering, it is unclear by what process the act of remembering occurs and who precisely is performing it, for as Paul Connerton notes, 'if we are to say that a social group, whose duration exceeds that of the lifespan of any single individual, is able to "remember" in common, it is not sufficient that the various members who compose that group at any given moment should be able to retain the mental representations relating to the past of the group'.[47] How, then, is it possible to move from social frameworks of memory and their creative potential to an understanding of a common popular memory based on second-hand experience, or from the memory which involves what Ricoeur calls 'close relations' to the 'public memory of communities to which we belong', without falling foul of a straightforward transposition of the properties of the individual remembering subject into the realm of the reified collective?[48]

Memory and mediated second-hand experience

Various attempts have been made to reconcile situated forms of remembering and public forms of commemorating or representing the past. In addressing the question of how public memories transcend the lived experience of people in social groups, Connerton claims that Halbwachs's explanations for the communication or transferral of 'collective' memories are anthropomorphic and formulaic, leaving us with 'no explicit sense that social groups are made up of a system, or systems, of communication'. As an instance of this problem, Connerton notes how Halbwachs accounts for the cross-generational transmission of memory in terms of 'intervals', which in this case are temporal but can also be considered in relation to what differentiates social groups in any given present. This illustrates the problem because it demonstrates 'an inability to pinpoint the characteristic acts of transfer'.[49] In discussing such acts, Connerton considers the role of social and cultural rituals as communicative acts through which memory is communicated between generations. This entails a shift in emphasis from Halbwachs's notion of the collective memory of social groups as a repository of products, to acts of repetitive remembering 'in common' which, by definition, have to be performed. For Connerton, 'societies remember' through commemorative ceremonies such as religious liturgies, and broader forms of bodily practice such as the use of culturally specific gestural vocabularies.[50] Connerton's account of the ritual bodily communication of memory across temporal and spatial intervals provides a first step in attempting to recover public memory from the conceptual cul-de-sac that

Halbwachs led us into. It does so by foregrounding the social processes and communicative practices that allow memories to circulate within and beyond social collectivities over time. Public memory is therefore not independent from lived processes of remembering, but has to be actively performed through them.

While highlighting the general problem of the communication of shared memories over time, Connerton's focus on embodied ritual does not move our discussion squarely into the realm of mediated second-hand experience. As a further step towards this we can turn to the distinction Jan Assmann makes between communicative and cultural memory in attempting to develop an account of the extra-individual nature of remembering that incorporates material culture as well as embodied ritual. For him, communicative memory 'includes those varieties of collective memory that are based exclusively on everyday communications'.[51] This refers primarily to remembering performed in its regular contexts, and having a temporal horizon limited to three or four generations. In contrast to the proximity of communicative memory to everyday lived experience, 'cultural memory is characterised by its distance from the everyday'.[52] This is to characterise cultural memory as a series of fixed temporal references or 'figures of memory' which 'preserve the store of knowledge from which a group derives an awareness of its unity and peculiarity'. For Assmann, cultural memory involves two main dimensions or modes:

> first in the mode of potentiality of the archive whose accumulated texts, images, and rules of conduct act as a total horizon, and second in the mode of actuality, whereby each contemporary context puts the objectivised meaning into its own perspective, giving it its own relevance.[53]

Where Connerton attended to the reproduction of collective memory through ritual and embodied performance, Assmann emphasises two key features of cultural memory: firstly, the role of objectivised forms of culture in transmitting memory beyond the individual by determining the temporal horizons of second-hand experience for the group; and secondly, through the loosening of these objectivised pasts from their contexts of production or reproduction, their recontextualisation in the current social frameworks of understanding belonging to the group. In this sense continuity with the past can be established in the present across preceding crosscurrents of change.

Assmann suggests that these objectified cultural forms are brought to bear in social life in individual engagements with the past by noting that these objects 'do not have a memory of their own, but they may remind us, may trigger our memory because they carry memories which we have invested into them'.[54] Memory of this kind exists in disembodied ways, and requires re-remembering or re-embodying in the present in lived acts of remembering, but for Assmann it is 'objectivised culture [which] has the structure of memory' that transcends the temporal intervals identified by Connerton.[55] Yet where Connerton's account of ritualised remembering builds in a sense of how the forms of memory that extend beyond the individual are realised in social life through lived practices of bodily repetition, how Assmann's cultural repositories of meaning are re-embodied and their mnemonic meanings realised in everyday life is less clear. He merely suggests that 'these objects of cultural memory are deployed in the present to fulfil two functions: a '*formative* one in its educative, civilizing, and humanizing functions and the *normative* one in its function of providing rules of conduct'.[56]

For both Assmann and Connerton cultural or social memory would seem to involve the reproduction of temporal meaning in the present. While objectivised culture clearly is not conceived of as having a memory of its own, for Assmann cultural artefacts act as triggers or reminders because 'they carry memories which we have invested into them'.[57] This conceptualisation emphasises the crucial role of media and material culture as vehicles of memory, but it does not make clear the extent to which mnemonic meanings of material and mediated culture are unstable and contested. It is certainly the case that 'there are clearly demonstrable long-term structures to what societies remember or commemorate that are stubbornly impervious to the efforts of individuals to escape them'.[58] Nevertheless, even as the communication of shared pasts across time is emphasised, there is a danger of the individual rememberer becoming serially folded into collective group memory rather than standing in an active relation to or even creative tension with it.

While the mnemonic agency of the individual subject in each of these accounts is certainly alluded to, in neither account is there a fully developed sense of how cultural repositories of temporally oriented meaning, in either ritual or textual form, are reconciled with our own experiential memory and actively incorporated into our individual and social understandings of the past. In Assmann's account in particular, we are presented with a sense of cultural repositories of memory as static and unchanging over time, providing a 'total horizon' for remembering. This excludes any sense of the extent to which cultural texts and objects move between public and private domains, along with the shifts in temporal meaning that can accrue in this movement, never mind in any broader fluctuations of valuation, taste or concern which might also follow. As Annette Kuhn has suggested, our personal engagements with the past are populated by a heady mix of private memory traces such as the personal photograph, and public representations of the past such as films or news photographs.[59] Any neat division between these realms immediately becomes problematic when we examine everyday remembering in practice. Instead of seeing popular memory as involving the subsuming of the remembering I into a remembering we, we need to see the exteriorisation of memory and its circulation in social and public domains as involving a dialogue between the autobiographical memories of the experiential I and the shared cultural forms and processes of the remembering we.

In the late 1990s, Susan Crane called for the individual to be written back into collective memory.[60] The trick to be executed is to manage this without falling into the trap of methodological individualism. José van Dijck's concept of personal cultural memory does this neatly enough through its concern with the ways in which personally owned textual forms and objects – photos, diaries, letters, souvenirs and so forth – are able to 'mediate not only remembrance of things past' but also 'relationships between individuals and groups of any kind'. This concern leads to the concept, for personal cultural memory focuses on the value of cultural items (of any kind) in coming mnemonically *between* individuals and collectivities while also 'concurrently signifying tensions between private and public'. Media technologies, which have become increasingly important as vehicles of remembering, 'help constitute a sense of the past – both in terms of our private lives and of history at large'. It is because of this 'mutual shaping of memory and media' that the concept places dual emphasis on individual acts and cultural norms in order to highlight their altercation.[61] Rather than seeing collective memory as a straightforward aggregation of individual memories, we can now see it as embracing the practices and processes of representing the past as these continually emerge from our individual uses of cultural texts and objects within particular social frames of remembering.[62] This enables van Dijck to define cultural memory as 'the acts and products of remembering in which individuals engage to make sense of their lives in relation to the lives of others and to their surroundings, situating themselves in time and place'.[63] The concept of personal cultural memory departs not only from the notion of collective memory as a discrete entity, but also from the binary separation of everyday social memory and public memory transmitted via mass media or acts of national commemoration. Van Dijck positions objectivised memory products at the intersection of the individual and collective, so moving away from the conception of collective memory as a fixed repository of shared memories towards a view of it as a shifting variety of products and practices. Mnemonic practices 'are always simultaneously individual and social', while mnemonic products 'gain their reality only by being used, interpreted, and reproduced or changed'. Collective memory is thus 'something – or rather many things – that we do, not something – or many things – that we have'.[64]

We have now arrived at a way of conceiving of collective memory which incorporates both elements of first- and second-hand experience and indicates how we might move between them. Media representations of the past are sites for the creative articulation of the relationship between individual experience and shared understandings of the past. While acknowledging the normative dimensions of cultural frameworks in determining what is remembered and how, as for example with the conventions of family photography, van Dijck argues that these conventions can be diverted and used in unintended or unforeseen arrangements. Social and cultural frames of remembering are not always transposed neatly into the realm of individual remembering; they may lead to the production of novel memory-texts and the creative interpretation and reinterpretation of public representations of the past in individual autobiographies and their different formations of readership. Via self-produced media forms such as weblogs we populate our shared memory with mediated forms of personal experience exchanged across time and space. The mnemonic imagination is clearly at work in their production, allowing an integration of personal experience with social frameworks of remembering and cultural forms of expression. As van Dijck notes, this process is fundamentally creative. The reinterpretation and re-presentation of experience using existing cultural codes and frames involves meaning being constructed and reconstructed, shared and communicated in successive presents. Our past experience is imaginatively reworked into textual memory products using interpretative schemata and social frames particular associated with the different groups to which we belong during the life-course. In this ongoing process we are not only continually achieving our narrative identity, but also continually contributing to and drawing from the identities of those collectivities to which we are affiliated.

In understanding the latter dimension of this process attention needs to be paid to the ways in which experiences-as-product circulate. This involves considering the action of the mnemonic imagination in the reception of these personal cultural mnemonic texts. Van Dijck uses the example of reading on an Internet site the entries of 'mentally ailing parents who try to share their intimate mental and physical ordeal with their children, partners and other loved ones, as well as with anonymous readers', and hoping that 'they are responded to in kind'.[65] What she does not discuss is how this response might occur. It is clear that a significant other, whose past and future is bound up with our own, might respond to our demands for our past to be recognised, understood and reconciled into their own understanding of the present, but on what basis would an unknown other, a remote stranger, respond to our mnemonic demands? One answer to this question lies in the mnemonic imagination, for it is there we find the capacity to respond 'in kind' to a (temporally or spatially) distant interlocutor and synthesise this public mode of second-hand experience into a shared understanding of the world. We are able to remember 'in common' with another person by imagining their experience, communicated to us in representational forms, or 'mediated memories'. As digital media platforms increasingly bring us into contact with the pasts of others in mediated form, van Dijck argues that memory 'may become less a process of recalling than a topological skill, the ability to locate and identify pieces of culture that identify the place of self in relation to others'.[66] The mnemonic imagination underpins this topological skill in allowing us to create new temporal meaning, not only from our own pasts, but also from those of others as they are communicated to us in mediated forms. Using the mnemonic imagination in this way provides important groundwork for empathy.

As a conceptual framework, personal cultural memory deliberately privileges private memory objects regardless of their level of public recognition.[67] While this has allowed an exploration of how personal memory is communicated, secreted and articulated through representational practices which induct memory into an economy of mediated memories, it doesn't provide a fully developed account of the ways in which we engage with the pasts of others presented to us in these products. For van Dijck the object of these processes of collective remembering is ourselves, as we have 'to constantly align and gauge the individual with the collective' by integrating and reshaping our images of self, family and community.[68] This leaves unaccounted for the role of media texts existing outside of our personal 'memory shoebox' in expanding our temporal horizons to incorporate the past of the distant other. In her short account of the Abu Ghraib photographs taken in 2004 of the abuse of Iraqi detainees, van Dijck skims over the 'horrendous political message' of the images to discuss their value in illustrating that 'cultural memory is forever distributed, perpetually stored in the endless maze of virtual life'.[69] While the distributed patterns of public memory are of course important, van Dijck seems to defer an exploration of the ethico-political relations that this may or may not foster to a celebration of their circulation. While she talks of personal cultural memory as creative in the sense that we synthesise our personal experience with social and cultural frameworks of representation, she stops short of accounting for the new temporal meanings that are generated when we are confronted with the radical difference of the past of the distant other. Without a sense of what happens to mediated representations once they enter the distributed maze of communication, we cannot explain how we remember 'in common' with members of social groups to which we do not belong, and we cannot go beyond this to explore the ethical frameworks which structure this mode of engagement.

Public media texts circulate and therefore speak beyond the boundaries of the social groupings which they represent, entering into our personal remembering in paradoxically intimate ways. In this sense collective memory involves not just a dialogue about the past between the remembering 'I' and the collective 'us'; it is a dialogue that also includes 'them' and 'their' past. Any hard-and-fast distinctions between personal and mass media in the digital age are problematic to say the least, but it is necessary to account for the role of those representations not produced privately or for private purposes which enter into a mnemonic network of communication. While van Dijck accounts for the composition of a public memory which flows outwards from the everyday personal practices of cultural representations, public memory operates across the spectrum of representational forms, from the intimately mediated family photograph to the publicly produced and distributed television docudrama. Our contact with either or both of these forms can involve a confrontation with the past of the other.

Alison Landsberg has suggested that at the interface between an individual viewer and mediated representations of the past which are not our own, audiences can 'acquire new memories'. Historical narratives are not simply viewed passively; potentially at least, they enable the viewer to take on a felt understanding of a past through which they did not live. These second-hand memories 'are able to shape a person's subjectivity and politics'. On the basis of what they offer, 'unexpected alliances across chasms of difference' can be constructed, allowing people to 'respond in kind' to the experiences of others.[70] Where van Dijck views digital technologies as allowing us to engage more intensively in the practices and processes of remembering ourselves and the groups to which we belong, Landsberg sees mediated technologies as providing opportunities to problematise or expand our very notions of belonging. Yet what is missing from Landsberg's account is a mechanism by which these new memories are taken up and integrated into the political perspectives or subjectivity of the individual rememberer. Without understanding how these transformative meanings can be realised, the implication is that they inhere in the text and are somehow imposed on individual viewers.

The mnemonic imagination provides a viable alternative to this assumption as it is a flexible mechanism by which the temporal meanings of the texts can be reconciled with the existing experiential memories of the viewer, and in this process lead to the creation of new meanings in the present. The mnemonic imagination is the route by which experiences and subject positions can be encoded in these cultural texts, as it provides the capacity to recall and creatively synthesise the disparate elements of experience into a qualitatively new semantic whole such as a film or book. It is also the means by which these semantic wholes can be synthesised and understood by viewers, readers or listeners in relation to their own past experience, and with reference to contemporary social and cultural frames of reference. It is the imaginative quality of a response to the past of the other that signals a move beyond simply listening to and recognising an account of another's past experience, to instead develop some sense of what that experience may have been like at that time. This can form the basis for our action in the present and future. Empathy can only ever be partial, but striving for it 'enables people to see and act differently'.[71] The Romantic poet Shelley identified this 'going out of our own nature' as the basis of moral good. We should, he counselled, 'imagine intensely and comprehensively' and put ourselves 'in the place of another and of many others'. The significance of this can be consolidated by reference to its opposite manifestation, exemplified in the callous ruthlessness of Graham Greene's fictional psychopathic gangster Pinkie Brown, whose imagination hasn't awoken at all: 'That was his strength. He couldn't see through other people's eyes, or feel with their nerves'.[72] Empathy, then, as Dorothy Rowe has recently observed, always involves a leap of the imagination.[73]

Paul Frosh considers the engagement with mediated second-hand experience to be inevitably imaginative since the viewer is repositioned by the mass-mediated representation of the past of another as a mediated witness. This interaction between text and witness involves an 'imaginative engagement with others within an impersonal framework of "indifferent" social relations, creating a ground of civil equivalence between strangers that is morally enabling'.[74] In his historical exposition of the nature of witnessing, John Durham Peters highlights the obligatory and ethical nature of witnessing as an act. He argues that

> Testifying has the structure of repentance: retroactively caring about what we were once careless of … To witness is to wish that the record of the past were more whole, and to grasp this lesson now is to live vigilantly, to make the present worthy as we imagine contemplating it from a future point.[75]

It is clear from this way of thinking about witnessing that it involves both the capacity to recollect the past and the imaginative capacity to view that past from a projected point in the future. This would suggest that mediated witnessing of the experience of others has the potential to allow us to recollect that past and from it project future possibilities and expectations. This imaginative absorption of the experience and expectation of others can, just as it does in relation to the synthesis of our personal experiences and expectations, provide the grounds for a critique of the present and action within it. It allows us to do this based on the ethical demands made on us by experiencing the otherness of alterity.

It would of course be naïve to suggest that every film about the Holocaust, every image of starvation, or every literary narrative of deprivation, immediately spurs us into action in the present. We can choose to ignore as well as respond to the ethical demands made on us by the experience of others. The mnemonic imagination might not be deployed to synthesise first- and second-hand experiences, or to provide us with an empathetic relationship with other people's pasts. These possibilities can be closed down as well as opened up and it is precisely this closing down of the action of the mnemonic imagination that we will consider in Chapter 6. However, recognising the potential of representations of second-hand experience to reconstruct temporal relations between self and other in this way allows a rehabilitation of mass media texts and images as resources for engaging with the past. It acknowledges the possibility of an ethical response to them in which imagination is intermediate between self and other. Recognising the importance of the interaction between imagination and memory makes us able to realise that possibility. It is also by addressing the action of imagination in the process of remembering that it becomes possible to account for the relationship between individual and collective memory.

Imagination synthesises personal experience and produces self-identity, but it is also the means by which we interpret and assimilate the experiences of both proximate and distant others and move through time together. Imagination is, then, a precondition not only for individual memory, but also for collective memory.

The contested space of popular memory

In attempting to explain the role of second-hand experience in remembering without succumbing to the tendency to reify collective memory as a property of groups, we have turned to communicative processes to explain the relationship between lived social practices of remembering and the public accounts of the past that transcend individuals and small groups. This involves a twinned dynamic of communication. Firstly, socially experienced pasts are mediated from within the groups and networks in which they were experienced. The employment of cultural conventions of representation, such as that of the wedding photograph or the family portrait, loosens these experiences from the specific social situations of their production, enabling them to circulate in textual form within and beyond social groups, populating a shared 'public' memory. These processes are creative insofar as they involve an active synthesis of first-hand experience with the second-hand knowledge of representational conventions, and in this way are articulations of the self-in-relation-to-others. This is a process by which first-hand experience is turned into public second-hand experience. The second dynamic is the institutional mediation of social experience. It is through this irreducibly public process that the pasts of ourselves and others are represented by others. In the construction of the period drama or museum display, different pasts are communicated to us and enter into our historical understanding in various ways. For this reason we agree with Jeffrey Olick that it is impossible to invoke '*the* collective memory of an entire society'.[76] Instead popular memory is a process of remembering in common which involves the reciprocal action of both of these communicative dynamics.

These dynamics are not, in themselves, popular memory. They are the continuous operation of popular remembrance. It is the mnemonic meaning generated from them that constitutes popular memory as the product of remembering in common. This is not held in the texts, nor is it held by individuals – it is in the discursive space between them that popular memory exists, energised by the action of the mnemonic imagination. Popular memory operates through a discursive space in which we remember in common using cultural resources in two senses: the conventional systems of meaning which structure the ways in which we communicate our pasts and the symbolic resources which represent the second-hand experience of others. Within this discursive space, it is the mnemonic imagination which enables us to recognise and reconcile the past of the other and to situate our own pasts in relation to theirs. Popular memory is then the interspace of dialogue activated by the mnemonic imagination, between the three objects of memory identified by Ricoeur: ourselves, our close relations, and distant others.

As Fentress and Wickham have noted, 'the moment we "think" our memories, recalling them and articulating them, they are no longer objects; they become part of us. At that moment we find ourselves indissolubly in their centre'.[77] We have demonstrated in this and the previous chapter that it is the action of the imagination which allows us to assimilate our experience into our narrative identities. But we do not only 'think' our own memories. Through the reception of texts representing the past experience of others, we 'think' the memories of others and in doing so place ourselves in some relation to their pasts. This is not a passive absorption of meaning. We do not simply adopt the memories of others as would seem to be implied by Landsberg in the apparently straightforward way in which prosthetic memories 'become part of one's personal archive of experience'.[78] Their meaning has to be constantly revised and renegotiated in relation to our existing and ongoing understandings of the past and the narrative identities contingent upon them. Popular memory involves the bringing into relation of our own pasts and that of others, rather than the folding in of the past of the other into our own memory. This is crucial, as it is the discursive space between 'our' pasts and 'theirs' that allows the opportunity for historical critique, and action in the present based upon it.

This bringing into proximity our own past and the past of others can be likened in part to Bergson's simultaneity of times, in that to understand and experience my own duration I must do so in relation to the time of others.[79] It is in the indeterminate space between the times one experiences that temporal meaning is produced, but in Bergson's characterisation temporal awareness seems to be an organically arising condition. In contrast, popular memory involves a 'complex process of cultural production and consumption' that includes 'the persistence of cultural traditions as well as the ingenuity of memory makers and the subversive interests of memory consumers'.[80] Proximity to the time of the other is not itself sufficient to remember in common. The connections between these pasts have to be performed as their relation to one another imagined by the rememberer. In this sense the discursive space of popular memory is continually contested as the competing interests of the rememberer in the present, as well as the structures of meaning inherent in the textual renderings of the second-hand experience, are always implicated and require continual negotiation.

Rather than constituting a utopian space for unchallenged mnemonic synthesis, popular memory and the communicative practices that it involves are structured by the normative demands of representational conventions and the power relations that permeate social life. In the first instance, not all experience and understandings of experience enter equally into the discursive realm of public memory, and so become available as second-hand experience. For example, while the combat experiences of men in the Second World War abound, women's experiences of war occupy a relatively marginal position on the fringes of popular memory. Representations of their respective experiences are structured from within as the gendered politics of the family contribute to a hierarchy of narratives, shaping the communication of memories from personal experience into public discourses. Similarly, ideological conventions pervading institutional practices of representation in both the remembered past and the remembering present lead to the routine marginalisation of women's experience. We are not, of course, faced entirely by closed systems of communication. Particularly with the advent of digital communications technology, there are other modes by which alternative and minority experiences can enter into the public domain, providing opportunities for these experiences to be heralded within popular memory. The discursive space of popular memory is, then, increasingly complex. We have the opportunities to be brought into proximity with a diverse range of temporally different and distant pasts.

As the presence of multiple second-hand experiences does not in itself constitute public memory, the social locations and frames of meaning specific to remembering practices are always implicated in the ways in which mediated second-hand experiences are imagined. To enter into the realm of popular memory these second-hand experiences must be imaginatively taken up in the ongoing dialogues between self and other which constitute this space. This, in part, refers to the widely ignored issue of the reception of mediated representations of the past, an awareness of which is precisely what steers us away from the reified notion of *a* collective memory. As Ricoeur noted, 'it was in the personal act of recollection that the mark of the social was initially sought and then found', and it is in the discursive action of individual remembering that remembering in common is performed.[81] Imagining the pasts of others in acts of reception is at the heart of the creative potential of popular memory as a temporal network of self–other relations, for it is within the frames of these interrelated pasts that future action is seeded. Of course, as we have already suggested, the presence of the past of the other in public discourse does not guarantee that we will act creatively or ethically on the basis of the imagined past of another or others. The action of the mnemonic imagination is one of synthesis and negotiation. When we find our own past implicated in the suffering of another, is our narrative identity thereby radically reconstructed through a creative reinterpretation of our own first-hand experience in order to incorporate the imagined past of the other, and provide the grounds for an ongoing ethically sound relation with them in the future? Or on a routine basis do we selectively refuse to imagine the pasts of others where they disrupt our own narrative pattern of memories and the meanings we have attributed to our experience? The answer is, of course, context-dependent, and neither outcome is guaranteed. The reinstitution of the individual in the realisation of remembering in common at once brings both the potential for creative ethical action, and a capacity to fail in that responsibility.

4
The Reclamation of Nostalgia

Cross-temporal contrasts

Our discussion of the ways in which personal and public memory interact and inform each other can be usefully extended by exploring the case of nostalgia. The close interweaving of individual and collective processes of remembering is central to nostalgia. What it involves may be deeply felt by particular people at particular times, but the meanings it is given are dependent on a broader social narrative about past and present, change and discontinuity, temporal distance and difference, innovation and estrangement from what innovation has brought to any given contemporary period. Individuals who feel and express nostalgia act as witnesses to what has over the course of time been junked, cast peremptorily aside and rendered seemingly unreachable from the present, but rather than speaking independently, they express feelings about the effects of this as members of a specific generation or social group who feel temporally displaced, strangers in a new world that seems radically disconnected from an earlier one. So in discussing nostalgia, we have to consider the public and personal as interdependent and closely influencing each other even if we do make certain relatively clear distinctions between them. That is how we approach this particular form of remembering here, but our main purpose goes beyond this in arguing for and supporting the reclamation of nostalgia from a consistently negative view of it as a modern malaise. Such a monolithic view is generally unhelpful in thinking about both memory and history.[1]

It is axiomatic to our main purpose in this chapter that nostalgia is not considered as a singular or unchanging phenomenon. Although we have already begun to characterise it as involving a sense of cross-temporal

112

alienation, the extent and manner in which this is felt, experienced and made sense of is highly variable. Nostalgia is dependent on a sense of temporal dislocation, and inevitably there are times when this is felt primarily as drastic loss. Here is the voice of Borjanka Santic speaking, at the age of 70, of the destruction of the sixteenth-century Stari Most bridge at Mostar during the Bosnian War: 'I enjoyed my first kiss on that bridge. I remember even now the stars and the moon shining down. I remember how I dropped stones into the clear water. Now that has all been wiped out.'[2] There seems in this statement only to be intense sorrow arising from the double loss of a past event and the historic landmark with which it was associated – a kiss intimately joins two people together just as a bridge joins two sides of a river and symbolically expresses this – and perhaps there are also certain aspects to the recollection that are peculiar to the cruel vandalism of war. Almost the opposite of this recollection of a bridge whose demolition seemed to dissever past and present are the nostalgic evocations in George Gissing's *The Private Papers of Henry Ryecroft*. There the charm of old English place names is considered 'unspeakable', and the exquisite 'quiet of those little towns, lost amid tilth and pasture, untouched as yet by the fury of modern life, their ancient sanctuaries guarded, as it were, by noble trees and hedges overrun with flowers', brings back memories of 'golden hours' with 'a passion to which I can give no name.'[3] As well as exceeding the power of verbal expression, nostalgia is often described as involving bittersweet feelings, but as these two examples show, sometimes the bitterness outweighs the sweetness, and sometimes the sweetness pervades any sense of bitterness at what time has swept away. The variation between bitter and sweet is considerable.

It is important, then, that we recognise from the outset the many forms which nostalgia can take. It is not amenable to an absolute or fixed definition. Yet even when its semantic reduction is not as severe as this, the meanings associated with it are often narrowed down and confined to whatever serves the aim of a particular writer or commentator. That is certainly the case when the term is deployed in a comprehensively negative, if not pejorative manner. Such uses of the term prevent us from tackling the complex and in some ways contrary features of nostalgia. Its significance as such has contributed to an abiding preoccupation with memory and remembering, but the reductive associations which have grown up around occurrences of nostalgia have in many ways obscured this.[4] More than that, they have led to the neglect of nostalgia as a pervasive feature of modern cultural dynamics, whether in philosophy, sociology, anthropology or social and cultural history. This is what we need to turn around.

Nostalgia is by no means necessarily stultifying. There are various ways in which it can attain an active cross-temporal presence. The nostalgic impulse has, for example, helped develop and sustain our modern fascination with autobiography and memoirs, biographical novels and fictional life-histories, with their characteristic focus on how particular lives can be made to cohere across the experience of continual breaks with the past, how losses and gains across time are handled and assimilated, and how private worlds move within and against the alternating currents of change in national and transnational worlds. Nostalgic interests and investments help as well in fuelling the enthusiasm for local history and regional folklore, which among similar provincial activities and interests represent a desire to hold onto something which is past, or not lose hold of it entirely because it is past, and time must move on. They do not only involve the preservation of the past for its own sake. They may also signal a collective desire to reconnect with what has apparently been lost or reassess what has apparently been gained. Both reconnection and reassessment bring the past into a dynamic relationship with the present, opening up the possibility of critique in the movements made between them.

This kind of desire demands a sense of contrast between two different periods. Nostalgia highlights this sense and throws it into sharp relief. This is clear in the opening verse of Blind Alfred Reed's most famous song, recorded in 1929. Reed was an early twentieth-century West Virginia singer/songwriter and fiddle-player whose work is an interesting combination of reactionary and progressive elements. His songs show conservative attitudes as he looks back to the past but also display a willingness to protest against current social ills and injustices and look ahead to better times.

> There was once a time when everything was cheap
> But now prices nearly put a man to sleep
> When we pay our grocery bill
> We just feel like making our will
> I remember when dry goods were cheap as dirt
> We could take two bits and buy a dandy shirt
> Now we pay three bucks or more
> Maybe get a shirt that another man wore
> Tell me how can a poor man stand such times and live?[5]

This openly nostalgic verse is structurally dependent on steep temporal contrast – 'there was once a time ... but now'; 'I remember when ... now we' – and these yesterday/today comparisons prepare the ground for, and give extra rhetorical force to, the final, concluding line: 'Tell me how …?' Nostalgic expression always turns on these kinds of comparative assessments across time, and everyone is bound to make such assessments because everyone lives in and through time and is witness to successive waves of social change. It is for this reason that nostalgia is an unavoidable quality of remembering to which we are all at times subject, sometimes through sharp temporal gradients in our experience, as for example when you look at your daughter as a young woman and recall the moment of her birth, or think of her as a little girl, sometimes through small, apparently inconsequential items, 'little fragments of the everyday, things which, in such and such a year, everyone of more or less the same age has seen, or lived, or shared, and which have subsequently disappeared or been forgotten'.[6] The contrasts on which nostalgia hinges may be far more stark at points of social upheaval and transition, but 'in all sorts of ways mementoes and survivals mark a widespread concern for and sentimental treasuring of the past, of personal, communal and national heritages running through so much of everyday life'.[7]

Yet nostalgia is not historically universal. It is epoch-specific. Nostalgia is a direct consequence of modernity and the sharp divergence between experience and expectation which we have already seen is one of its key characteristics. It arises out of modern and modernising societies, and shows us some of the important ways in which people respond to their continually changing material and symbolic environments. Nostalgia is both existentially and socially valuable as a way of trying to understand change, to reconcile it with the remembered past and relate it to particular strands of continuity in the present. Those who criticise it out of hand would doubtless agree that nostalgia is a response to broad structures of social change and transformation, but continue to deride it as undesirable and disabling. Undoubtedly there are cases where nostalgia may be both. We shall deal in the next chapter with some of the ways in which it can be manipulated and exploited, and regressive versions of it produced which undermine the strength of tradition as a resource for the future, but that is by no means the whole story that can be told about nostalgia.

As we argue in this chapter, there are forms of nostalgia which are activated by the mnemonic imagination and so can work in ways that involve a quite different interaction between past, present and future. When it does it may well move beyond compensation for mourning over loss and instead represent a more active effort at reclaiming what seems lost. It may lead to a questioning of the changes that have caused the experience of loss and severance across time, or to a more sceptical view of the compulsive fostering of change, and whether this is indeed a social good that should always be espoused. There may be times when nostalgia has deserved the bad name it has earned, but nostalgia and what underlies it are not unchanging, and what is involved in vernacular nostalgic practices may be sharply divergent from commercialist appeals to nostalgia or the nostalgic spin that is given to the production and marketing of cultural commodities of one form or another. Nostalgia can just as readily be about how imagination reactivates memory and seeks to connect personal experience with widely shared feelings about the relations of past and present. Most positively, it can be about keeping certain alternatives open within the public domain and keeping alive certain counter-narratives that rub against the grain of established social orthodoxies and political pieties.

Nostalgia is also a distinctive form of remembering because it always involves an affective dimension, which remembering in itself may not, and sometimes does so quite acutely, as for example with its sonic catalysts when a piece of music evokes a scene from one's homeland left several years before, or awakens a longing to be immersed again in an earlier moment of one's life. Perhaps, in the more indefinite manner noted by Fernando Pessoa in one of his poems, an 'old and uncertain tune' from a tavern across the street makes 'one suddenly miss what I'd never missed'.[8] Such feelings are characteristic of nostalgia and central to the temporal aesthetics within which it is configured. It is in part because of these aesthetics that nostalgia may be positively valued or critically devalued, but in every case this only confirms that nostalgia is never uniform: how it is evinced and assessed is always specifically coordinated in time and space and so variable in its experiential scope and significance. This is an important stricture as it helps us avoid the temporalised polarity between progress and nostalgia that has proved so baneful in the past. Such polarity has usually arisen where positive conceptions of progress and development in modernity have been seen as dependent on an open-ended future quite divergent from what has happened in the past. Nostalgia has then been cast as their conceptual opposite, viewed as trading in a past that is passive and foreclosed, and showing a sharp loss of faith in the future. As such it offers only sentimental escapism and bland consolation. This approach to the nostalgic impulse is conceptually dependent on the increasing divergence between experience and expectation that has grown up in modernity and late modernity. We want to turn it into reverse and see nostalgia instead as emerging in opposition to their divergence. We want to conceive of nostalgia as representing a desire or inclination for transactions with what has gone before which are responses to the increasing acceleration of temporal movement and change in modern times. Nostalgia is expressive of how we feel about such movement and change, about what has been lost or what continues to exert a strong emotional tug on our hearts and minds.

We have insisted that nostalgia can become manifest in various kinds of ways, its meanings and values being dependent on specific social and historical contexts, and its expressions and representations varying according to topic, genre and communications medium. Now of course if this were comprehensively true we would not be able to think of it as a common category of remembering, in some way or other applicable across different contexts and modes of representation. So if we regard nostalgia as always in some way a response to the changing configurations between past and present in modernity, we need to think of what makes it recognisable outside of its particular manifestations, and what general component parts its composition requires, even as their relations change and are modified from one situation to another.

Bearing this in mind, we conceptualize nostalgia as a composite framing of loss, lack and longing. These three constituents have differing temporal orientations. While longing is an orientation to the past from the perspective of the present, lack is oriented to the present and an absence within it. By contrast, loss is longitudinal as it involves a movement or transition from the past to the present. It is when these differing temporal orientations are combined in some way that nostalgia occurs. This comes about roughly in the following manner. To begin with, the experience of loss creates an awareness of lack, and feelings antecedent to nostalgia may then arise out of the realization that the lack cannot be made good because what has been lost is now unregainable. It is because something has ceased to exist and in that sense disappeared into the past that nostalgia is possible, but this lack in itself is not a necessary precondition of nostalgia. It is when the lack is allied with longing for what is lost that nostalgia comes into being. Nostalgia may then involve a longing to return to what was, but it may also be combined with an awareness that we have changed since then and so would not now be able to see what once was as we did in first living through it. It is in the synthesis of loss, lack and longing, which may be different in any given example, that nostalgia comes into being.

This synthesis is possible via the action of the mnemonic imagination as it grasps together these multiple temporal orientations to what has been, what is no longer, and the longitudinal movement between these two moments. It is this capacity of the mnemonic imagination to produce a composite of loss, lack and longing that makes it possible to reclaim nostalgia as a mode of memory which is not singularly oriented to the past or manifest in a paralysing longing for it. Longing, albeit in varying degrees, can be motivated by lack in the present and lead to a sense of loss, but in recognising the relationship between an unregainable past and a deficient present, the grounds for change are prepared. The past becomes a reference point for critique of the present and, as a result of this, for possible transformation in the future. As the mnemonic imagination brings the horizons of experience and expectation into view of one another, the recollection of a positive past is always partly oriented towards the present and future. Narratives of change are only possible when the different temporal tenses are brought to bear on one another. It is only in instances where the mnemonic imagination fails to be brought into play that longing becomes unmoored from its accompanying elements, cast adrift from the attendant orientations to the present or change over time that are characterised by lack and loss. This denuded form of nostalgia is robbed of its transformative potential by a univalent orientation to the past. It is condemned to a futile attempt to breathe life into a long dead past, rather than generate new temporal meaning through a synthesis of the past with the other temporal tenses.

The synthesis of loss, lack and longing is not necessarily an individual act relating to personal pasts. While the mnemonic imagination grasps together the temporal tenses allowing loss, lack and longing to be recombined in the composite act of nostalgic remembering, it also facilitates a second movement. As we saw in both Chapters 3 and 4, the mnemonic imagination moves us beyond the boundary of our own experience, enabling us to engage with second-hand experience and to synthesise our own experience with that of others. We are able to draw on pasts that we share or even those that are not our own in making sense of the present and orientating ourselves to the future. It is in this way that the mnemonic imagination allows collective loss and lack to be registered, and pasts that have not been experienced to be longed for. Remembering these second-hand pasts, just like those we have experienced first-hand, can involve similar composite blends of loss, lack and longing. To recognise another's loss and lack, to empathise with their longing and to be able to creatively reconcile it with our own, is the precondition for ethical social action. This creative response to the loss experienced by others or experience of loss we might feel when brought into proximity with another person's past, means that nostalgia can help sustain the relations between self and other in and through time. Nostalgia has the potential to be a transformative mode of remembering in both the individual and collective realm.

Nostalgia results from our perception of a lack of connectedness across time, the disparities between 'then' and 'now', and so represents an attempt to use memory in an imaginative manner by trying to make new retrospective linkages across what have come to seem like differently experienced worlds. While, as Edward Casey notes, the world of the past associated with nostalgia is 'the past of a world that was never itself given in *any* discrete present moment', the nostalgic mnemonic imagination is not necessarily trying to recapture a moment that never was in any temporally separable sense, but rather to respond to the impossibility of return.[9] In grasping together loss, lack and longing, the unregainable past becomes a source of meaning, not in its separation from the present, but through a recognition of its direct relationship to the other temporal tenses. It is because of the impossibility of return that what we take from the past can imaginatively pose certain possibilities for the future. Whatever memories we retain, we cannot reenter the time to which they relate because we have reworked our memories over time and we ourselves are no longer the person whom we remember in them. They may evoke nostalgic feelings about the past, and generate certain regretful longings within us, but these feelings should help us realize that we can only carry them forward in our experience of temporal loss. Regardless of what we gain or lose, we carry the past within us in order to move forward into a different future. In light of this, the nostalgic mnemonic imagination is concerned with using memory for the sake of presenting alternative options to the ones before us, or showing us remedies for deficiencies within the present. The longing in this may stem from a sense of lack caused by loss, but it is not necessarily the hopeless longing – the longing without hope – which the critics and detractors of nostalgia have claimed most characterises it. The nostalgic mnemonic imagination may foster a form of longing that is quite compatible with hope, and it is because of this that we can talk of the past as a source of aspiration.

Shifts in sense, fluctuations in meaning

According to a now rather stale joke, nostalgia is not what it used to be. This is quite literally the case, as we can see from attending to the historical semantics of the term. 'Nostalgia' derives etymologically from the Greek *nostos* – return home, and *algos* – pain. Their lexical conjunction is attributed to the Swiss physician Johannes Hofer, who used it as a diagnostic label in the late seventeenth century for what was then considered a psychosomatic disease with symptoms ranging from melancholia and weeping to insomnia and anorexia.[10] The affliction, which at its extreme could lead to suicidal depression, was related to prolonged and usually involuntary absences from home, two key categories of people suffering from it being soldiers and female servants. Following Hofer, the term became so much an established part of accepted nosology that by the late eighteenth century 'people began to be fearful of extended sojourns away from home because they had become conscious of the threat posed by nostalgia'.[11] Gradually, over the next two centuries, 'nostalgia' became semantically unmoored from its clinical association, subsequently entering into both academic and popular vocabulary as a term referring to emotional yearnings for the past experienced by particular individuals, and later at a collective level to the commercial appeal to such yearnings in a broad range of cultural representations. As the meanings of the term changed, and particularistic identifications with home or birthplace declined, so in later psychiatry the emphasis of attention moved to questions of failed adaptation to 'the new society which the individual must live in' and goals of successful 'reintegration into an existing milieu'.[12] By the time debate over the condition and diagnostic uses of the term disappeared from medical discourse in the late nineteenth century, two important shifts had occurred.

The first of these is that its metaphorical application, as a sort of homesickness for a past left behind, had become its dominant meaning in ordinary parlance. This involved a move from spatial dislocation to temporal dislocation, as for instance in connection with the sense of feeling oneself increasingly a stranger in a new period that contrasted negatively with an earlier time in which one felt, or imagined, oneself at home. The metaphorical use was always aided by the multiple crossovers of sense between people's mundane orientations to time-space coordinates, as for example in the commonplace deixical uses of the phrases 'here and now' to denote the immediate, located present, and 'distant past' to denote the opposite of temporal proximity, yet over time that which the term stood in for became what was predominantly meant by the actual term itself. The second shift of meaning suggests that in standing in for a previous malady, nostalgia in its latter-day usage became associated with something different to its original symptoms, which were obviously far more drastic than those associated with feelings of nostalgia for a past time. Few people today cry uncontrollably, lose sleep or refuse to eat because of these feelings. They may indeed weep when thinking back fondly to a past occasion involving experience with a loved one who has since passed away. This may happen as we are looking through old photographs or hearing again a piece of music that became hallowed as 'our tune', but it is far more usual now for this to be handled with commonplace mechanisms of coping with, or assimilating painful memories, and for our response to such memories not to become pathological. There is nevertheless a sting in the tail of this classificatory change from spatial to temporal dislocation. It comes to us as a semantic hangover from its uses in medical discourse – on the one hand the sense that nostalgia is, if not a disorder, then certainly an emotional or intellectual weakness, and on the other the resemblance of nostalgia to homesickness in its affective registration.

Although its historical meanings and manifestations have changed, we can also see another line of continuity in the question of separation. This somewhat neglected force of modernisation accompanied its attendant developments, including industrialisation, urbanisation, rationalisation and ruthlessly calculated efficiency in the means of capitalist production, for it led to the severance of many people from their previous patterns of life in rural communities and the development of a huge sense of distance in their memories between time then and time now, in the present or more recent past. Such massive disruption and sense of loss, in contrast to the more settled ways of life where past and present had co-existed in a more or less even balance, led to what Richard Terdiman identifies as a crisis of memory at the start of the nineteenth century, a crisis with long-lasting consequences.[13] That crisis was in many ways first realised in the change of social environment from country to city, and perhaps explains the significant increase in medical attention to nostalgia in the first half of the nineteenth century, with the condition being taken as a pathological response to disruption between past and present, and in this sense a forerunner of the *maladies de la mémoire* that would preoccupy psychiatrists and neurologists in the later part of the century. Nostalgia in this sense was then seen as 'resulting from an excess of desire for the past, from the longing to return to a specific and crucial place in one's past'.[14]

As a matter of judgment, this raises the question of what constitutes excess. There is no definitive measure of this and so considerable variation in how its threshold is seen and assessed, with the relativism involved in turn inducing the need for distinctions between such desires and longings. For example, in the mid-twentieth century, when the latter-day meanings of the term had become well-nigh established, Beardsley Ruml could still hark back to acute and violent forms of nostalgia (in the classical sense of the term) while clearly recognising the need to qualify this by referring to emotional responses to the past in 'ordinary experience' which he called 'nostalgic sentiments'. These he associated with the concomitants of *gestalt* transformations, so clearly was not discussing such sentiments in the contemporaneous perception of their cheap, melodramatic evocation. The reference was instead to the generation of such feelings because of some interruption or disturbance in the time-binding force which characterises any human *gestalt*, linking past and present experience and giving them quality and form.[15] In modern or modernising societies, such interruptions and disturbances are common enough experiences. Most people confront them at certain junctures in their lives, but again there is considerable variation in their strength and consequences, so leading to different degrees of intensity in feelings of nostalgia and whatever ensues from them.

These different degrees depend on the manner in which the trio of components which make up nostalgia – loss, lack and longing – are combined in any specific response or set of responses to social and historical experience. The form which nostalgia takes can never be forecast in advance of such experience because this depends upon the extent to which these components, in their variable combinations, interrelate in their syncopating rhythms with each other. While manifestations of nostalgia are therefore always a matter of the manner in which loss, lack and longing are felt in relation to each other, it is the relation between them which counts. Without it nostalgia itself would be indistinguishable from grief, lamentation or remorse on the one hand, and desire, aspiration or greed on the other, all of these being in some way or other responses to perceptions of lack. In longing for what is lacking in a changed present, nostalgia for a lost time clearly involves yearning for what is now not attainable, simply because of the irreversibility of time, or because the lost time is associated with somewhere which no longer exists. There may be pathos in this, but the feeling is not necessarily forlorn, as Richard Eliott has shown in his study of Portuguese fado, with its characteristic quality of *saudade*. So, for example, the lower Mouraria district of Lisbon, once home to various *fadistas*, was demolished by the city planners of the Estado Novo during the second quarter of the twentieth century. Yet in fado there remains a critical nostalgia that stubbornly hangs on to a vision of what was and maintains 'the hopes and alternative futures of the past'. Fados 'have become stand-ins for the vanished architectural delights as the remembered city is restored in the lines of songs and the resonance of *guitarras*'.[16] So as we noted at the outset, nostalgia cannot be pegged solely to sentimentalist yearning because feelings of regret for what time has brought may become linked to how we view various possibilities for change in the future. By standing in witness to what time has wrecked, nostalgia may retain ways of using the past as a paradigm – or, more modestly, a set of exemplars – for the future. When the mnemonic imagination activates the response to loss, the experience of it may be turned to creative ends and connected to an alert regard for new opportunities. Feelings of loss can become commingled with a sense of social gain or liberation, or with efforts to regain what has been lost in new ways that positively engage with the process or consequences of change. This is quite different to a monopoly of attention to the future.

Of loss and acceleration

The temporal emphasis in modernity has always been on relentless supersession and movement beyond existing conditions and circumstances, leaving little or no space for dealing creatively with the experience of loss. Nostalgia arises in situations which seem to be discontinuous with what has gone before, where we struggle to make connections across time and in that sense may feel dispossessed. In extreme circumstances – and modernity has certainly generated such circumstances at particular points of radical social transition, starting with the French Revolution – the sense of loss may seem catastrophic.[17] The experience of loss is certainly endemic to living in modernity, regardless of whatever version of it applies in any particular time or place. Whether through war, revolution or regime change, mass involuntary migration and emigration, or less dramatically through social mobility or social redevelopment and the dispersion of existing communities built up over time, change and attendant feelings of loss have altered how the past is seen and considered. Modernity has changed the very conception of loss along with some of the compensations offered for it, such as nationalism, invented traditions, new-fangled commemorations, and the preservation of folk songs and folk tales from a rurally oriented preindustrial past. This changed conception of loss has grown concomitantly with modernity's own transformative scope. In both personal and public senses, loss and the sense of lack that follows in its wake remain connected with the characteristic features of modernity, including its relentless uprooting and erosion of time-honoured stabilities, along with its continual generation of temporal difference and separation of past and present onto radically distinct planes of historical periodicity. The connection is not only with the extent of temporal dislocation, but also the temporal pace and acceleration of social and cultural change.

Historical acceleration radically alters our apprehension of time, introducing what Todd Gitlin has called 'a new velocity of experience, a new vertigo', which is in part associated with the construction and reconstruction of events by the mass media.[18]

Temporal value in modernity is placed on what is temporary. This can involve a sense of disorientation from continuity or durability, increasing our feelings of perturbation by cutting away the grounds for active dialogue between past and present. Response to relentless change and increasing acceleration is characteristic of the experience of modernity, but the extent and pace of change vary along with the degree to which we may have to accommodate it. Experience of change, loss and feelings of estrangement from present circumstances fluctuate in intensity, yet regardless of that, how we deal with any nostalgic impulse remains difficult because of the lack of positive valence to attach to it. Such lack only increases our sense of perturbation. This has become a major stumbling block. In what has become the standard view, the sense of cross-temporal loss and alienation, being negatively valued, has simply to be overcome, regardless of the pain and pathos that may be involved. Nostalgia is castigated as a dumb refusal of the experientially new, an irrational desire to hold onto what is irretrievable. This is a simplistic, one-dimensional conception of nostalgia which, by accusing it of idealising the past, reinforces modernity's own idealization of the future. Is it simply irrational to want to question this new velocity of experience, to seek palliatives to this sense of temporal vertigo, to argue for the need for slow time? Is it simply dumb to reject an insistently positive valuation of the temporary and transient, to desire imaginative reengagement with past events, earlier times, or previous conjunctural moments?

These are of course rhetorical questions, but we pose them because we do not conceive of nostalgia as simply turning one's face backwards from the storm of the future. As we shall continue to argue, nostalgia may entail a powerfully felt need to regain, in relation to what is to come, at least a putative continuity and coherence in response to experience of the fragmented modern or late-modern environment. Nostalgic impulses are then integral to attempts to forge viable alternatives to the acceleration of historical time. They seek to forge alternative temporalities which are not a function of speed by mining the strata of certain past sedimented experiences or developing a form of dialogue with the past that is based on recognising the value of continuities in counterpoint to what is fleeting, transitory and contingent. More modestly, they may represent attempts by people 'to bring what is absent into the present in order more fully to integrate their lives', and so constitute signs of 'hope, or promise, that they can, for a moment, place themselves in the track of their former selves'.[19] For those who see nostalgia only as a uniform modern malaise involving mawkish attachment to the past, reverencing the old for old's sake, and dwelling only on memory once past miseries have been removed, such hope or promise is either illusory or impossible.

With equal cultural pessimism, Fredric Jameson believes an active relation to the past via continuities has become unachievable in late modernity because of another form of loss. The loss of a sense of historical location means that we float through a series of presents that are undifferentiated and without depth.[20] Paradoxically, this can be connected to an earlier stage of modernity in the West, as indeed Jameson himself did in an earlier piece of writing when he characterized Walter Benjamin's work as being 'marked by a painful straining towards a wholeness or unity of experience which the historical situation threatens to shatter at every turn'.[21] This straining is inextricably related to the quest for continuity across memory and so to mastery of our experience, a process Benjamin associated with traditional storytelling and contrasted with the way in which the contents of our daily newspaper are serially forgotten. We could see such forgetting as akin to the depthless presents against which nostalgia represents an imaginative resource, yet Jameson seems himself to have forgotten his own recognition that 'there is no reason why a nostalgia conscious of itself, a lucid and remorseless dissatisfaction with the present on the grounds of some remembered plenitude, cannot furnish as adequate a revolutionary stimulus as any other: the example of Benjamin is there to prove it'.[22] The conditions for furnishing such a stimulus have certainly changed since Benjamin's time, but just as certainly they cannot be said to have deteriorated to such a degree that a nostalgia conscious of itself is no longer possible. We should instead seek to carry forward Benjamin's responses to modernity and the effort after temporal connectedness in the face of the historical forces that seek to thwart it. Media representations of the past may well be integral to contemporary temporality, but to see in this relationship only a narcissistic presentism, or a drastic loss of engagement with historical time, is analytically the consequence of the intellectual allures of negative certainty.[23]

Looking backwards, seeing forwards

Modern radicals have had a troubled relationship with nostalgia. They have not dealt at all adequately with experiences of loss and lack and the longings for the past that arise out of them. This was a result in the first place of what happened to prevailing notions of nostalgia once it had declined as a condition in its classical symptoms. Gradually the term became used to designate the construction of a past exorcised of all pain and difficulty, along with a misplaced personal yearning for the past thus idealised. There was also a transference of reference from pain to pleasure, so that for example where the consumption of nostalgic media representations induces sympathy or longing, these are associated with pleasurable feelings rather than with desperate suffering. As nostalgia shifted in form towards temporal dislocation, these developments contributed towards its increasingly negative reduction. Imaginative and critical uses of nostalgic experience were then absorbed into this reduction which, at the same time, helped to underwrite the longer-term valorisation of the horizon of expectation. Radical commitment became equivalent to an unrelenting trek towards it.

One aspect of modernisation is that leaving your place of upbringing or country of origin becomes more and more common. This brings with it a shift from disturbance to exhilaration, except of course when departure is enforced. The disappearance of classical nostalgia can then be explained in light of this shift, as increasing centralisation, the growth of new modes of travel and communication, and the decline of particularist identities and forms of belonging, helped reconcile people to being uprooted and becoming disconnected from places dear to their memories. Being space-bound came to be associated with being culturally parochial. These gains in becoming modern could then stand in testimony to the ideological triumph of progress. Belief in the inevitability of linear progress forwards to an improved future was bolstered by the generation of its antithesis, so that even as it switched from a psychological disease to a cultural condition, nostalgia's association with the past facilitated its becoming negatively *othered* as the conceptual opposite of progress. Relations between past, present and future, increasingly configured in terms of ever sharper disjunctions between the 'was', 'is' and 'will be' tenses of time and movements across time, allowed nostalgia to be represented as defeat in the present and retreat from the future.

In the annals of progress, time marches inexorably forwards and is irreversible, and where a dogmatic belief in progress entailed an ardent longing for the future, nostalgia as its paired inversion entailed only an ardent longing for the past. It was then as if nostalgia arose only in compensation for refusal to invest hope in the horizon of expectation, as if it could only exist as a safe haven from the steady destruction of manifestations of the past in the name of progress. Among other things, this rhetorical framing of nostalgia has always allowed 'advocates of industrialisation and modernisation to dismiss the complaints of their opponents as products of distorted memories and aberrant emotionality'. It has also helped them 'to silence the victims of modernization – to render their emotional experiences suspect (even to themselves) and undermine their confidence in their memories, their unhappiness, and their hopes'.[24] As Peter Fritzsche has observed, 'an ominous ideological operation is at work' when positive responses to 'traces of another time are condemned for their sentimentality and dismissed as "irrational, superfluous, and overtaken"'.[25] Nostalgia in the de-pathologised senses in which it is now invariably used retains the legacy of this rhetorical framing, with radical intellectuals buying into its containment and marginalization, so looking askance at attachments to the past and viewing feelings of loss with deep suspicion.

In an important paper, Alastair Bonnett has shown how twentieth-century radicalism 'became characterised by an attitude of hostility to nostalgia', widely condemning it 'for its conservative affective register', yet despite such hostility 'it could never entirely rid itself of this chronic facet of modernity' precisely because 'under conditions of rapid social change political resistance tends to be articulated through emotional attachments to a disappearing past'. He argues that radical anti-nostalgia represents the predominance of a technocratic and scientific paradigm. This is in marked contrast to early to mid-nineteenth-century radical groups such as the Spenceans and Chartists, for whom 'the past was an obvious resource for the critique of unwelcome social and technological changes and for models of a better society'.[26] This remained the case with certain socialist writers and intellectuals of the late nineteenth century, William Morris being a key figure in this respect and one with whom late twentieth-century radicals have had a troubled relationship.[27] The main reason for this has been the socialist and Marxist endorsement of the horizon of expectation and its attendant devaluation of the space of past experience, with nostalgia being considered undesirable not only because of its association with illusory attachments to the past, but also because it was regarded as conducive to a destabilising loss of action in the present. The underlying theme of much nostalgia critique has thus been of a future-oriented present as the locus of action and a past-oriented present as the refuge of ethical passivity and political quiescence. Nostalgia in this view is a 'paralysing structure of historical reflection'.[28]

The single feature which spoils Raymond Williams's excellent study of English literary representations of city and country is an unquestioning

acceptance of nostalgia in this sense.[29] As well as buying into this ortho-
dox conception of anti-nostalgia, he fails to locate the phenomenon
specifically within modernity and recognise that as a response to the
troubles and travails of urban life, it is not all of a piece.[30] William's
critical project is, in the main, one of demystification, showing how
nostalgia obscured the injuries of material appropriation, class inequali-
ties and social deference in the countryside. There can be no objection
to this in itself, even if it is largely dependent on rationalist historiographical conceptions of the past and people's relationship to it, and
does ignore the appeal of pastoral in the face of capitalist depredations.
There nevertheless remains an unresolved tension in the book between
ideological exposure and fondness for the past, with Williams showing
a fine understanding of the experience of dispossession and loss, but
not of the nostalgic feelings that are so often their consequence. Despite
this irresolution, as Marcos Piason Natali has pointed out, Williams is
himself prone to localist nostalgic longings. This is clearly shown in a
passage early in the book, when he thinks back to his village upbringing
in the Welsh border country:

> Thus at once, for me, before the argument starts, country life has
> many meanings. It is the elms, the may, the white horse, in the
> field beyond the window where I am writing. It is the men in the
> November evening, walking back from pruning, with their hands
> in the pockets of their khaki coats; and the women in headscarves,
> outside their cottages, waiting for the blue bus that will take them,
> inside school hours to work in the harvest. It is the tractor on the
> road, leaving its track of serrated pressed mud; the light in the small
> hours, in the pig-farm across the road, in the crisis of a litter; the
> slow brown van met at the difficult corner, with the crowded sheep
> jammed to its slatted sides; the heavy smell, on still evenings, of the
> silage ricks fed with molasses.[31]

Such a passage would fit snugly into a novel that displays nostalgic
engagement with particular conceptions of past rural life, but the lyrical
evocations here need to be reconciled in some way with the idealism
that is elsewhere the object of critical analysis. Of course responses to
the development of industrial capitalism and the large-scale urbanisation it required have repeatedly led to rather idealist versions of a
pre-commercial age, all the way back to Goldsmith and Cobbett, but
with some writers, at least, these lines of response were made out of a
tested perception of a deficient present, and obviously were not entirely

without foundation and not in every case simply a cause of lament and complaint. Nostalgia cannot be generalised as merely illusory. In the case of Cobbett, for example, we may acknowledge, along with William Stafford, that *Rural Rides* is a nostalgic book, and that Cobbett is, to some extent at least, vulnerable to the argument put forward by 'defenders of progress, and of the market economy he detests ... that poverty would only be cured by the growth of industry and commerce'. But Cobbett was not 'disabled by his nostalgic stance', as Stafford claims.[32] He was enabled by it, for a nostalgic conception of better social relations and conditions in the past is what facilitated Cobbett's social critique of Old Corruption, and lent to it such force and conviction. Looking back with fondness to the rural past was, in Cobbett's case, politically motivated.

The question of how to view nostalgia for the rural past prior to the Industrial Revolution has become aligned with the now common thesis, stemming mainly from Martin Wiener, that Englishness and English national identity are rooted in the anti-industrial pastoralism of the late-nineteenth and early twentieth-century period.[33] Peter Mandler summarises the thesis in the following way:

> Nostalgic, deferential and rural, 'Englishness' identified the squire-archical village of Southern or 'Deep' England as the template on which the national character had been formed and thus the ideal towards which it must inevitably return ... 'Englishness' reversed the modernising thrust of the Industrial Revolution and has condemned late twentieth-century Britain to economic decline, cultural stagnation and social division.[34]

Mandler contests this, arguing that not only in England but also across Europe, modernisation and nostalgia have often been complementary, 'causing little cognitive dissonance'. Within England towards the end of the nineteenth century, 'a swooning nostalgia for the rural past' was the preserve of a small, articulate *derrière-garde*; the nation at large had 'come to terms with its urbanity'.[35] This is a salutary counter to the anti-modern Englishness thesis, suggesting that Jan Marsh's judgement on the rural nostalgia of the late nineteenth century, made at more or less the same time as the publication of Wiener's influential book, was all along more accurate: 'the anti-industrial manifestations described here ... soon fell into obscurity, overtaken in the twentieth century by political and economic events of far greater significance'.[36] The wide-ranging literature on Englishness sees it as a mythical construct to which many adhered. The value of Mandler's historiographical critique lies in revealing the Englishness thesis as itself containing various elements of recent construction that do not stand up to the countervailing evidence which shows that English culture of the late nineteenth and early twentieth century was as forward-looking as it was backward-oriented.

The key elements here are the interaction of these temporal attitudes and the extent to which the mnemonic imagination operates within it. Let us take just one manifestation of this. Where nostalgia is excessively self-oriented, this may suggest that the mnemonic imagination has failed in initiating any move towards sympathy with, and insight into, the perspective of others, so enabling nostalgia to operate individualistically or carry convenient ideological meanings which bolster a collective *amour propre,* as for example when imperialist nostalgia involves 'mourning for what one has destroyed', so that 'putatively savage societies become a stable reference point for defining (the felicitous progress of) civilised identity'. Renato Rosaldo adds to this: '"We" (who believe in progress) valorise innovation, and then yearn for more stable worlds, whether these reside in our own past, in other cultures, or in the conflation of the two'.[37] Such nostalgia may also be projected onto first nations people, as Michael Brown has noted: 'Today, white Australia needs Aboriginal Australia to keep alive the dream that there exist, somewhere not impossibly far away, forms of lived experience that retain the magical holism shattered by modernity'.[38] Self-serving manifestations of nostalgia contrast with nostalgic enterprises where mnemonic imagination has a definite presence, however problematic that may be. An interesting example is provided by the various initiatives that developed in the 1970s and early 1980s dedicated to encouraging working-class people in Britain to put into writing memories of their own lived experience.

The working-class autobiographies that emerged from these initiatives were undoubtedly shaped by the various concerns and investments of the middle-class activists and intellectuals who helped to produce them. This led to considerable debate in the early 1980s about the nature of this relationship: 'what was at stake was the very meaning of these autobiographical projects'. For their enthusiasts, 'they empowered people to share their personal experiences of the past', while for their critics, 'such projects were limiting because they rarely encouraged any analysis of the experience captured'.[39] It is true that many of the accounts that were produced were saturated with nostalgia for the working-class neighbourhoods and community spirit characterising them that had been obliterated by post-war slum clearance and 'planning blight'.[40]

The values associated with this lost world of mills and corner shops had already been established before these working-class writing projects got under way, as for instance in Richard Hoggart's famous 1950s treatment of everyday life in Hunslet between the wars. What linked writers like Hoggart and those who facilitated working-class writing in the 1970s was their social mobility through education. This clearly rendered 'problematic their relationship to the community they left behind', as it did the 'extensive discourse of nostalgia' they helped to establish.[41] In spite of this, those involved did not all stand at the same invariant distance from the working-class communities whose loss was being so much lamented, and these kinds of projects were developed in a broader cultural and intellectual context that featured such developments as 'history from below' and the oral history movement, both of these involving a revaluation of ordinariness in experience and a respect for the voices of the dispossessed. For some as well, experience of displacement from family background through educational advancement provided grounds for sympathy with those experiencing displacement as a result of the loss of those stable patterns of social life associated with the traditional working-class communities of northern towns and cities.

These adjacent developments show the mnemonic imagination actively at work in one way or another. That is why they cannot simply be characterised as self-oriented forms of politicised research, any more than the worker-writers can be simply characterised as analytically naïve. The nostalgia for traditional working-class communities that runs through so many of the autobiographies and local histories of the 1970s and early 1980s was generated by massive social change, and change on such a scale is often the catalyst for nostalgic remembering and reassessment. This applies all the way back to Haussmann's grand-scale redevelopment of the Parisian landscape in the early nineteenth century: the destruction of what the playwright Victorien Sardou described as 'the things which once constituted our own little world' was 'a prolific generator of urban nostalgias'.[42] The most looming empirical feature of this scale of change and development in Britain was the destruction of those very places, associated with their own little worlds, that were so deeply associated with the memories that were being recreated.[43] The writers drew upon their own mnemonic imaginations in order to bring forward what was being most valued from the past and offset it against the bleakness of the period in which they were penning their accounts. If the work of mnemonic imagination here often took the form of nostalgia, this was hardly surprising given the prevalent sense that a drastic severance had been made between past and present. What is important is that the nostalgia involved was trying to find a way to look forwards as well as backwards, or rather a way to see forwards by looking backwards. It is through the mnemonic imagination that nostalgic resignation to what has been lost in place is reactivated into nostalgic resistance to what has been taken out of place over the course of a given period of time.

We can see the mnemonic imagination working via nostalgia in a similar way in Northern Ireland. In a fascinating study of a rural community in County Tyrone, Ray Cashman has shown how, through oral narrative, popular song and verse, and collections of material objects standing metonymically for the past, Tyrone men and women, both Catholic and Protestant, express 'a sense of loss coupled with a perceived acceleration of change over the past century that is considered unprecedented and destabilising'. Again, we may see a loving attention to material objects from the past as providing only a form of compensation for this sense of loss and of time continually speeding up, but we need to change this functionalist interpretation for a symbolic one in which an affective regard for aspects of the past manifests a way of registering one's own evaluative discernment of temporal difference. The fast pace of change may make it difficult to evaluate change, 'to discern true loss (such as a decline in neighbourly cooperation) from at least provisional improvements (such as modern conveniences of transportation and communication)', but nostalgic practices of one kind or another do facilitate 'a reclamation of individual agency' in the face of the juggernaut of progress and modernisation. They give to these women and men 'a temporal perspective necessary to become critics of change, and more or less willing participants'. Nostalgia provides them with a way of taking stock of rapid change, and is 'eloquent of a determination not only to remember, but also to reconsider – to leave a conceptual space between now and then, to resist, if nothing else, the finality and conclusiveness of the changes wrought over the past century'. This is not a passive or unthinking form of nostalgia, a reactionary romanticism that is uncritical of the past, for as one of Cashman's informants put it: 'A lot of things were for the better and a lot of things were for the worse'. Cashman's ethnography offers evidence of the nostalgic mnemonic imagination involved in actively weighing up what is worth salvaging from memories of past times and what is not, what may be carried forward into the newer generation and what in the present may be considered regrettable, worthy of criticism or in need of being tempered by a different set of values. The mnemonic imagination operating through the threefold optic of nostalgia offers 'a substantial number of people critical equipment for living in an unfamiliar present and ... for shaping a more desirable future'.[44]

Cashman shows how nostalgia operates for particular individuals in enabling them to gain some purchase on temporal movement and temporal shifts, interrupt the incessant pitch forwards in trying to find some space for reassessment, and exercise a sense of personal agency 'by implicitly questioning the notion of progress and deciding for him or herself which aspects of change to embrace'. Specific people can thus identify the uses of nostalgia for themselves, yet along with this are more collective uses, as in voluntary associations of one kind or another which, in the case of Northern Ireland, may challenge divisive representations of the past with 'alternative narratives, reformulate identity in local rather than sectarian terms, and use the contrast between past and present to inform action taken in defence of community'. These are important points of observation, for they show that when put to such uses, 'nostalgia becomes a register for critical (that is, judicious) thought that may inspire critical (that is, vitally important) action'. They also suggest that analytical work on nostalgia has been considerably tilted towards negatively assured judgement of it on the part of deskbound critics. Nostalgia can certainly be exploited or turned to reactionary ends, as we shall see in the next chapter, but we need to correct this imbalance and move to a more refined conception of it as a distinctive form of individual and collective remembering. Cashman points out quite rightly that 'many academic critics have overstated their case about the universally uncritical nature of nostalgia', and that this is due, at least in part, to the fact that they do not engage in ethnographic fieldwork.[45] Empirical research in the field, investigating everyday forms of memory and remembering, is vitally needed if memory studies is not to become overburdened with speculative commentary or untested theorising. While there are relatively few signs as yet of a move in this direction, what is heartening is the rethinking that is going on around nostalgia, with greater recognition now being given to its use as a resource in everyday critical assessments. It is to the consideration of some further examples of this than we now turn.

Critical nostalgias

It has been central to our argument that nostalgia can only be properly conceptualised as a contrary, and even at times contradictory phenomenon, so that we can see it at different points of the spectrum of its manifestation as being driven by utopian impulses – the desire for reen-chantment – as well as melancholic responses to disenchantment, or as being a shifting mixture of both, with an emphasis sometimes falling more on loss and aching regrets over an ensuing lack, and sometimes more on the uses of memory as providing critical points of vantage on the present and fruitful ways of reorientating for the future. Longing is not confined to any single temporal plane. It is therefore far too simplistic to call nostalgia 'a flight from the present', as Harry Moody has described it, precisely because it can be so variably charged.[46] Among other ways of approaching it, it can be considered 'as convey-ing a knowing and reflexive relationship with the past, as a yearning for a better but irretrievable past, or, in more sceptical accounts, as emblematic of an engrossing but ultimately fabricated approximation of the past'.[47] Contrary to such interpretative possibilities, Tony Blair's observation that 'countries wrapped in nostalgia cannot build a strong future' demonstrates only a latter-day vapid investment in the horizon of expectation, with scant regard for where countries come from histori-cally in their contested pasts as they move towards that horizon and negotiate it.[48] Politicians are at times prone to superficial or opportun-istic pronouncements on nostalgia even though it is clear that it can be reflexively engaged with and is always ill-served by being set up as the straw target of futurist rhetoric.

Further to this, if we conceive of nostalgia in the ways we have been arguing for, it becomes inappropriate to see it as necessarily operating with the dichotomous before/after scenarios of classical sociology and critical theory. Either implicitly or explicitly, where nostalgia has been characteristic of elitist criticisms of mass culture, a stark historical divide posits premodern art as having 'an organic relationship to the commu-nity expressing ritualistically its natural forms of production and social relationships'.[49] The folk society paradigm in anthropology and folk life studies relied on exactly such an assumed organicism and in some cases supported an anti-modern reaction to so-called mass culture in ways closely allied to imperialist nostalgia.[50] This does indeed idealise a preindustrial past and is reliant on traditional/modern sociological binaries that make little sense of nostalgia for industrial working-class communities in Britain or early post-war suburbia in the United States. If nostalgia is always based on contrasts, it is important that we avoid polarising these and so do not forget the cross-temporal movement they generate.

In recent rethinking of the concept of nostalgia, there is a tendency to set up, if not binary oppositions within nostalgia, then at least radical separations between psychologically healthy and unhealthy, or politically desirable and undesirable forms of the phenomenon. This is difficult because there are often conservative official nostalgias and what Jennifer Ladino has referred to as forms of counter-nostalgia, which are 'ambivalent, ironic, localized, contingent, and potentially subversive' in the way they tactically reappropriate and resignify the forms of official nostalgia. Ladino distinguishes counter-nostalgia from the anti-nostalgia of literary critics like Williams, whose expository critique seeks closure through condemning nostalgia as 'a totalizing, romantic, and oversimplified narrative approach to a complex socioeconomic past'.[51] Such a description seems far more applicable to official forms of nostalgia, and yet, while Ladino is quite scrupulous in noting that official forms and forms of counter-nostalgia are mutually dependent, with any pairing where one is counter to the other there is a danger of posing the two in terms of a straightforward moral or political choice. We are back then with an either/or dilemma rather than uncertain movement between them.

The same danger hangs over Svetlana Boym's study of post-communist cities where nostalgia has been widespread, and nostalgic expression among writers and artists of the Soviet diaspora. It is in order to develop a more nuanced understanding that she approaches our relationship to the past via two kinds of nostalgia which she says are 'not absolute types, but rather tendencies, ways of giving shape and meaning to longing'. On the one hand, restorative nostalgia does not recognise itself as nostalgia since its transhistorical conception of the past is posed as the unassailable truth, as in assertions of national memory and identity; it also 'offers a comforting collective script for individual longing' for wholeness and continuity, the reestablishment of stability or stasis. On the other hand, reflective nostalgia dwells meditatively on history and the passing of time, turns away from the national past to a creative, more open-ended interaction with local collective memory, with the elective affinities that thrive in the space of cultural experience between individual and environment. Restorative nostalgia reconstructs 'emblems and rituals of home and homeland in an attempt to conquer and spatialise time', whereas reflective nostalgia 'cherishes shattered fragments of memory and temporalises space'.[52]

This is certainly suggestive, particularly in the way reflective nostalgia bears various resemblances with what we have been referring to as the nostalgic mnemonic imagination. In conceptual terms, the nostalgic mnemonic imagination approaches the relationship between past and present as transactional, shows a temporalised disposition as it roves

between individual and collective memory in a quest for cultural dialogue, and seeks to ensure that the threefold elements of nostalgia continue to move in dynamic interaction with each other. Yet it remains
unclear how these different forms of nostalgia emerge or are fostered,
and when set up as sharply opposed prevailing tendencies, we are witnessing once again the proclivity among analysts of nostalgia 'towards
dividing the category up into acceptable, progressive forms and unac-
ceptable, conservative forms'.[53] This obscures the ways in which
restorative and reflective forms of nostalgia may interact, 'the two forms
working dialectically rather than in binary opposition to each other'.[54]
It is clear that in her case studies and throughout the book as a whole,
Boym is concerned principally with reflective nostalgia. Much of the
interest of her book derives from this, but our broader point is that the
reclamation of nostalgia has to include rethinking the range of various
forms in which the phenomenon becomes manifest; it has to see its
manifestations as shifting, at times being blurred across analytical distinctions; and it has to work out from the acknowledgement that while
distinctions are vital, as heuristic devices they need not be used to make
clear-cut demarcations according to a priori aesthetic, moral or political
criteria, and that where such criteria are necessary, we need to know
who is drawing them up and who is applying them.

Counter-nostalgias are of critical importance, not least because they
provide those politically left of centre with a means of reassessing
their romance with the future, and reconnecting with what was once
central to the radical tradition, but what counts most of all is who is
using them to refuse the erasure or neglect of particular pasts and con-
test official nostalgias, in what alternative ways nostalgia is used as a
psychological and cultural resource, and how they facilitate remaking
the linkages between individual and collective memory. In his study
of how residents of two Cape Town communities remember apartheid
and how their memories are very much shaped by loss and resilience,
Sean Field sees nostalgia as 'an imaginative process of finding words to
make sense of memories laden with uncomfortable images and feelings
evoked in the present but linked to what has been lost from the past'.
Those who experienced forced removal and relocation have used the
time associated with the period before this happened as a means of
assessing change, but the destruction of the social world in which they
grew up has been experienced '*as if* the inner self is being fragmented
or *as if* "all is lost"', and so in response 'many protect themselves by
psychologically splitting off parts of the self to create imaginary places
framed by nostalgic memories'. Such memories both provide a way of

'holding together' an 'imagined whole self', and of imagining a better future 'which results in popular memories that look backward *and* forward with ambiguity'.[55] The key noun here is ambiguity, for in looking backwards to see forwards the relations between loss and longing are not perceived and responded to as simply a matter of instrumentally deciding between 'good' and 'bad' nostalgias. Retreat and retrieval are elements in 'every nostalgic vision', and this ambivalence needs to be kept in mind 'when considering the many ways in which nostalgia has been institutionalized in Western societies'.[56] The process of retreat and retrieval is one of affectively registering loss and temporal displacement *and* imaginatively engaging with the otherness of the past as a locus of possibility and source of aspiration.

With this interactive process, nostalgia becomes an action rather than an attitude, showing how the politics of nostalgia are realised in its applications rather than being inherent in the affective phenomenon itself.

'Nostalgia' is a term that enables the relationship between past and present to be conceived as fragile and corruptible, resilient and bountiful. Since it 'responds to a diversity of personal needs and political desires', and 'may be put to use in a variety of ways', it can serve reactionary and critical imperatives.[57] What distinguishes critical nostalgia is that it is concerned not just with what was, but also with what could have been and what could be. It derives not from the desire to return but from knowledge of the impossibility of return, and in the face of that seeks to uncover and assess which aspects of the past may act as the basis for renewal in the future. Nostalgia is then not so much a search for ontological security in the past, but rather a means of taking one's bearings for the road ahead among the manifold uncertainties of the present. Released from its negative connotations, it marks 'an effort to discover meaning in one's life, to understand oneself better by making comparisons between the past and the present, and thus integrating experiences into a larger schema of meaning'.[58] When integrated with the mnemonic imagination, nostalgia may be associated with desire for engagement with difference, with aspiration and critique, and with the identification of alternative ways of living in modernity or of the ways of living which modernity lacks. At the same time nostalgia represents an attempt to grapple with discontinuities and abrupt shifts in time. For each of us, nostalgia informs the imaginative effort to connect who we were with who we are now, and reflect on the ways we have changed. As we use our mnemonic imagination to think of our successive selves and how they somehow interrelate in terms of a life-narrative, the associated feelings may indeed be called nostalgic sentiments, but it would be quite inappropriate to describe them as *merely* nostalgic or sentimentalist. So too with the memories of such events of remembering, when these are reawakened on subsequent occasions. Such forms of remembering do not offer safe refuge from the present, for they make us aware of the complex interweavings of different threads of time even as we think back fondly to what has been or once was, and so harbour certain longings for what is irrevocably gone by. These forms of remembering act through the mnemonic imagination in both forward- and backward-looking directions, carrying elements of the past onward in ways which enrich or enlarge the future.

5
The Foreclosure of Mnemonic Imagining

Armchair nostalgia

In the last two chapters we have been discussing the relations between processes of social remembering involving individual participants and the public and popular forms of representing the past that are common in contemporary societies. Nostalgia as a mnemonic field grants us the opportunity to do so because it shows how individual remembering, when catalysed around the composite sense of loss, lack and longing, is embedded in broader social narratives concerned with past times and present times, with what has been gained and what has been sacrificed that should have been saved. Nostalgic remembering can involve feeling the absent presence of what has been lost in an acute and reflexive manner, and when the mnemonic imagination is able to move actively between its three components, this can be turned to critical account in relation to present times. It may foster the appropriate impetus for creative renewal by the way past cultural elements are drawn upon and reworked. When such impetus is felt, what arises from the interactions of loss, lack and longing is a different sense of possibility, one which is formed around what could be done differently, but in light of what has been done before. The legacy of past deeds, practices or values is then seen as a social resource which is important not just because it ensures continuity across time, but also because it can reorient us in the present, provide a new set of directions for moving forwards, and so help shape the future.

The future doesn't come into being through forgetting, through denying or dismissing the past. When the present is judged to be in some way deficient, the imperative concern is with forward-looking uses of the past, of the past as a source for funding the future. Uses of the past in this way have always to be critically negotiated and imaginatively engaged, whatever element of the past is in the frame, but the equally critical and imaginative identification is with what has been passively or actively set aside and neglected in the present. Illustrating this, the demands of certain subaltern groups for social justice and a fairer future are fostered, at least in part, 'by vigilantly returning to the past, reinvestigating the past over and over again in order to find places and moments of resistance to oppression that might open up a better future'. For many such groups, the past has long been a locus of possibility and source of aspiration, of providing a way of imagining 'present impossibilities becoming possible in the future', for 'the future opens into otherness only insofar as the past does too'.[1] For example, during the nineteenth century among farm-labourers in the English southern Midlands, a dialogic ballad extant from the seventeenth century attained classic status in oral tradition as a result of its historically renegotiated meaning and value. By being associated with the distant past and contrasted with the increasingly ascendant capitalist organisation of agriculture, the ballad, which extolled the virtues of honest husbandry, became used as a component of social critique and challenge to social injustices in a rural world growing more and more destructive of labourers' interests and welfare. The ballad helped to 'construct and maintain a defiant self-respect in the face of a dominant class's contempt, which is in itself a vital element in the effort to create new and better ways of thinking and being'.[2] When the past provides a source of aspiration in this way, nostalgia becomes an action rather than an attitude, with the mnemonic imagination as the generative agent turning past into possibility.

This always requires the right conditions and contexts in which it may be brought about, and there are various ways in which they may be undermined or eroded. Nostalgic experience or feeling may become stunted, with the mnemonic imagination unable to fertilise the relations between longing and the sense of lack and loss. This does not necessarily follow from the transformation of cultural creation into commodity production, but the tendential logic of commodity production is for the use-value of a commodity to be subservient to its exchange-value. The consequence of this is that if the past has consumer appeal, the past will be marketed, or if the association of a product with a past image or style helps sales of it increase, that is what will be promoted, in both cases regardless of what consumers themselves do with the ensuing products in their own uses of them. Commercialist uses of past cultural elements are commonplace in modernity, as for example in the recycling processes that occur in fashion and clothing, furniture and interior design, and then in the promotion and advertising intended to help sell various commodities. These devices generally isolate longing from awareness of loss and lack since they seek to convert longing for some aspect of past times or past experience into the forms of longing necessary for consumption. Hence the appeal in advertising to previous stages in life, especially childhood and youth, or to past lifestyles where 'people, products or settings of consumption are harmonized around a unified impression'.[3] The emphasis is then on the relationship between cultural texts and audience expectations of the materials of everyday life becoming lodged in the creation of 'surfaces of meaning through the manipulation of association and evocation'.[4] Commodities have of course to be sufficiently reenchanted by their adornment with past associations and appearances that longing can be channelled into its satisfaction by consumer acquisition, but this can be quite separate from feelings of loss and lack in the present. As Arjun Appadurai has noted, 'nostalgia, as far as mass merchandising is concerned, does not principally involve the evocation of a sentiment to which consumers who really have lost something can respond'. Instead, 'these forms of mass advertising teach consumers to miss things they have never lost'.[5] It is not so much cultural elements with a tangible reference to the past that are then in play, but rather a vague or diffuse sense of pastness which is used as an attractive gloss for the product or service being promoted. This opens up a debilitating distance between loss, lack and longing and so makes all the more difficult the effort of the mnemonic imagination to bring them into active conjunction in a forward- as well as backward-looking way. This sense of pastness rather than of memory itself has been dubbed armchair nostalgia by Appadurai, by which he means 'nostalgia without lived experience or collective historical memory'.[6]

In this chapter we shall be looking at some of the ways in which consumerism and promotional culture are central to the ideological production and perpetuation of what such armchair nostalgia involves, but we should also note at the outset that the conditions necessary for it are provided and abetted by modern communications technologies of production and consumption, transmission and reception, recording and replay. From the late nineteenth century, these technologies have usually been credited with breaking down the barriers of space and time, bringing people and cultures into increasing contact with each other, and continually abbreviating the time it takes for messages and data to be transmitted. The consequences of this are generally considered beneficial and progressive. Obviously they have their virtues, but highlighting them has the effect of obscuring the ways in which they have exacerbated certain existing spatio-temporal distances, and created new forms of symbolic distance. So, for example, the distances within time and space in which these technologies are implicated seem in some ways inversely proportionate to the distances across time and space which armchair nostalgia so ably exploits. Past cultural forms are brought back to us in the present, in some cases such as film or recorded music with a seemingly high degree of exactitude, but what is lost is the sense felt in lived cultural experience of how they are closely informed by the past of which they speak. Likewise, without prior engagement with particular cultural forms or subsequent enquiry into them, we generally gain only an inkling into how the elements of the past they convey have a bearing on the present. Added to this, when we see an old documentary photograph from the 1940s, watch an old romance film from the 1930s, or hear an old hillbilly record from the 1920s, the sense of temporal distance between 'then' and 'now' is exacerbated by our awareness of all the other moments or intervals of seeing, watching and listening that have occurred across time in the consumption of these cultural products. The anonymity of consumption which this involves means that we can only orient our own act of consumption across time to the originating product itself, and not also to the originating context or to what has intervened between 'then' and 'now', as we would in an active cultural tradition. It is this cumulative process of temporal dissolution which mass merchandising preys upon, and out of which only that generalised pastness prevails as the aesthetic allure to a cultural commodity. Such is the artfulness involved in divorcing pastness from the past that even the present can be represented with the requisite stylisation to make it appear to have already passed by, and so be misrecognised as now no longer here. The result is what Fredric Jameson calls 'nostalgia for the present'.[7] The peculiar twist in this is that the consumer then consumes the present, as past, within the present. In what amounts to a weird temporal contortion, it is as if the present had gone way out of date but has now fortuitously come back into fashion.

Memory and modernity

The cultural technologies which convey as well as help create the conditions for armchair nostalgia have of course been characteristic features of modernity. This leads us to the initial question we want to address in this chapter, which is whether memory itself has changed under conditions of modernity. These conditions include continual alteration, and how societies remember has certainly been transformed as a consequence of this, but the key issues are in what ways and to what extent? Here we encounter a grand-scale thesis which argues that collective memory has suffered a breach of such magnitude that it is now radically distinguishable from memory in earlier periods of history. The major contention in this thesis is that, under the regal sign of progress, historicism has replaced an authentic relation to the past. Since the thesis sits adjacent to our concern with what can happen to nostalgia when its relationship to lived experience and collective memory is dissipated or severed, it provides us with a convenient stepping-off point in our consideration of the ways in which nostalgia becomes regressive.

The writer most associated with its various claims is Pierre Nora, who makes a key distinction between traditional lived milieux of memory and modern *lieux de mémoire*. In the former, social experience and collective memory are seamlessly integrated, whereas the latter are sites or locations of memory which acquire a memorial significance following a fundamental rupture with the past. Nora formally defines a *lieu de mémoire* as 'any significant entity, whether material or non-material in nature, which by dint of human will or the work of time has become a symbolic element of the memorial heritage of any community'.[8] As this catholic definition might suggest, such sites include not only historically significant places and monuments, archives, libraries and museums, but also any of the huge range of items of popular culture which provide reconstructions of the past. This obviously involves considerable variation, yet despite this, according to Nora, all they represent are vestiges of the past. They can only offer us a residual sense of what was once socially and culturally meaningful. The reason for this is that these sites are no longer integral to a lived mnemonic community; they are evidence only of historical disruption and loss. It is perhaps important to note at this point that Nora's project was generated during a period in French history when a national mood of loss, doubt and depleted confidence was pervasive. There were various reasons for this, including the political decline of the Left, the shrinking of France's international status, and decades of rural depopulation. Together they created the sense that what had previously belonged to the realm of lived memory seemed to be slipping inexorably into historical time, moving further and further from the present. This was perhaps especially the case with rural France, the heartland of the agrarian ideal of *la France profonde*. Hence the effort to embrace what was being lost, to map the contours of French collective memory and national identity, in a seven-volume publication of encyclopaedic proportions – in what became, ironically,

a 'scholarly *lieu de mémoire* in its own right ... a reverentially acknowledged object of admiration' that was in itself 'worth a journey'.[9]

Lieux de mémoire are thus the evidence of this loss of lived memory,
memory as an integral part of everyday life and cultural process. In early
modernity, historical consciousness as it was then coming into being
supported a national memory, but in late (or post) modernity the relationship between history and collective memory has collapsed. Memory
for Nora has been usurped by history; their previous 'close fit' has been
broken and this, along with a new antagonism between them, has
been central to the subsequent development of modern sensibilities.[10]
Nora gives force to this argument by characterising *milieux de mémoire*
as real or genuine environments of memory, in contrast to which our
contemporary obsession with the places, objects and media in which
'memory crystallises and secretes itself' is a substitution for 'memory
entwined in the intimacy of a collective heritage'. As he puts it in the
same essay: 'If we still lived among our memories, there would be no
need to consecrate sites embodying them'.[11] Public, popular, exterior-
ised and dispersed representations of the past have replaced lived social
memory, and 'what we take to be flare-ups of memory are in fact its
final consumption in the flames of history'.[12] Less flamboyantly but no
less histrionically, Nora asserts: 'We speak so much of memory because
there is so little of it left'.[13]

We want to begin by noting some of the problems raised by this thesis.
Its own nostalgic quality is not in itself one of these, but the conceptual
framework through which this nostalgia is mobilised is most definitely
a problem. It is so because of the abrupt contrasts on which it relies. The
thesis is in this way a latter-day version of the temporal dichotomies of
classical sociology. These similarly asserted a severe, if not total rupture
between modern and premodern societies, so relegating 'community'
and 'tradition' irrevocably into the past while also lamenting certain
ills as endemic to modern society. Nora's thesis is in direct lineage with
classical sociology. There is a clear extension from the observation
that traditional forms of community have disintegrated as a result of
industrialisation, urbanisation, mass migration and the growth of communications media, to the claim that the consequence of such developments is that social memory is no longer rooted in everyday experience:
the 'less memory is experienced from within [such communities], the
greater its need for external props and tangible reminders'.[14] Likewise,
lieux de mémoire are the residual traces of lost or moribund traditions,
or evidence of traditions that have been 'invented' in compensation for
such loss and decline: '*lieux de mémoire* exist only because there are no

longer any *milieux de mémoire*, settings in which memory is a real part of everyday experience'.[15] Quite obviously the nature of 'community' and 'tradition' in the West has radically changed over the past two centuries, but the problem with such a conception of the historical transformations of modernity is its reliance on stark conceptual polarities. These pose a sense of historical dichotomies between 'then' and 'now' which are far too schematic for dealing with such contingencies as the symbolic valuing of 'community' or 'tradition' in inverse proportion to their residuality.[16] Arguments predicated on claims of historical rupture create an indisposition to attend in a more measured way to institutional structures of continuity across time, and an inability to grasp in a more subtle manner the complex interactions between continuity and change of which memory is only one, albeit critical element.

The functionalist emphasis in Nora's thesis on the purposes of memorialisation distracts attention from the tensions that may exist between the official commission of public sites of remembrance and private responses to them.[17] We do not all appreciate or value the multiform items of memorial culture in the same way or for the same reasons. Nora argues that the 'fear that everything is on the verge of disappearing, coupled with anxiety about the precise significance of the present and uncertainty about the future, invests even the humblest testimony, the most modest vestige, with the dignity of being potentially memorable.'[18] This identifies an underlying relationship that can obviously be found in modern, ever-changing societies where there is a marked tendency at times for everything that is solid to melt into air, but it suggests a social uniformity of response and investment that can empirically be gainsaid by any local ethnography of remembering practices, and it obscures the politics of evaluation and judgement that are so often implicated in decisions about *what* is memorable and worthy of preservation. The modern need to objectify collective memory in public monuments and reliquaries 'does not so much indicate the death of another, more natural memory as it does the presence of a certain hierarchy of memory activities, in which "enduring" (and properly documented) testimonials take on the greatest value and cultural prestige'.[19] This is perhaps especially the case in relation to nationalism and its need for nation-binding symbols and rituals that distract from unjust social divisions or oppressive social relations.

Nora makes a similar point in asserting that the acceleration of history generates the need to stockpile, piously and indiscriminately, 'any visible trace or material sign that might eventually testify to what we are or what we will have become'.[20] It may well be that the 'scale of collecting increases in inverse proportion to our depth perception', and obviously museums and to a large extent archives of various kinds are specifically modern responses to social change in modernity.[21] This is precisely because the pace and scope of such change creates a strong awareness of the need to conserve the past in ways that do not arise in more stable societies or historical periods, but they are not in themselves wholesale substitutions for memory or compensations for the utter loss of *milieux de mémoire*. Such milieux are not totally eradicated by modernity even if in many ways they have been altered and we have developed a more historical sensibility than was the case in the premodern past.

A further problem, no less important than those already identified, is that the negative valuation of *lieux de mémoire* proceeds from an assumption that there was an ideology-free, unmediated memory that predates them. This is an erroneous assumption. Memory has never been unmediated since it relies for its communicative realisation on forms of signification and representation, in language, discourse, images or physical objects. Consequently there is not and never has been any direct or authentic access to the past, in French peasant culture or anywhere else. Nora's *milieux de mémoire* are an abstract idealisation, a ruralist anti-modern myth bred of his fatalist rendering of the troubles and travails of being modern. By essentialising collective memory, Nora 'equates memory with authenticity, continuity, and presence and history with discontinuity, mediation, and absence'.[22] It is a classic folkloric manoeuvre.

Our position throughout this book is that all remembering involves re-presentation or reconstruction of some kind, occurring in a changed and changing present that continually modifies our relation to what is remembered, and how. There are three key features of this which need to be kept in mind. Firstly, what distinguishes processes and practices of remembering is that these reconstructions are performed in different ways, or in different modes; secondly, lived and mediated modes of remembering coexist in everyday life and so should be considered in their interaction with one another rather than one being used a priori as a template of evaluation of the other; and thirdly, it is not the case that *lieux de memoire* necessarily command only one mode of identification. As reception studies in media and communications research have demonstrated, the meanings of mediated representations are multiple, and these polysemous significations are situationally negotiated by audiences, made sense of and integrated into their ways of understanding the social world in which they live. Meanings are not imposed on audiences; meanings are made in the interpretive space between audience and text. This is equally the case with the temporal meanings taken from texts or objects of memory. Public representations of the past only become popular memory when they are actively used to remember in common among those we are in more or less continuous association with. Nora has no way of taking this process into account because of his narrowing down of modern memory towards its commemorative function and the preferred readings of memorialisation. Consequently in the long run he fails 'to view the local within the national' or 'the anchoring of memory in community'.[23] For Nora's 'memorial culture' there can only be a consensual fit between individual and collective memory at any level.

A notable feature of Nora's account of the changes to memory in modernity is its quality of assertive generalisation and unqualified extensiveness. So, for instance, he refers to modern media of communication as chief among the culprits in the construction of a present that becomes manifest as a continual series of successive moments in which their historical relation to each other is never established. We would certainly agree with this up to a point since it echoes our earlier concern that while modern communications technologies may bring us into close proximity with the past through documentary film or recorded songs, we experience it as a cultural fragment dislocated from its place in and across time. In Nora's view, this tendency is exaggerated in a memorial culture where moments from the past are commonly regurgitated but with little attempt to uncover and explain their relations across time. What are then on offer for mass consumption are 'recycled images and sounds emptied of any historical plenitude'. For Nancy Wood, this may seem convincing in general terms as a characterisation of contemporary media, but in Nora's hands it is 'too sweeping in scope and too hasty in its outright condemnation of the media's ideologising role'. She illustrates this by pointing to the ways in which certain historical events such as, in France, Vichy and the Algerian War, may return to haunt the 'era of commemoration' 'courtesy of the resources of the modern media'.[24] We need not look only to nationally troublesome events of this scale to see the truth of this point. We can illustrate it as well with reference to the more quotidian mnemonic value often found in modern media.

In her study of radio sound in everyday life, Jo Tacchi has shown how it is used to make fluid cross-temporal connections which, in line with much of what we said in the previous chapter, she refers to as nostalgic. Although such connections may be felt in sensory and affective modalities that do not necessarily require linguistic expression or rationalisation, they are experienced as a positive social practice which 'does not interfere with the present, but enhances it'.[25] They may involve memories of a deceased mother, or that haunting experience when you hear again after many years music first encountered in another period of your life. Radio seems a highly congenial medium or site via which reconnections with such memories can be made. It is crucial to Tacchi's approach that she recognises the varying ways in which nostalgia can be manifested. She draws on the distinction made by C. Nadia Seremetakis between the American notion of nostalgia, which is characterised as 'trivialising romantic sentimentality', and the Greek notion of *nostalghía*, which is understood as desire or longing with a burning pain to journey back and so expunge the painful experience of exile.[26] In the Greek notion the senses and affects associated with this intense feeling are aesthetically and culturally integrated, whereas the senses in transatlantic modernity are often separated and experienced in isolation from each other or become disembedded from lived everyday experience. To the extent that they become objects of perceptual acquisition or units of media consumption that are not assimilated into the temporal rhythms of our lives, this lack of connection is in line with Nora's argument about the modern fate of memory and the role of the media in contributing to this. The American construction of nostalgia forecloses the possibility of the past having any transformative role in the present while the Greek conception evokes a range of bodily experiences in connection with the past and allows the past a transactional role in the present.

Two points readily emerge from this example. Firstly, while historical value may have been drained from certain mass cultural products and media transmission may involve temporal disconnection rather than engagement, the media can also facilitate and foster acts of remembering which return us imaginatively to some past event or scene. It is a question of particular cases and individual merits rather than any magisterial cross-media pronouncements. The second point is that the distinction Tacchi makes between two alternative forms of nostalgia is not one that necessarily relies upon an idealisation of *milieux de mémoire* that are then used in absolute contrast to their debased historical descendants. Making such a distinction enables us to think critically about the different potential and realisable power of one form of nostalgia over another, and about the variable ways in which nostalgia facilitates or obstructs cross-temporal connections between past, present and future. That is why it is important, and why it is at odds with the rigid separation of forms of nostalgia into 'good' and 'bad' camps when this is largely based on preference, proclivity and taste. These obviously provide close-at-hand templates of discrimination and evaluation, but the position we have taken is that it is more productive to consider the degree to which nostalgia is expressive of a desire for creative reconnections between past and present, or is able to cater for such a desire, rather than to try and gauge what it says of the aesthetic values (or lack thereof) of any individual nostalgic. Such reconnections are possible when the mnemonic imagination is allowed the space in which to move backwards and forwards and so facilitate transactional movement between past and present. This is nostalgia of the kind we have argued stands in clear need of reclamation from a generalised negative evaluation of the phenomenon, and as such it is obviously quite different from 'trivialising romantic sentimentality' in its manifestation as escapist fantasy about the past.

We hope by now to have firmly established that nostalgia can move in quite alternative directions, having 'a culturally specific historicity and a wholly contingent aesthetic efficacy' as a 'vehicle for knowledge and experience'.[27] This returns us to the question of whether certain forms of nostalgia present a threat to memory in its vibrant connections with experience, or to the workings of mnemonic imagination in the ways we have identified them. For all the problems with Nora's aspersions on modern memory, they do have a redeeming value in helping us focus on this question. His thesis about the relationship of memory and historicist thinking in modernity makes us attend to the ways in which we relate to representations of popular memory, and makes us ask if there are certain integral limitations or drawbacks in how they are constructed and deployed. We might well ask, in light of this, whether there is not at least a degree of validity in Nora's claim that we have entered into a paradoxical moment in history where memory is all-pervasive, yet with no vibrant connection to lived processes of remembering in specific social groups or communities. The sense that the popular memory which is so abundantly present is ersatz because 'real' memory has vanished is in some ways not that different from the criticism that is often levelled at certain commercially produced forms of nostalgia, including indictments of their 'trivialising romantic sentimentality', but in another, more interesting sense Nora is pointing to the consequences of highly selective images of the past standing in for a fuller account and so restricting the way to developing a more complex historical understanding. Although Nancy Wood is quite right in saying that Nora's condemnations of modern communications systems and their ideological practices are far too peremptory and overgeneralised, it does at times seem that with certain media representations of the past, 'moments of history are plucked out of the flow of history, then returned to it – no longer quite alive but not yet entirely dead, like shells left on the shore when the sea of living memory has receded'.[28] The point can be taken up in reactionary ways, but it nonetheless describes what often happens when items of cultural heritage or representations of the past are presented or packaged in such a way that they are reduced to readily identifiable images only half-alive with meaning and more or less moribund in the way they connect with the past, or rather permit connections between past and present to be generated.

Retrotyping

This is a form of mnemonic representation which we want conceptually to identify as retrotyping. To recapitulate: in rapidly changing societies, nostalgia is inevitable and perhaps also necessary, both individually and collectively, yet it is generally seen in a negative light, as escape into an idealised past and a loss of faith in the future. This is not necessarily the case, which is why we spent the previous chapter outlining certain progressive uses of nostalgia or identifying progressive elements within nostalgia. According to whatever form it takes, the emphasis can fall on different aspects of nostalgia's constituent elements. This is the case when longing is singled out and seductively aroused in the effort to sell a commodity, make a media product more appealing, or render a political message more seductive. The regressive versions of nostalgia which often result from its exploitative uses are our main focus in this chapter, and we want specifically to look at retrotyping as a collective form of regressive nostalgia. The consequence of retrotyping is generally to reduce the past to a limited repertoire or set of stock images. It involves the production or reproduction of memorial objects or signs whose potential for creative memory has been radically depleted. As we shall go on to discuss, retrotyping also imposes restrictions and constraints on the mnemonic imagination. There are various ways in which it is manifested, so we shall start by discussing a couple of mundane examples which most people will have encountered.

Over the past 30 years or so, it has become fashionable in pubs and restaurants to see framed photographs of the late-nineteenth or early twentieth century hanging on walls in strategically located places. The retrotyping function of these wholly generic images is to provide an aesthetically generalised impression of pastness and so create the sense of the venue having been habitually frequented by generations of fond patrons. The photographs no longer relate to any specifically known individual, as they did in their initial uses; the passage of time has allowed these associations to be stripped away. Their previously unmistakable manner of signifying an intimate family member or close friend has been replaced by this now unrecognised person being employed merely as a vague gestural reference to some past that is symbolically evoked as the past only via style of dress or peculiarity of hairstyle. Such images are only half-alive in meaning, having been torn out of their previously lived context; any active meaning they bear is at best generic. The mood or feeling they are meant to impart is a romanticised nostalgia for a past just slipping over the far historical horizon, almost but not quite beyond recall, their grainy monochrome quality speaking of an apparently outmoded communications technology whose historical associations are with steam trains and bathing machines.

A similar retrotyping function is served by second-hand books often loosely arranged in alcoves or on shelves at the back of a padded settle. They have probably been purchased by job-lot, and are positioned in no discernible order, with manuals on woodworking skills sitting promiscuously alongside old travel books or novels by authors whose names have faded into obscurity. There is tremendous pathos in both these examples. This generally goes unacknowledged when what prevails is their function as background décor. As such they provide a retrotypical air of old-fashioned domesticity, of home life before the days of television or even radio, a cosy and comforting ambience that reassures because of their collective association with past family togetherness and an autodidactic attempt to 'improve the mind'. As mnemonic inscriptions or cultural repositories they are meaningless; empty shells left on the shoreline of a receded time. Generically old photo-images and old books in these contexts are forms of designer pastness, and retrotyping always operates through such easily identifiable formulas for signifying pastness. These all-too-ready formulas are then intended to work closely with a predictable emotional register that puts customers at their ease and helps them feel relaxed and in the right frame of mind for enjoying their time while 'eating out' or having a convivial drink with friends.

Such topographically engineered forms of nostalgia are akin to kitsch in providing 'vicarious experience and fake sensations' of the past, for the kitsch past is not personally remembered, it has no identifiable points of reference, it no longer connects to any former period of anyone's life, it registers only the weakest sense of loss at what time has erased, and the sensations of pastness it offers are unconnected to any actual past.[29] Of course these nostalgic forms do not *necessarily* operate in this way. Publicly displayed photographs may have a local reference, may refer specifically to a village or town, with a particular example perhaps showing the public house in which it hangs as it stood in a former period, with people gathered outside in their best clothes for some festive occasion. They may then serve to foster a sense of local belonging or of connectedness within a place-community across the vicissitudes of time.

Books are another matter. The book is of course one of the earliest forms of prosthetic memory, for it enables us to record and remember things that we would not necessarily be able to do ourselves, and transmit these across the generations, so we can for example read of someone's upbringing in 1930s Cairo or experience as a child labourer in the 1840s Potteries.[30] Within your own lifetime the books on your shelves remind you of when you read them, so that when you take them down again they bring back not only what you took from them but also the period in your own life when you first traversed their pages. That kind of autobiographical connection is utterly severed when books become merely a pleasant backdrop to the business of eating and drinking, their associations even in popular memory being only of the most attenuated kind. When it is just their outer spines that signify, the words of which they are composed have stopped living, and mnemonically they work only as retrotyping.

The retrotyping that results from consumerist packaging of the past may, like kitsch, be intended in all seriousness, or advanced as a self-conscious, ironic aesthetic, as for example in the use of reproduced posters from wartime periods announcing 'Your Country Needs You' or warning that 'Careless Talk Costs Lives'. But whereas the kitsch of one period may acquire a different aesthetic value as time passes, in a creative recoding of its historical reference, retrotyping operates by attempting to fix the historical reference so that it yields only its prepackaged sentiment, and so restricts subsequent playful adaptation. The latent message is that this sentiment is sufficient; we need take nothing more from it. In this sense retrotyping is a mode of stereotyping the past in that it has a marked tendency to homogenise the traits of people in particular periods, as for example in depicting middle-class Victorians as repressed prudes, or to heavily stylise the social experience of those periods, so that working-class life in Victorian London inevitably becomes depicted in stock Dickensian manner. Where there is lack of conformity to these traits or experiences, there is then a strong pull to orient description and assessment around the essentialist definition.

Retrotyping is a one-way form of projection backwards from a contemporary perspective. It builds walls rather than bridges between past and present because it does not want to encourage interchange between them; it only wants to project its predetermined view of the past on the walls it erects. Retrotyping is also similar to stereotyping in providing ready-made short-cuts, clichéd signs of generality that inhibit movement from common references to a historical period or past social group to the effort of relating to particular people and the attempt to understand how, while individual in various ways, they were conditioned by their historical time and circumstance. It is a form of representation counterposed to fluidity, variation and ambivalence. As with stereotyping, retrotyping is, often enough, highly selective, highly stylised, highly prescriptive, yet while stereotyping can work at an interpersonal level as well as a mass mediated level, retrotyping is more of a problem for popular memory than for individual remembering.

This is easily discernible in the retrotypical transfer of a vehicle of individual or family remembering into the realm of popular memory. The merely generic sense of pastness that results is of the same order of representation as when images or sounds from the past are used as a commodity aesthetic. We have illustrated this with the consumerist reuse of old photographs, and we want to continue with this particular form of visual communication not only because it has long been a chief carrier of memory in local and small group contexts, but also because it illustrates how retrotyping works on a macro-social, even global scale. This happens largely through a small number of multinational agencies which buy up, store and sell the reproduction rights of a vast number of photographic images. These are taken up and reused in advertising, marketing, multimedia and other realms of consumer culture. Whether clients want pictures of domestic harmony or commercial amity, the trade is usually in formulaic images which draw on and help reproduce social and cultural stereotypes. To some extent this tendency has been weakened by digital storage, since this can cater more easily to niche-marketing, but the overall context is still that of a globalised visual content industry with an annual turnover of $1–2 billion worldwide.[31] As Paul Frosh has shown in his study of this industry, stock photography is an increasingly powerful force in contemporary visual culture; it is no longer simply the cheap alternative to assignment photography. The images are stock in two senses: they are kept 'in stock' according to a standardised system of photographic practices and then sold on as cultural commodities; and they are 'stock' in possessing the predominant quality of being 'instantly recognisable iconographic combinations which rely upon, and reinforce, "clichéd" visual motifs and stereotypes that are drawn from a far broader cultural archive or image-repertoire'.[32]

Stock photographic images directly foster nostalgic retrotyping, and Frosh illustrates this with reference to certain classic black-and-white photographs of kissing couples from the 1940s and 1950s which were recycled in the 1980s 'on anything from posters to jigsaw puzzles'. Two examples he mentions are Eisenstadt's kissing sailor and young woman in New York at the end of the Second World War (1945) and Doisneau's lovers outside the Hôtel de Ville (1950). The history of the couples or the history of which they were a part – in the former case 'the most self-destructive conflagration produced by modernity' – are irrelevant except in terms of the standardised 'period feeling' in which they are frozen; their embraces are no longer perceived as evidence of 'an impulse springing from the flux of their environment and the strength of their feelings'. Romantic stock photographs, whether playful or meditative in manner, invite you to 'become who you are' within the embrace of consumer culture:

> [T]hey materialise normative social hierarchies of sex, sexuality, race and class, mobilising these same hierarchies as aspirational values in the service of commodity consumption, and do so under cover of the ultimate principle of *non-instrumentality*: romance as the free play (in the case of playful images), or authentic self-disclosure (meditative images), of unfettered individuals.[33]

Stock nostalgia works through citation and repetition which then foreclose mnemonic imagining by constraining any interactive movement between past and present, inviting instead only the passing glance. Nostalgic retrotyping channels response into an immediate act of consumption, and the effect of this is to thwart the mnemonic imagination in its effort to use the past in temporary disengagement from the present, as a source of critical reflection on current historical conditions. Contrary to the examples we considered in the previous chapter, retrotyping is a case that clearly shows how 'nostalgia too easily mates with banality, functioning not through stimulation, but by covering up the pain of loss in order to give a specific form of homesickness and to make homecoming available on request'.[34] Retrotyping fosters the illusion of feeling at home in a world that is constantly changing.

Retrotyping by bread alone

Covering up the pain of loss is a characteristic feature of nostalgic retrotyping. The appeal is instead to a deeper sense of pleasure in what is claimed to endure, but this immediately becomes ironic when advertising is involved. It is ironic because, where an acute sense of loss is endemic to capitalist modernity because of its unsentimental insistence on continual transformation and development, advertising, one of the key lubricants of consumerism, finds ways to exploit this by sentimentally numbing the pain of loss, not least through counter-assertions of durability and reliability. The retrotypical appeal is then entirely backwards and only for the sake of being linked to acts of consumption. Well-known examples of this in Britain are the series of advertising campaigns conducted by the bread manufacturer Hovis (Premier Foods). The early 1970s television ads made by Ridley Scott, the famous film director, are particularly renowned, especially the 'Boy on Bike' sequence which featured Gold Hill in Shaftesbury, Dorset. The ad shows a young lad pushing his bike, its wicker basket laden with loaves of bread, up this steep cobbled hill with its quaint cottages huddled on either side of the street. The background music chosen for this, the *largo* from Dvořák's Symphony No 9, rearranged for brass, enhances the old-time atmosphere and their combined effect is then capped as the boy reaches his last place of delivery at the top of the hill and says, in fondly wistful recollection: ' 'Twas like taking bread to the top of the world'. This has been voted Britain's favourite ad of all time.[35] The predominant sense of its resolutely backward reference is that symbolically 'the top of the world' is to be found in the bucolic depths of the English past, in a more stable and secure time where all the retrotyping markers are in place: bicycle, boyhood, bread, happily combined with careless exercise, caring elders, carefree times.

Twenty years later, in 1973, a series of print ads for Hovis bread 'purveyed nostalgia through sepia-coloured images and old-fashioned, colloquial language' where the conversationally familiar narration was always 'from the point of view of an old(er) person, looking back to his or her youth'.[36] The title and the accompanying text to the right hand side of the picture is in rather antiquated mock-handwriting supposedly done with a fountain pen. The style deliberately mimics homemade photograph albums of the early twentieth century and plays upon the pleasure of looking back through such albums to pictures of one's youth. In one example, entitled 'An Honest Crust', a man remembers the red poppies in the wheatfields 'from those harvests before the war'; the laborious process of weeding them out was relieved by breaking for dinner, when Freda, the farmer's daughter, brought tea round in a pail.

> She'd just dip in a mug and pass it to us and we'd give her bunches of poppies in return.

> Dinner was cheese and maybe a pickled onion, with doorsteps of
> fresh farmhouse bread. I'll always love the taste of crusty wholemeal.
> Speaking of which, have you tried Hovis's Wholemeal with kibbled
> malted wheat?
> There's no mistaking that glorious taste of harvest, washed down
> with Freda's thick, hot, sweet tea.
> Freda's tea? Well yes. You see, I married her.

Wholesome work, wholemeal bread: the combination is of goodness
in food and goodness in those pre-mechanical days before the war, red
poppy days when you laboured outdoors in the sunshine and ate with
a hearty appetite in the fresh air. Not only that – the nostalgic contriv-
ances of the ad are doubled by the happily predictable twist at the end,
which turns the narrative into a love-story, and blends the lifelong mar-
ital fidelity of the couple with the biblical associations of honest labour
and honest bread. These are all encapsulated in the title of the ad. The
promotion of Hovis's Wholemeal is incidentally slipped into the mono-
logue, almost as an aside, and yet the bread acts as a synecdoche for the
golden past and the enduring marriage to which it led, one probably by
now celebrated in a golden wedding anniversary. The golden past which
Freda's husband celebrates is also at one with an England embalmed in
the myth of Old England where tranquility and virtue reign, larks are
always ascending and lilacs wait to be gathered in the spring.

   Another example from the same period, called 'Best in Show', tells
of how a man's mother baked her heart out in preparation for the village fete, using malted brown flour 'from a recipe discovered by monks
in the days when people knew what was good for them'. Her sample
loaf went into the competition for 'best in show' where it was pitted
against Tina Dade's chrysanthemums, old Maurice Mallyon's marrow
and Farmer Diplock's gander.

> Most sporting, they were. Tina and Farmer Diplock both asked for
> the recipe. Maurice said he'd never tasted bread like it.
> No more did I for years afterwards, until one day I picked up a loaf
> of Granary from Hovis, baked with special flour same as my mum's.
> Just one wonderful malty bite and once again I heard the uncon-
> trollable excitement in the judge's voice.
> 'Aye', he said, 'this'll do'.

The ad again associates the goodness of the product with a rosy rus-
ticity summed up in the peculiar country surnames and the dour

understatement of 'this'll do' when what is being referred to was bread that tasted like no other, bread which can, in one wonderful bite, bring back the judge's verdict on his mum's baking, except of course that this is now a bite from a loaf of Hovis's Granary. The two products, the home-made and the factory-manufactured, are almost unnoticeably yoked together across time in this sub-Proustian moment, and this is then clinched in the strapline that follows all these short narratives: 'As good today as it's always been'. So times are turbulent and ever-changing, people sink into debt or struggle through divorce, motorways are built across otherwise open countryside, fast-food chains open for people who don't know what is good for them, yet you can always rely on bread as good as the kind mum made that triumphed in the village fete over flowers, vegetables and livestock. 'And by extension, Hovis bread is also the "best in show"'.[37] The ad thus borrows retrotypically on the sense of an idyllic rural past of home baking, cottage husbandry, family solidarity and community values.

The original Hovis wheatgerm loaf was developed in 1886 by Richard 'Stoney' Smith. In 2008, Hovis commissioned a television advert to celebrate their product's longevity. The ad is 122 seconds long, with one second for each year of the product's lifetime simultaneously covering 122 years of political history in Britain. It is called 'Go On, Lad' and it starts with a baker saying this to the Hovis boy as he picks up the bread from the baker's shop in 1886, and then turns to start time-travelling across the succeeding years to the present. Through his eyes we retrotypically sample key moments in the nation's twentieth-century story: scenes of confrontation involving militant suffragettes at one end of the century and militant striking miners at the other; soldiers marching off to the trenches in World War One, houses bombed out in World War Two; a street party in celebration of the Queen's Coronation, a 1960s car passing by with flags and scarves streaming patriotically from the open windows in celebration of England's only World Cup victory. Throughout these scenes we see retrotypical markers such as a Bakelite radio from which a snatch of Churchill's famous rallying wartime speech is heard, a horse and cart in a cobbled street, posters telling of the sinking of the Titantic. At the end of the film the Hovis boy arrives home in contemporary-looking clothes and sits at the kitchen table with his loaf, and we hear his mum ask from another room: 'Is that you home, love?' The same strapline is then seen on the screen: 'As good today as it's ever been'. Enduring in value, the dependable Hovis loaf transcends all the years of suffering and strife, and the Hovis lad moves through them all to show just how dependable the product can be in helping raise healthy children who run errands for their mother and smile quietly to themselves at the end.

The implication of this epic ad is not only that bread acts as a retro-type of care, affection, nurture, community and a healthy lifestyle, but also that consumer culture is far more reliable and trustworthy than all that happens in the continual upheavals of social and political life. Consumerism is equated with civic culture; the two merge in unchallenged harmony. In addition, as a result of the process of retrotyping which samples historical details as if through an interest in costume or colloquial speech rather than in pursuit of political meanings, the scenes involving bitter disputes have somehow lost their bitterness, becoming instead a cause for a wry smile or a touch of wit, as for example when the Hovis boy stands centre-screen in between opposed ranks of miners and police in the 1984/5 Miners' Strike. A northern-sounding miner asks jocularly: 'Eh lad, in't it past yer bedtime?' The historical significance of the miners' struggle is drained away, as it is with the marching suffragettes. Indeed, history itself is transformed into token signifiers of change which confirm the retrotypical continuities which somehow ensure that we all arrive safely home and, in the end, are able to smile quietly to ourselves at what endures and helps unify this old country.

The 2008 Hovis commercial has been much admired and considered as exemplary of creative advertising, yet the ways in which it cleverly marshals its combinations of images and sounds only strengthens the effectiveness of its retrotyping. It appears to acknowledge moments of conflict and struggle but it strips them of the suffering they entailed and, in its seamless move from one dramatic scene to another, makes them historically equivalent to moments of celebration and expressions of community spirit. The level of equivalence becomes that of nostalgic pleasure, nostalgia without the pain. This is a direct result of retrotyping's concealment of the pain of loss in nostalgia, and its creation of an illusory sense of the good things in life continuing despite the ever-rolling stream of disruption and transformation in modern life. The effect of retrotyping and the regressive nostalgia of which it is a key device is to make it more difficult to reconnect with the past or to use the past to think critically about all that has changed and is changing.

Memory boom or memory bust?

Retrotyping deals in selective parts, never in wholes; it offers only disconnected fragments of the past. These are repackaged for their immediate short-term consumption, having been plundered from whatever database or archival source seemed handy, and how they are interconnected in the historical process, or how we may draw on the past to expand our historical awareness, are issues of no interest as they do not relate to the values or principles of the market. Retrotyping plays on our longings while ignoring the sense of loss and lack that informs nostalgic longing when it becomes a source of critical reflection in the present. The consumerist forms of nostalgia which are the consequence of this exacerbate the experience in modernity of living life in fragments. The acceleration of social and environmental change combined with the problems of semiotic and informational overload in media-saturated cultures are among the contributory factors leading to this fragmentation of experience, and the difficulties of then assimilating experience into an ongoing life-narrative in the longer term. This can create the sense of contemporary life floating free from the past, becoming unmoored and temporally adrift. There is nothing inevitable about this and it can be countered in various ways, but retrotyping always adds to these difficulties because the atemporal fragments that are its inflated currency do not correspond to lived first-hand experience or to shared social memory. As the cultural historian Peter Fritzsche has put it, the 'interiorised voice and vernacular location of nostalgia has been made nearly obsolescent by the mass media's ability to package and repackage the past in a way that facilitates its omnipresence but diminishes its pertinence to particular lives'.[38]

We may quibble with Fritzsche's claim of near-obsolescence – indeed, the whole of our previous chapter has demonstrated that this is not yet the case, despite the stern admonitions of elitist cultural critics – and we may also want to argue that the mass media cannot be subject to such a sweeping generalised reference that would yoke *YouTube* together with *The Antiques Roadshow*, or put the BBC's *The Last Tommy* on a par with the iconic image of Marilyn Monroe holding her skirt down while standing over an air-vent.[39] That is why we are trying to be more specific in identifying the problem as one that is not to do with the media *tout court*, but with a recurrent tendency in media culture to reductive retrotyping. It is nonetheless the case that retrotyping's stimulation of consumerist forms of nostalgia make it less likely or less tenable that the critical voices of vernacular nostalgia will be heard, at least in any amplified media form. This undoubtedly baffles any contestatory power they may garner, and it is because of this that we need them more than ever in order to help us remember and engage with the otherness of the past, and so counter retrotyping's inherent tendency to make the foreign country of the past seem entirely compatible with the familiar homeland of the present. This regression to the present is reinforced by the fragmentary structure of so much media scheduling, as we jump from watching news bulletins through soap operas to comedy shows on television, or read a newspaper's hotchpotch of stories and features, letters and obituaries. These provide an abundance of at-hand information that is difficult to distil into longer-term knowledge. Added to this is the habitual eschewal of complexity, so that to a great extent an 'argument that cannot be summed-up in a single sentence has no media value'.[40] Within this jigsaw puzzle of representations whose scattered pieces rarely fit together are a broad range of references to the past, but all too often they work in a retrotypical way because correspondences between them are left hanging and coordinations across them are neglected in the market-driven compulsion to move on to the next item of consumption.

Media retrotyping is a major contributor to the 'fragmentation and privatisation of social memory processes', so that while we may note continuous references to the past in image and information disseminated on a broad scale, in Geoffrey Cubitt's summary these 'relentlessly blur the distinctions between different phases of past experience, between past and present, between reality and simulation, between knowledge and entertainment, and between what is experienced personally and what is experienced vicariously, on which the individual's participation in a stable formation of social memory depends'.[41] Blurring, fragmentation, loss of coherence, jigsaw pieces failing to come together: consumerist retrotyping contributes to all these features of media representations of the past. The question that follows from this is whether these obstacles to mnemonic imagination necessarily result in social amnesia.[42] This question takes us back to Nora's thesis that we attend so much to memory because it is so much diminished. Increasingly, other critics and scholars have also made the claim that we are fast losing the ability to develop and sustain collective memory in any significant way. Eric Hobsbawm, for example, has written that young people now 'grow up in a sort of permanent present lacking any organic relation to the public past of the times they live in'.[43] For Fredric Jameson, we have lost all sense of the transactional value of the past in the present because we no longer have any sense of historical location and are locked into an endless succession of depthless presents.[44] Both these views lend support to Nora's argument about the emergence of a memorial culture and the reasons underlying it, while also endorsing Adrienne Rich's claim that 'nostalgia is only amnesia turned around'.[45]

That of course is a nice quip, but it can hardly help explain the paradoxical relationship between cultural retrotyping and its undermining of the possibilities of critical nostalgia gaining purchase on the one hand, and the huge contemporary preoccupation with memory on the other.

There are various different strands that would need to be brought together to develop such an explanation, as for example the intensely felt need to regain and reassess our pasts in their localised dimensions in reaction to the forces of globalisation. But it is the paradox that most needs explaining, and Paul Connerton does this in relation to the structures of time which undergird the contemporary political economy, pointing specifically to the temporalities of consumption, careers, information production, and the production of modern spaces. It is these together which lead to the post-mnemonic culture he claims we are living in, that is characteristic of a modernity which systematically forgets.[46] Consumerist retrotyping reinforces these structures of time and contributes to this forgetting even as it seems to be remembering. It does so because the past is not being attended to as a source of guidance in the present, claimed through cultural entitlement or inheritance, but rather as a decontextualised source of material that can be sampled at will in order to support any set of interests or purposes in the present. This feeds into memorial culture in its paradoxical relationship with an amnesiac culture because the public fear of memory loss 'is awkwardly expressed in the taste for the fashions of earlier times, and shamelessly exploited by the nostalgia-merchants', so that 'memory has thus become a best-seller in a consumer society'.[47] The past is, in other words, a good sales pitch. Patrick Hutton elaborates on this handsomely:

> Collective memories in societies of late capitalism are enthralled in the process of memorialising, but often in the guise of meretricious advertising. We may not perceive the connection readily. But memorialising has come to be intertwined with a beguiling publicity that enhances the appeal of the commodities of a consumer society. We have learned to consume memories much as we do commercial goods. As we look back on the past from the perspective of late modernity, once-nurturing nostalgia has been transformed by the sirens of Madison Avenue into the fluff of newly minted kitsch.[48]

Inasmuch as there is then a divergence between first- and second-hand experience, consumer culture exacerbates this and increases the difficulties of integrating them with each other, particularly where the first is remembered as the existential fabric of a life-narrative and narrative identity, and the second is reconstructed as part of the alluring aesthetic gloss of commodities for sale in the marketplace. The irony of nostalgic retrotyping in this is that it opens up a distance in the present from the people, scenes or events which are represented or which are the object of reconstruction.

Andreas Huyssen has observed that the critique of cultural amnesia is invariably directed to the media as well as to consumerism more generally, while it is the media in all their variety which make memory so abundantly available to us. This may be another aspect of the paradox we are discussing, but as we have hinted before in this chapter, it is too convenient to blame the media in any general sense, and as Huyssen points out, there must be something else at stake 'that produces the desire for the past in the first place and that makes us respond so favourably to the memory markets'. The way Huyssen attempts to explain what is at stake connects back to the claim he makes in *Twilight Memories* for a gradual shift in the conception and organisation of temporality in late modernity. This closely relates to one of our major concerns in this book. It is different to that put forward by Connerton, but complementary to it. The claim made by Huyssen is that the faith in historical progress which caused the divergence between experience and expectation in modernity has now declined, if not broken down. The gist of this claim is that where previously investment in the past declined in inverse proportion to investment in the future, this has now been reversed. Hence the memory boom, as he has felicitously described it.[49] Earlier forms of critical nostalgia may be understood as responses to the weight of faith placed in the future as the only dynamic realm of time to which our energies in modernity should be devoted, but the ideology of progress towards an ever-improving future no longer carries the force it did previously, and in Huyssen's view this means not only that we are experiencing a profound sense of pessimism and doubt about the possibility of human or civilisational advance in the early twenty-first century, but also that we are 'living through a transformation of the modern structure of temporality itself'. To this he adds: 'The more we live with new technologies of communication and information cyber-space, the more our sense of temporality will be affected'. Huyssen adduces various unfortunate causes of this, but he does not simply adopt a position of cultural pessimism in reaction to them. Significantly, he sees the memory boom as potentially a healthy way of responding to this profound shift of temporality. It is, for him, 'an expression of the basic human need to live in extended structures of temporality, however they may be organised'. In other words, the intense surge of interest in memory over the past 30 to 40 years derives from the same impulse that we have identified with critical forms of nostalgia. Both are in close alliance in that they represent the need for temporal moorings and amount to a struggle against temporal dissolution, particularly 'in a world of puzzling and often threatening heterogeneity, non-synchronicity, and information overload'.[50] It may well be that the kind of consensual collective memory for which Nora is nostalgic cannot now be recreated, but we nevertheless attempt to counteract the fear of forgetting and disappearance 'with survival strategies of public and private memorialisation'. Even if we know that such strategies 'may in the end themselves be transitory and incomplete', we still need 'to anchor ourselves in a world characterised by an increasing instability of time and the fracturing of lived space'. In short, the 'faster we are pushed into a global future that does not inspire confidence, the stronger we feel the desire to slow down, the more we turn to memory for comfort'.[51] Nostalgic retrotyping provides that comfort, but depletes the strengths of mnemonic imagining in its engagements with historical process and historical difference.

Where does all this leave us? The theses and arguments we have sampled in this chapter are all interesting vehicles to travel in for a while, particularly as they take us between unqualified pessimism at our ability to retain and learn from the past (the memory bust claim) and qualified optimism that the contemporary fascination with memory may have some redemptive force in the face of regressive nostalgia (the memory boom claim). The two claims are clearly related and the paradoxical qualities of the relationship between tendencies to cultural forgetting and obsessions with cultural remembering do need to be carefully considered. Here we find Huyssen a good deal more persuasive than Nora or Jameson, and more compatible with our own pattern of argumentation about creative memory and the mnemonic imagination. Ultimately, though, there is something unsatisfactory about all these grandstanding historical theories of memory, and that is their tendentious nature, and their use at times of evidence that conveniently suits their case. The arguments they advance are, in the main, speculative. They attempt to make historical pronouncements about a historical time in which we're still immersed, a perilous exercise at best. It would help considerably if their ideas and claims were tested empirically, so that, for example, with media representations of the past which are subject to negative critique, for whatever reason, this is followed through with an audience study to see what people belonging to different social groups and categories make of what they consume, and how they go about relating their media consumption to their social experience. We hold our own hands up here, for this stricture equally applies to our discussion in this chapter of consumerist retrotyping and the obstacles it creates to mnemonic imagining. Symbolic constructions cannot be conceived outside of social relations, and media representations of the past are part of a communicative process between producers and consumers that is conditioned by those relations. Retrotyping seems to us reductive in the way it attempts to close down the meanings made of its representations and to obstruct the movement of the mnemonic imagination between the constituent elements of nostalgic experience. This is what we have argued, particularly in relation to certain characteristics of commodity aesthetics, but we cannot be certain of our analytical understanding of retrotyping without investigating further into how it operates not only in the text but also in the interpretive space between producers and consumers, text and audience.[52] As Alon Confino and Peter Fritzsche have stated, when images of the past are analysed as if they are 'circulating in an autonomous sphere of representations', the emphasis 'is on how memory represents social relations, but not how memory shapes them'.[53] This is a current major weakness of memory studies, and we need to find ways of breaking out from the tendency to 'read off' from a text or produce 'cultural' readings without relating them to studies of media reception and ethnographies of cultural process and practice outside of the sphere of representations.

6
Creative Memory and Painful Pasts

Thickets of thorns

The major preoccupation of this book has been with how memory and imagination operate in conjunction with each other in a necessary alliance that helps us develop our understanding of temporal processes and maintain the past as a dynamic presence within an ever-changing present. We have introduced the concept of mnemonic imagination in order to show this alliance in operation both in personal life and in public culture. The concept encompasses the fertile ways in which memory and the imagination are interactive, working on each other in various manifestations. They require each other in moving beyond their own limits as we think of the patterns of change and continuity in our sense of ourselves over time, and the diverse ways in which the past is represented and used as a resource in all aspects of cultural life. The mnemonic imagination is vital for the many different forms of everyday creativity that help to give our lives structure and purpose, meaning and value. Some of these are developed further and receive more formal recognition as artistic or cultural attainments, in genres that run the gamut of artistic expression from popular song to musical theatre, from the novel to installation art, and from documentary film to folk museums; but the mnemonic imagination operates across otherwise quite distinct cultural forms and fields, and is not circumscribed by any particular realm that, for whatever reason, may be hierarchically elevated above others. Its value and significance are not specialised in that way. The mnemonic imagination is integral to all our thinking about past, present and future, and the manifold ways in which they are interrelated across first- and second-hand forms of experience.

This is to speak in a somewhat idealistic manner. That is why, in the last chapter, we dwelt at length on one particular way in which the mnemonic imagination can be thwarted or stunted, for consumerist ret-rotyping acts to ensure our thinking of past, present and future works in unrelated ways, restricting movement between them and imparting only a regressive value to nostalgic experience. In this chapter we deal with other ways in which the mnemonic imagination may be closed out or allowed little space in which to flourish. There may be areas or aspects of past experience which remain a source of pain and disturbance in the present, certain memories which we flinch from because of their hurtful or injurious associations; there may indeed be particular times in the past that are denied to conscious forms of recall even though they con-tinue to haunt us and exert a debilitating influence over us. In focusing here on painful pasts, we want to explore at least some of the ways in which they cast a baneful shadow across the present and throw up a thicket of thorns around the mnemonic imagination. Our intention is to give fuller recognition of the fact that the mnemonic imagination is not a free agent, always able to rove at will across the landscape of the past and make of its characteristic structures and topographical features entirely what seems to be appropriate within the present. That is never the case, since it is bound in varying degrees by what is given from the past as well as what is needed in the present. There are in addition to these constraints certain damages that may have been inflicted on the relationship of memory and sense of selfhood, particular cataclysms in the past that continue to reverberate in the present, and tie down or block access to the mnemonic imagination in a far more constrictive manner. Painful pasts can resist creative remembering, and it is this resistance we want to explore here.

Such pasts are not all of a piece in the ways they restrict the opera-tions of the mnemonic imagination. A central concern in our explo-ration of them is the need to make important qualifications in the severity of their influence over the present, and the degree of impact they have on the scope of the mnemonic imagination in its uses of the resources memory bequeaths to us. Though it may seem a rather obvi-ous point, painful pasts are painful in different ways and with different outcomes. We feel it important to make this point because it seems often to be overlooked when such pasts are discussed with reference to inflated terms or exaggerated claims. We pay considerable attention in the chapter to painful pasts which are in some sense knowable and assimilable into life-narratives, and those which are not, and so can-not become part of the story we tell of ourselves and our identities as individuals. We are also concerned with how painful pasts that are specifically individual and those which have presence and influence far more extensively in collective memory need also to be subject to more scrupulous distinction. As we shall see, it is perilously easy, and thus very common, for them to be cavalierly run together in ways which damage our understanding of them. This is in various ways not only conceptually slipshod but ethically irresponsible as well.

Our final chapter moves beyond these concerns to a broader discussion of how we are able to come to terms with painful pasts and assimilate them more fully into the present and future. We examine the ways in which mnemonic imagining is able to develop a transactional relationship across the temporal tenses and give a more full-blooded identity to the presence of the past when certain painful areas of remembering have to be negotiated. We hope to show how the value of the concept of the mnemonic imagination extends to these struggles in overcoming and consciously engaging with those sources of pain that continue to disturb us as we move through our lives. The pivotal issue here is how, despite this continuing disturbance, memory can become a creative resource once again, so reducing if not actually annulling the pain of the past, and enabling us to turn towards the future in a less daunted fashion. Our expansion into this broader discussion follows the shift we have taken between the first and second parts of the book where we have gradually turned from thinking about individual remembering to more collective forms of memory and the attendant contexts that inform and sustain the processes and practices of remembering in everyday life. Painful pasts and their influence on everyday remembering are not confined to those who have directly experienced them. In our relations with each other, the pasts of certain individuals may have secondary consequences for other individuals, often in an intergenerational passage between those who are older and those who are younger and have to negotiate their own formation as individuals in the shadow of their elders' pasts. Painful memory can be inherited, and we try to give at least some outline of what this involves.

The emphasis is thus on second-hand experience and how memory relates to what has been called postmemory or memory that is transferred in various ways from one subject to another across different historical locations. We focus first of all on second-hand experience that is situated, becoming central to memory and identity in concrete forms in different families and communities. We then turn our focus to second-hand experience of painful pasts that is mediated to us, as for example in photography or film, the novel or historical account. It is here we return, finally, to the issues of ethics and the ethical relations involved in our engagement with the painful pasts of other people and other groups. This is not only a matter of appropriate response, though that is an important aspect. It is also a question of what is ethically entailed in our relations with the painful pasts of others, and what role the mnemonic imagination can be said to play in them.

Trauma, collectivities and communicative limits

Throughout this book we have argued that the distinctively modern project of thinking about one's life in autobiographical terms involves, over the course of time, not only revisiting past experience and retuning its meanings within a changed present, but also imaginatively connecting and reconnecting the different stages and directions of past experience into a more or less coherent narrative structure. The autobiographical project presupposes the ability to trace and weave our memories together into a life-narrative, so turning lived experience into the assimilated experience that is vital to the patterned coherence across time we seek to fashion.

This process is not always possible. Certain events or encounters within lived experience may prevent it in some way, blocking access to memories of them or hiding the memories away so they are not available for conscious retrieval. A modern term for designating such problems is 'trauma'. What it denotes is a condition of individual psychic damage of such severity that the person who suffers from it is unable to make experience storyable and knowable. Trauma entails a failure of the autobiographical project because it produces experience that is not amenable to assimilation. It is an engagement with the past in the absence of the mnemonic imagination. The self of the traumatised victim cannot remember itself to itself, and cannot imagine itself whole.

Various forms of traumatic experience have arisen as a source of suffering in the modern period. 'Shell-shock' is a notorious example. This is a response to the horror of wartime experience. It was first described as such by the British psychiatrist Charles Myers in 1915, and is now indelibly associated with the psychological stress and pain caused by what was endured by men fighting in the trenches of the First World War.[1] It may indeed have involved the experience of being near to, or seeing comrades blown apart by an exploding shell, but the term was used generically and so covered subsequent response to other forms of military experience, such as bayoneting another man or hearing a fatally wounded man calling repeatedly for his mother. Experiences of this kind may of course have been cumulative, rather than relating to a single incident, but their traumatised victims were certainly widespread: in late 1916 it was claimed that up to 40 per cent of the casualties from heavy fighting zones were cases of shell-shock.[2] They led not only to mental disturbance, but could also cause physical paralysis, as for example in making a man stammer uncontrollably or be struck mute; become unable to walk or use his hand; or exhibit involuntary spasmodic movements where the traumatic experience seemed to act like a suddenly uncoiled spring inside someone's body.[3] Such examples show how severe the damage to mind and body could be, yet trauma is a difficult condition to understand because it involves both an inability to forget, with an uncontrollable past making terrifying intrusions into the present, and an inability to assimilate the past within a broad duration across time because what cannot be realised as such, acts as it were in utter scorn of the victim's present and future needs. Trauma embraces both radical cross-temporal discontinuity, and radical temporal continuity heedless of the biographical continuousness of change.

In this sense, Jay Winter captures the trauma of shell-shock well in calling it a severance of the links between an individual's memory and identity, so compromising his integrity 'because of what he has felt and seen and what he continues to feel and see', whether through nightmares, sudden flashbacks or 'unwitting reenactments' that haunt the victim because they cannot 'be interpolated in a story of before and after'.[4] He adds to this that shell-shock in the First World War reconfigured both popular and medical notions about memory because it called into question the ways in which memory was conventionally understood. In writing of the disruptions to identity in cases of war neurosis which he encountered in the South Pacific during the Second World War, Erik Erickson likewise saw these as involving a loss of 'the ability to experience oneself as something that has continuity and sameness, and act accordingly'. The men involved 'knew who they were; they had a personal identity', but 'it was as if, subjectively, their lives no longer hung together – and never would again'.[5] So while acknowledging that the trauma could become manifest in various ways, what now seems clear is that overcoming the difficulties of assimilation of front-line experiences is dependent on the mnemonic imagination being able to rebuild the links between memory and identity, to realign the 'before and after' elements of a life-story with what has so drastically intervened between them. Though aspects of it appear to remain beyond any articulation, the ability of many men to reorient themselves to these elements seems to have been crucial in coming to terms with their wartime experience and in some sense moving beyond it.[6] Even so, this was not straightforward, with remembering often requiring some special tack or manoeuvre, such as dwelling on points of ironic detail or action.[7] Refusing to speak of the war while unwillingly remembering it was perhaps the most general response among veterans in the aftermath of the First World War, while for those who did give expression to what they recalled, there was always the fear 'that as soon as a memory forms it immediately takes on the wrong light, mannered, sentimental as war and youth always are, becomes a piece of narrative written in the style of the time, which can't tell us how things really were but only how we thought we saw them, thought we said them'.[8]

Just as there were different causes and different symptoms of shell-shock, so there were disagreements about how to distinguish between genuine psychological injury and malingering, and with those who were diagnosed as genuine victims, about how to treat them. Should, for example, emphasis be placed on 'reliving' the originating experience so as to produce an appropriate emotional abreaction, or on consciously integrating that experience into longer-term memory so that a traumatised veteran could achieve a 'resynthesis of the forgotten memory ... overcome his dissociated, fractured state and accede to a coherent narrative of his past life'?[9] Despite the varying responses among physicians and psychiatrists to shell-shock, in more general cases of traumatic dissociations or amnesia it can be argued that there is still a valid distinction to be drawn between neurotic, uncontrollable repetition of the past and conscious assimilation of the past into a temporally ordered narrative of its unfolding. In Judith Herman's concise summary, the 'goal of recounting the trauma story is integration, not exorcism'.[10] It is only subsequent to this that the mnemonic imagination can engage in open dialogue between past and present, and draw effectively on what is needed from the past within the present. This is of course dependent on therapeutically finding a way of bringing into the light of imaginatively holistic memory the initiating horrific situation. It is a hazardous process, and one that carries various moral and ethical implications, but without it the severed links between memory and narrative identity cannot be reconnected, and agentic self-representation remains impossible.

It is because remembered experience is constitutive of our successive selves as these inform our sense of identity through time that the distinguishing feature of traumatic experience is its denial or severe inhibition of this process. Repression or mnemonic dissociation as a self-protective response to trauma then makes forgetting rather than remembering the crucial process, a point for which Ireneo Funes provides exemplary reinforcement.[11] The inability to turn experience into conventional narrative and give it expressive form can lead to a cumulative exacerbation of interpretive difficulty and disruption for the individual subject involved, for it is not just the originating pain and hurt that causes trouble within a life story, but also how this plays 'a decisive role in a person's perception of life afterwards, interpretations of subsequent events, and ... memories of preceding experiences'.[12] It is because of such continuing repercussions that traumas can become abiding sources of suffering or, as William James once put it, 'thorns in the spirit' with which the human subject must struggle to live.[13] Yet despite the psychological scars that may remain, the remarkable ability of many combat veterans and other victims of terrible events to avoid traumatic suffering and find some way of moving on is testimony to the power of the mnemonic imagination, and it is because of this that we can distinguish between the resilient handling of traumatic events, leading to stronger personalities and subsequent personal growth, and less successful responses to severely disruptive events which lead to mental disturbance and the psychic problems now associated with post-traumatic stress disorder.[14]

Resilience and moving on can take various forms. Ronnie Janoff-Bulman has usefully explained the coping processes associated with post-traumatic growth and attendant schema change in terms of either gaining strength as a direct result of what an individual has suffered, adopting new, and in some ways more negative assumptions about the world in order to withstand further possible tragedy, or existentially reevaluating what is of greatest significance in the life of the survivor.[15] All of these subsequent reorientations are signs that the mnemonic imagination has found ways of responding to traumatic experience and moving beyond it, albeit always as a changed person. This does not alter the fact that trauma, in the shock it causes to the memory system, along with its associated forms of disorder, thwarts an individual subject's capacity to remember the past in a relatively coherent manner – coherent, that is, for the sake of a recognisable continuity of self – and articulate this in narrative form to others as an integral aspect of everyday social interaction. In its disunion of memory and identity, trauma denies an individual subject's need to connect back with the past and make it validly usable in the present, though as we have insisted, responses to trauma and their subsequent manifestations range considerably in severity and so vary widely in how they may be observed.

It is in light of this that we should make a further distinction between trauma as an anti-memory syndrome and the devastating experiences and painful pasts to which, in greater or lesser degree, individuals accommodate themselves in their memories. Devastating experiences may come to seem mnemonically indelible, as for example in the First World War when a young officer described the following incident in his field diary:

> Up the road we staggered, shells bursting around us. A man stopped dead in front of me, and exasperated I cursed him and butted him with my knee. Very gently he said 'I'm blind, Sir,' and turned to show me his eyes and nose torn away by a piece of shell. 'Oh God! I'm sorry, sonny,' I said. 'Keep going on the hard part,' and left him staggering back in his darkness.[16]

Even without the aid to memory provided by his written account, such an experience would have readily returned to disturb his post-war days. Likewise, painful pasts may have long-lasting repercussions, as for example in Thackeray's reference to the brutal system of corporal punishment in the Prussian army:

> The French officer I have spoken of as taken along with me was in my company and caned like a dog. I met him at Versailles twenty years afterwards and he turned quiet pale and sick when I spoke to him of old days. 'For God's sake', said he, 'don't talk of that time; I wake up from my sleep trembling and crying even now'.[17]

The old days can thus continue to oppress and disturb, and the force of this soldier's plea not to call them back, even two decades later, is a measure of the extent to which this can apply, but he could at least consciously acknowledge and give expression to their enduring consequences. That is quite different to the temporal disseverance caused by a traumatising experience, and it is upon this difference that Freud's notions of 'acting out' and 'working through' depend, regardless of the difficulties of understanding quite what either involves.[18]

We have already referred to examples of acting out, which occurs when an individual compulsively relives a traumatic experience with heightened sensitivity because of an inability to recognise its origin and repetition, while working through means developing an interpretation of such experience in order to overcome 'the resistances to which it has given rise' and allowing 'the subject to accept certain repressed elements and to free himself from the grip of mechanisms of repetition'.[19] This enables us to see that trauma is not directly locatable in a particular 'violent or original event in an individual's past, but rather in the way its very *unassimilated* nature – the way it was precisely not known in the first instance – returns to haunt the survivor later on' (our emphasis). For this reason, 'the impact of the traumatic event lies precisely in its belatedness'.[20] The 'numbingly traumatic event does not register at the time of its occurrence but only after a temporal gap or period of latency, at which time it is immediately repressed, split off, or disavowed'.[21] This entails more than disturbance of the memory system because trauma is a compulsive acting out of the past in the absence of mnemonic imagination. The synthesising capacity of the mnemonic imagination is redundant and in this situation the past cannot be reconstituted and made to serve the interests of the remembering self. It is only in the complex movement from acting out to working through that the subject regains the scope necessary for the mnemonic imagination to rove between temporally differentiated events and experiences and reconnect them in the context of present needs and circumstances. For this reason the primary conceptual value of the term 'trauma' lies in the enormous difficulty of engaging in conscious memory with a shocking event or series of such events in an individual's experience, and in the process of working through from the psychic reaction to the trauma towards the healing stage in which an individual is able to fully articulate the experience.

The term in this sense is indispensable, but its currency has been much debased. The problem begins when the concept and the notion of working through are extended to their applications at broad collective levels of violence and suffering, involving large agglomerations of people (communities, nations, entire social categories). Such extensions involve huge but unexplained leaps from clinical senses of the term to putative forms of collective experience, as for example in such usages as 'screen trauma' or 'traumatised societies'.[22] In literary studies and culturalist versions of psychoanalysis, the underlying premise is that links can be examined 'between the inner world of memory and the external world of historical events by focusing on the experience of pain', and that 'nations – like individuals – must work through grief and trauma'.[23] This premise is untenable. Pain cannot provide such links – it can only be experienced by individual bodies and psyches – and nations in themselves cannot remember any more than they can think or feel. In these indiscriminate applications, the term 'trauma' is being used rhetorically, but this flies in the face of the extreme difficulties individual trauma sufferers have in openly confronting their past experience. Such profligate usages damage our understanding of the relations between individual and collective memory as we have set them out earlier in the book. That is why we are now making a distinction between painful experiences which remain in some way expressible, and traumatic experiences which do not (until worked through) because they remain as recalcitrant traces of the past that cannot be satisfactorily turned into conscious recollection and so become properly knowable.

Of course what enables the extension from individual to collective via the term 'trauma' is metaphor, and the question that the metaphorical application of the term raises is whether applying the concept to collective suffering has any valid meaning in itself rather than solely as a rhetorical trope.[24] Used metaphorically, the term 'trauma' is certainly powerful and can be said to convey, at least in some measure, the immensity of suffering that is involved in war crimes or systemic racial oppression, but what is at issue here is not the validity of metaphor as a figurative device, for metaphors are integral to expressive form and often the first step to advances in conceptual thought. The issue is that of reading off from individual trauma into broad institutional spheres and public discourses where what are at stake are actually remembered events represented as traumatic for the sake of reparation or reconciliation, and not the problem of the amnesiac self. In a discussion of the complex issue of how to deal with individual and collective remembering in memory studies without recourse to binaries of public and private, or psychic and social, Susannah Radstone cites Christopher Colvin's essay on Truth and Reconciliation Commissions, such as that in South Africa, in which he complains that 'terms associated with personal memories of suffering are being deployed to describe the history of a nation'.[25] In the consequent 'therapeutic historiography', the 'key events of history are portrayed as a series of traumatic events', as if trauma is 'the hidden hand that moves history'.[26] History knows no such hand, hidden or otherwise, and can much more adequately be described as an interlinked pattern of intended and unintended consequences. In light of this it seems entirely reasonable for Colvin to conclude that 'psychotherapy is embraced privately by many as a means of individual recovery, but not as a guide for how the history of apartheid should be written'.[27] If the promise of memory studies is that of overcoming the memory/history divide, this is not the way that promise will be realised.

Conceptual vocabularies devised in the attempt to improve our understanding of psychic damage are ill-suited to the sociological analysis of collective forms of commemoration, negotiation of pasts poisoned by racist organisation, or media reconstructions of controversial historical events and episodes.[28] The use of such terms as 'trauma' in ways that go far beyond personal memory is nevertheless so much a part of recent directions in memory studies that it is commonplace and uncontentious. There is an enormous assumption here. As Radstone puts it, the 'recent burgeoning of work on traumatic memory and testimony to suffering may be at risk ... of assuming that terms best suited to the description of affects felt and not felt by an individual, or in play between individuals, can be applied to analyses of the diverse articulations of memory in the public sphere'.[29] This has in fact become a leading mistaken tendency in memory studies, involving an excessive stretching of memory in areas beyond the individual, and a general lack of explanation about what this analytical stretching may involve. It is an over-reaction to another analytical pitfall: that of asocial individualism, involving either an excessive stretching of individuality and an occlusion of the continual interaction between the individual and historically specific social institutions and cultural formations, or an idealised sense of memory as natural or unmediated. These tendencies are opposite sides of the same coin. Both obstruct the effort to rethink the relations between individual and collective memory and avoid the usual entrenched binaries in the process, never mind also reconceiving the conventional oppositions between memory and history and their different temporalities. As we have seen, studying collective memory is a crucial dimension of memory studies as a field, but trauma cannot conceptually be a part of that dimension because it is not available to collective remembering any more than it is to conscious recall by the individual. Applying it to social categories not only attributes agency and subjectivity to collective nouns; it also makes the concept available for rhetorical purposes that are not warranted by the condition of trauma itself.

Trauma is not multipliable. Its application as an explanatory grid for controversial or painful national and other collective pasts diminishes the status of the concept in therapeutic discourse. There it has the potential to contribute to a subject's ability to overcome neurotic symptoms through reconstituting certain past experiences and settling affective disturbances. When applied to collective pasts, the finite meanings and characteristics of traumatic experience become blurred and the specific nature of the pain and distress which underpins traumatic experience is obscured. What is then lost is the notion of trauma as involving experiences so radically disruptive to the self as to be unassimilable when using the social and cultural resources at our disposal.

Instead, trauma becomes an overused and imprecise descriptor for any past experience of a difficult, problematic or contentious nature. Where trauma is characterised as a collective experience, accounts of the injurious shared experience are already manifest and accessible through communicative and representational practice. This is now routinely overlooked. For example, Arthur Neal has suggested that the enduring effects of trauma on the individual resemble the enduring effects of a national trauma 'in collective consciousness'. He suggests that if individual trauma involves a range of 'maladaptive responses', including eating disorders and impaired memory, responses to national trauma likewise involve fear and feelings of vulnerability, while damage to the social system generates national discourse 'directed toward the repair work that needs to be done'.[30] Peculiarly, this is the opposite of trauma and its consequences, for it emphasises the possibility of reconciliation of an event or experience to conditions in the present. Neal suggests that the primary difference between individual and collective trauma is that collective trauma is shared with others.[31] But in order to be shared, painful experience has to representable, communicable, in some way knowable. Neal's usage contravenes the very criteria by which trauma is defined.

Specific cases of trauma do of course acquire definite social and cultural features. The experience of many women raped during the armed conflict in the Democratic Republic of Congo, for example, is traumatic not only because of the violence of the event itself, but also because of the disruption of social norms, conventions and values surrounding sexual relations and the consequent social stigmatisation. But trauma is not reducible to these features. In making this point, we take issue with Jeffrey Alexander's claim that locating trauma in individual experience constitutes a naturalistic fallacy which assumes that events themselves are inherently traumatic. His counter-assumption that any collective past, real or imagined, can be socially constructed or reconstructed as a trauma, either in real time or after the event, simply cannot be substantiated.[32] Coherent narrative reconstruction is precisely what is difficult for those suffering from trauma. By disregarding this defining characteristic of trauma, Alexander broadens the concept of trauma to the extent that almost all specific psychological meanings have been evacuated from it. He counters naturalistic fallacy with sociologistic fallacy. The unsuitability of the discourse of trauma to post-hoc cultural representation of a collectively experienced event has not gone unrecognised. Kristian Gerner's account of collective practices of remembrance and of cultural representation associated with the Hungarian Trianon Treaty, for example, acknowledges the inappropriateness of the term 'trauma' for organised cultural expressions of the historical past. Although characterising the event itself as a trauma, Gerner's explicit rejection of the concept of trauma as able to provide an analytical framework is commensurate with our assertion that trauma is not easily transposed into the realm of social communication and cultural representation.[33] The concept of trauma deals with the rhetorical failure of memory, rather than with remembrance's effective conduct as a mode of making sense of the past in relation to the present and future. If trauma is the name for events or experiences which are retrospectively uncontrollable, and so not amenable to being recognised as memory or articulated as narrative, the notion of traumatic memory as having rhetorical value for memory studies is illegitimate. To be rhetorical assumes that such memory is controllable, and can be rationally managed in human discourse. 'Trauma' is instead a term for the lack of such control. That is why we are arguing that trauma cannot be applied terminologically to all problematic or painful experience. It is only where the past is inaccessible, unassimilable and unavailable for the task of making sense of experience that trauma is a relevant analytical concept. It is inappropriate to talk of effective representations or accounts of the past as traumatic when they are functioning successfully to make the past knowable and usable.

When applied to collective pasts a number of dangers loom: firstly, the finite uses of language in analysing and treating traumatic experience may become dissipated and blurred; secondly, the experience of radical loss seems to disappear when trauma is appropriated as symbolic capital or vicarious thrill by those who have not been victims of it; thirdly, victim and witness may be elided, with those who suffer and those who see such suffering (as either first- or second-hand forms of experience) being run together in an indispensable first step to the rhetorical notion of collective trauma. Trauma has also been taken up as thematic of the failure of representation to bridge the gap between representation and reality.[34] Trauma is not concerned with a crisis of signification or representation in a broad philosophical sense, only in a finite psychological sense: it is not an epistemological problem. It can only be seen that way through its semantically unfeasible stretching in ways which do grave disservice to the victims of traumatic horror or violence, and are ethically irresponsible. The fashionable celebration of trauma in certain branches of cultural theory, as if it is the exemplary condition of postmodern culture, exhibits not only a flamboyant rhetorical opportunism, but also shows a breathtaking disregard for the traumatic experiences suffered by so-called ordinary people. When the interest lies only in what can be philosophically extrapolated from such experiences, the stake is no longer in the possibility of successfully working through traumatic experience for the sake of restoring some degree of mental well-being, but actually in the preservation of trauma as a definitive historical condition. Bizarrely, cultural trauma theory is completely incompatible not only with therapeutic discourse but also with the entire literature on trauma from Freud onwards.

The view that 'all history is trauma' because the past can never be known in its once-lived totality, and thus that 'history can be grasped only in the very inaccessibility of its occurrence', is misconstrued as a principle of the philosophy of history because it pathologises both historical process and historical practice.[35] It even begs the question as to how it is possible to write so prolifically about the past, which even historiographically challenged poststructuralists and postmodernist theorists succeed in doing. Trauma has little value for historical analysis because its conceptual focus is on disconnection and discontinuity. Although inevitably marked by silences, lacunae and forgetting, histories have to be understood in terms of the temporal interlinkings of past events and processes, their causes and effects, their patterns and consequences. 'Trauma' is a term for the absence of these interlinkings or an understanding of them, and just as it is only through remembering that past experience becomes meaningful in relation to our contemporary selves, so it is only through memory that we can tell the story of troublesome pasts and share with others at a collective level the nature of our pain. This requires an imaginative engagement with past experience, that 'thickening and deepening provided by the back-and-forth movements of consciousness that cause time present and time past to coexist in a complex temporal space'.[36] Forging transactional relationships between past and present necessitates the past being available for new uses in an ever-changing present, and this involves not only reflexively considering the past from our own perspective but also imaginatively engaging with the relations which others might have with particular pasts, or how they might view our own relations to the past. Imagining the painful pasts of others is the precondition for empathy, and empathy is itself the precondition for sharing such pasts, but even before mnemonic imagining of this kind can occur, any traumatic experience has to have been worked through, for without this there can be no empathetic engagement, whether of the mnemonic imagination or the historical imagination. It is only painful experience which can be co-performed discursively, and this is always dependent on the intersubjective relations of those involved. It is to these that we now turn.

Working through inherited pain

Responses to painful pasts, and to traumatic events after they have been worked through and assimilated into narrative form, are not limited to those who lived through them. These events reverberate through longer swathes of time. Their residual secondary meanings haunt the memories of those who succeed the victims and survivors. These pasts are inherited and to some degree inhabited by subsequent generations in a long trail of loss. This is not a legacy passed on in a monadic form. The tendrils of these distant happenings permeate the experience of those who come after, for whom loss 'seeps and winds like an invisible psychic link through individual lives, decades and generations'.[37] Painful memory of the past may be absorbed though a general emotional climate, but the precise nature of what is inherited and the way in which this is reckoned with over time remains unclear.[38] The question of whether or not inherited pain can be creatively brought to bear on the present by the mnemonic imagination, and whether this process can be considered a kind of working through at one remove, requires careful exploration. Clearly the paralysis of the mnemonic imagination that an original trauma might provoke cannot itself be inherited in any direct way. As we have already noted, while trauma is neither multipliable nor communicable in a conventional discursive sense, painful pasts are not hermetically sealed off from the world of aftermaths, whether this is after the Holocaust, after slavery, or after systematic torture. Pain does not reside singularly in the past, and its continuance or inheritance may be necessary if the past is to become transformative in its capacity to disturb or, as Benjamin suggests, arrest our flow of thought in the present to stimulate new meaning and action.[39] Although its meaning may solidify and to varying degrees stabilise with the passing of time, it is in the continuing ability of certain pasts to pierce through conventional narratives and demand the reinterpretation of comfortably accepted truths that their ethical potential resides.

   While the radical experience of pain can be a block to the action of the mnemonic imagination, inhibiting the assimilation of the past into coherent narratives and representational form, over time painful pasts may become intelligible at one remove for those who did not experience them at first hand. Their meanings may be to a certain extent communicated and to varying degrees reconciled with ongoing narrative identities.[40] What is unclear is precisely how the second-hand experience of pain is remembered at a considerable socio-temporal distance. In addressing this issue we return to the experience of the second generation of Holocaust survivors. The Holocaust is considered by many as a limit case, standing as the outer marker of extreme loss and suffering in modernity. By exploring second-generation accounts we can trace the ways in which the long trail of loss is articulated over time, and how painful pasts are brought to bear on the present. We can see the mnemonic imagination at work in making sense of inherited pain, opening it up for reconciliation with other aspects of experience and facilitating the creative reworking of painful pasts in order to bring them into a transactional relationship with the present and future.

The second generation of Holocaust survivors did not crystallise as an explicitly identified group till the late 1970s, but since that time the children of Holocaust survivors have given voice to their experience in a range of textual forms from artwork to films and novels. Initial analysis of their post-Holocaust experiences resulted in a somewhat polarised debate, with some asserting a straightforward transmission of psycho-pathologies from one generation to the next, and others resisting such determinist accounts, tending instead to underplay the impact of the Holocaust on second-generation identities.[41] Critical accounts of the second and, more recently, third generations have become more sensitive to the plurality and complexity of their inheritances.[42] It is in the memoirs and narratives of second-generation survivors such as Eva Hoffman, Lisa Appignanesi and Art Spiegelman that the forms of this inheritance are most intimately and sensitively articulated. Eva Hoffman succinctly conveys the way in which she became aware of her second-generation inheritance of memories through a series of hints and glimpses:

At first it was not rational interpretation, or information, or anything like memories; for even if survivors could recollect their stained spots of time precisely, such things cannot be passed on like some psycho-genetic endowment. The attic in my imagination, to give only the most concrete example, probably bore no resemblance to the actual attic where my parents were hidden. In fact, I had almost no information to go on, nothing that would allow me to put together a real attic in my mind. But what I did sense, as my mother talked about it, was the huddled hiding; the despair, the fear, my father's alertness to danger, my mother's deep resignation. Those were among the molecular elements of my early world as they were for so many of my background and generation.[43]

As she makes clear, Hoffman's parents' wartime experience as Jews in hiding was not transmitted to her wholesale, partly because she was not in receipt of a fully coherent set of memories. The knowledge she gleaned came in a fragmented, only partially reworked state; deeply felt but only half-grasped. The acuity of her feelings of despair and fear in the bristling shadows of her parents' experience were not matched by a more abstract understanding or communicable narrative of the past from which they flowed. The challenge faced by the second generation is signalled even in the title of Hoffman's memoir, *Lost in Translation*. The profound loss of the first generation – their entire families – is partly lost in how it becomes translated across the generations, but translation itself stands to make this into something understandable, communicable, and part of herself. It is a monumental task of construction and interpretation, as a result of which she could find or lose herself. This is the importance of the 'post-ness' of second-generation memories, for the Shoah permeates their experience and their accounts of it, yet always belatedly; it is never the experience that is remembered, but always some indirectness of observation or detail that has to be imagined and creatively engaged for the second generation to be able to 'liberate themselves from the thrall of the past … to place absence within the parameters of presence, death within the parameters of life'.[44] The task is one that goes beyond the recall of the first generation's experience, for it requires reconciliation or synthesis with their own. In her opening chapter, Hoffman places out before the reader the experiential and mnemonic strands of her first- and second-hand experience that have to be woven together in her post-Holocaust account. It is in their telling that the process of synthesis is achieved.

Hoffman writes of her post-war emigration, an experience common to many second-generation children; the moment of standing at the railing on a ship's deck, seeing the Baltic shoreline retreat in spatial distance and in time:

> I desperately want time to stop, to hold the ship still with my force of will. I am suffering my first, severe attack of nostalgia, or *tęsknota* – a word that adds to nostalgia the tonalities of sadness and longing. It is a feeling whose shades and degrees I am destined to know intimately, but at this moment it comes upon me like a visitation from a whole new geography of emotions, an annunciation of how much an absence can hurt. Or a premonition of absence because at this divide, I'm filled to the brim with what I'm about to lose … Of the place we're going – Canada – I know nothing.[45]

Here is the betweenness of her experience: the moment of transition between her Polish homeland and Canada, the unimaginable destination. It is this betweenness that she traces through her autobiographical experience, and in using it as a leitmotif in the narrative she is able to navigate discursively rather than completely reconcile the dislocations between old and new lives. Betweenness in the narrative does not occur at isolated moments in her past, but is the ongoing framework of memory which can be imaginatively applied to her past and through which her subsequent experience can be conceptually filtered. Her past remains irreducibly different to those born in the place to which she is removed. While later in life an American acquaintance describes a lost childhood paradise of material privilege, her own Eden was one of material struggle in immediate post-war Europe. In bringing these pasts into visible proximity in the present she inaugurates a dialogue between them, so opening a creative space for mutual engagement between herself and others, and between the different dimensions of her own experience: North American and Polish. There is a strange dialectic between presence and absence: the physical closeness and emotional intimacy of her relationship with her parents, the sound of their breathing in the next room, her father's physicality, the fragility of her mother's mourning; an overflowing presence that is accompanied by a vacuum, the dreams of a wizened *Baba Yaga*, the stories of her murdered aunt. The dead are intensely present, and simultaneously unknowable. The aliveness of her parents, the pleasures and vitality of domestic life and of her childhood experience, become inseparable from the tense penumbra of horror and death.

The experience in its temporal and spatial (dis)locations is characteristically second-generation, and what becomes increasingly clear is how, in both her account of emigration and of the presence and absence of close family, the mnemonic imagination is in play. It is the mnemonic imagination which allows the past child to be recalled but at the same time suffused with possibility, presented as a harbinger of the experiences of displacement to come. Hoffman positions this exiled child in a relation of continuity with her not-quite-in-place contemporary self at a New York party, and in doing so is able to make sense of her difference from the acquaintance with whom she talks. Threads of commonality around the experience of exile are creatively woven between them. It is the mnemonic imagination that allows Hoffman to assess the cargo of loss carried in her parent's lives, through which she conceives her own relation to them and her own sense of self. In her meditation on her sister being named after her murdered aunt and her own naming after her murdered grandparents, she feels herself and her sister as embodying the past while signifying their absence. She gives wing to her fantasies of her grandmother and lost aunt, and through these reconstructs a sense of her own narrative identity. While her inhabitation of loss is a burden of remembrance, her 'sense of the future returns like a benediction, to balance the earlier enunciation of loss', and in these cross-temporal movements the mnemonic imagination creatively reconstructs the past and orients her to the future.[46] This is not one moment of synthesis. It is an ongoing action of reconciling successive pasts and successive presents in their transition into the future.

In reflecting on her narrative, Hoffman calls it a project of translating backwards to retell her story in the language of the present. It is only in reimagining the past through this language that she is able to reconcile her successive selves to each other. It is not, as she herself notes, a return to an origin, but a creative act of bringing into view the disparate strands of her own experience, enabling a movement 'between them without being split by the difference'.[47] It is only via the action of the mnemonic imagination that this condition of multivalent consciousness which moves between past and present, here and there, oneself and others, loss and renewal, can be realised. As postmemory, narratives like Hoffman's take on a quality beyond belatedness; they acquire a critical distance, for their relation to the past is not straightforward recall; it involves 'imaginative investment, projection and creation'. While the intensity of the pain of the Holocaust 'threaten[s] to cover the whole landscape of imagination', making the construction of second-generation accounts a complex, hazardous task, they involve an 'uneasy oscillation between continuity and rupture' born of a combination of their own belatedness and the very pain that threatens to overwhelm them:

> For it seems that just as for survivors only full remembering could bring about catharsis, so for the second generation, only a full imaginative confrontation with the past – with the ghosts of the dead, with the humiliations the parents suffered, with the loss of what one did not know, and grief too deep for tears – can bring the haunting to an end.[48]

It is precisely this imaginative confrontation that we see in Art Spiegelman's *Maus*. His rendering of his parents' experience in cartoon form, where he uses animal codes to distinguish between ethnic and national groups, brings social frameworks of remembering to bear on his father's (and subsequently his own) experienced past; and, as we demonstrated in Chapter 3, it is the synthesising function of the imagination that allows him to move between personal experience and historical reality. While the horror, absence and loss that the Holocaust involves threatens to paralyse the imagination, in *Maus* we see it rehabilitated. The combination of the potent 'faithfulness' of memory to a terrible past in conjunction with the imaginative capacity to apply to it his acquired social frameworks of meaning involves interweaving an account of his father's past with the representation of Spiegelman's own role as his father's interlocutor. The account is undoubtedly, on one level, a history but the narrative structure, the visual puns and imagery provide other layers of meaning in which Speigelman seeks to locate his own identity in an oscillating relationship with his father's experience of loss.[49] Spiegelman was much less concerned with developing a verifiable historical document than with conveying his father's understanding of his experience and his own understanding of his father.[50] In his visual narrative he positions himself *in relation to* his father's loss in order to produce qualitatively new meanings of that painful past in the present. His father's experiences are reconstructed in order to explain his character and his relations with Art. In this sense there is an imaginative grasping together of his and his father's experience. Spiegelman imagines backwards and remembers forwards as he expresses the ways in which his father's past reverberates through his own experience.

Spiegelman's work brings into sharp relief the problems inherent in narrating painful inherited pasts.[51] In their creative treatment lies danger. It has been suggested that he has 'transgressed the sacredness of Auschwitz' in his use of a visual narrative, simplifying it into an easily knowable and consumable popular form.[52] Hoffman also notes the perils of postmemory when it involves trying to reconcile an inherited painful past with contemporary cultural forms or narratives: 'Making a "story" out of extremity – or wanting such a story – sometimes offers false and facile consolations'.[53] Undoubtedly all postmnemonic accounts tread this fine line. Each has to be judged on its own merits, but certainly for us the degree to which mnemonic imagining is able to cross-fertilise past and present and ensure both of a 'future content' is one measure of how this is being achieved.[54] Neither Spiegelman nor Hoffman seeks to 'fix' the meaning of the Holocaust, their parents' experiences of it or their ongoing relation to either. Instead, they render visible the unstable relations between the horrific past and the experience which follows it. In *Maus* the possibility of definitive meaning of or, as Levine suggests, burying the past and preventing its return, is subverted.[55] The creative postmemories of those who inherit painful pasts involve a configuration of the past and present into a particular constellation of meaning at a moment in time, but any arrest of meaning is only momentary in the sense that this involves seizing a memory at a precise moment, its particular meaning and arrangement being contingent on the 'moment of danger' in which it is grasped.[56] Their future content is never fixed but always a latent potential, ready to disabuse the present of its complacency.

In responding to the memory of the Holocaust, we all tread this fine line. Here, Marianne Hirsch makes an important distinction between familial and affiliative postmemory.[57] Familial postmemories belong and are articulated by those whose parents survived the Holocaust. Their inheritance is one that is based on what Ricoeur calls 'close relations', which position it in the interstitial space between individual and collective memory.[58] Affiliative postmemory involves other members of, in this case, the post-Holocaust generation. We too came after this tragic episode, but differ in our proximity to it. Our inheritance does not have the pained intimacy or barbed intensity of postmemory transmitted through organic familial structures. It is understood largely through the rendering of events in cultural forms, including those second-generation accounts that we have already examined. The question that emerges from this distinction is how far the mnemonic imagination can be considered to be at work beyond the margins of familial mnemonic transmission when we attempt to engage with representations of painful pasts? Outside the lived imprint of the Holocaust in which the second generation was raised, are our efforts to do so inevitably condemned to subjugate a faithfulness to experience to our desire for understanding these pasts as knowable and communicable? Unlike *Maus* and *Lost in Translation* as textual articulations of familial postmemory, this becomes more a question of ethical media reception. How, then, can we respond 'in good faith' to the representation of painful pasts in popular culture?

Responding to the pain of others

Painful pasts have become staple references in contemporary popular culture. The most cursory examination of recent Hollywood film reveals a fascination with historical disasters and horrendous crimes perpetrated against individuals and groups. Popular films such as *Schindler's List*, *The Boy in the Striped Pyjamas* and *The Reader* represent the Holocaust with varying degrees of verisimilitude; *Saving Private Ryan* and *Flags of Our Fathers* explore American experiences of the Second World War; while *Flight 93* and *Three Lions* present radically different perspectives on experiences of fundamentalist terrorism. For those of us who have no socially inherited knowledge of these historical events, the knowledge that we gain about them is most likely to be transmitted through our consumption of media texts and cultural commodities. In addition, references to these painful pasts have entered into political and popular discourse. As Jeffrey Shandler notes in relation to the Holocaust, 'it is regularly invoked in speeches by national leaders and on the editorial pages of major newspapers' as well as in everyday talk.[59] We have a long lineage of pain and conflict on which to draw when describing the latest horror: the Libyan conflict is likened to the most recent Afghan war, which in turn was likened to the second Iraq war, which was itself seen in relation to the first, and so on backwards in collapsing cards of historical precedence. The past pain of others pervades our everyday lives, but does its ubiquity and its representational location in cultural products mean that our responses to it are limited, even fatally compromised by our positioning as media consumers, or can our mnemonic imagination enable us to somehow engage with the experiences of others?

These questions are not in themselves particularly new. Susan Sontag was long concerned about the potential that photography possesses for its audiences to apprehend the pain of others.[60] In her early writing Sontag claims that images of atrocity have lost their ability to reach us; their ubiquity has rendered them powerless to move us to action. She argues that the kind of knowing produced through the viewing of an image is sapped of its ethical and emotional power.[61] In her discussion of Holocaust images Barbie Zelizer likewise claims that 'as memory proliferates in the public imagination, the act of bearing witness is growing thin', so that 'we leave the twentieth century with scrapbooks that are cluttered with snapshots of horror', which can push the horror from our memory.[62] This seeming paradox is symptomatic of the wider contradiction that is said to be at the heart of the modern memory boom itself: we turn ever more frequently to the past just as contemporary culture becomes increasingly amnesiac, unable to articulate a dialogical relationship with the past.[63] In her later work, Sontag questioned the inevitability of this amnesia and reconsidered what is lost and gained in the act of viewing images of other people's pain. She stepped back from her original claim to suggest that 'there are hundreds of millions of viewers who are far from inured to what they see on television'.[64] Her position shifted in acknowledging the possibility that although pain cannot be fully known through mediated images, we can be brought into uncomfortable proximity with other people's pain, and that our response to such pain cannot be determined absolutely by the image itself.

Mediated representations do not necessarily preclude creative engagements with the past, but such engagements require 'going beyond' the
image because 'the problem is not that people remember through photographs, but that they remember only the photographs'.[65]

In contrast to the argument Sontag makes in *On Photography*, Alison
Landsberg argues that media representations of painful pasts do not
crowd out memories of events but offer opportunities for the development of qualitatively new memories experienced by the consumers of
mediated representations. Distinguishing between sympathy and empathy enables her to see this ethical relation to another's pain as different
from the exploitation and violation of the pain and death of others that
Hoffman identifies in excessive identification with victims:

> While sympathy presupposes an initial likeness between subjects,
> empathy starts from a position of difference ... empathy depends less
> on 'natural' affinity than sympathy, less on some kind of essential
> underlying connection between two subjects. While sympathy,
> therefore, relies on essentialism of identification, empathy recognises
> the alterity of identification.[66]

An empathetic response does not conflate the victim and the viewer.
It does not involve a flattening out of the specificities of experience
or scales of suffering, but is produced precisely by bringing into view
differences of this kind. Bringing the pasts of others into proximity
without collapsing them into the experience of the viewer-at-a-distance
provides the condition for making qualitatively new meaning in the
present while at the same time developing a capacity to understand 'the
traumatic historical event through which she did not live and to which
she might not otherwise feel connected'.[67]

What remains less clear in Landsberg's account is precisely what
occurs in this moment of engagement and most importantly, what it
is that generates this creative mode of historically conscious reception.
She herself notes that imaginative interaction with the pain of others is
never guaranteed 'because of the mass media's standard mode of address:
a dissemination of pre-digested messages that require no active engagement or thought on the part of the individual'.[68] This would seem to be
a retrograde step away from a dual emphasis on the interaction between
text and audience, a retreat back to textual meaning as the final deter-
minant of historical apprehension. Inevitably some texts are more open
in the ways in which they bring past suffering into the present, but this
is not the whole story. It is also the extent to which audiences are able

to employ their mnemonic imagination to actively position their own experience in relation to that of others in their consumption of a text which contributes to the realisation of new meaning. Just as no representation of the pain of others can guarantee our active and empathetic relation with it, no text can ever close completely the possibility of affective and creative reception as its meaning is always produced in relation to the viewer's accumulated experiences and existing frames of expectation. The capacity of a representation to arrest and disrupt depends in part on the specific horizon it is brought into relation with.

Bringing the concept of the mnemonic imagination to bear on attempts to understand the extent to which the pain of others can be engaged with at a distance shifts the parameters of debate around mediated representations of painful pasts. Feature films in particular have become battlegrounds in arguments over the nature of representing horrific pasts. On the one hand the application of Hollywood's representational logic and aesthetic codes to horrific events has been criticised as trivialising and simplifying; on the other they have been considered to open up historical events for popular engagement. This debate is most widely articulated with reference to Spielberg's *Schindler's List* and Lanzmann's *Shoah*, summarised here by Andreas Huyssen:

> Spielberg's film, playing to mass audiences, fails to remember properly because it represents, thus fostering forgetting: Hollywood as fictional substitute for 'real history'. Lanzmann's refusal to represent, on the other hand, is said to embody memory in the proper way precisely because it avoids the delusions of a presence of that which is to be remembered.[69]

While Huyssen notes that this debate is premised on a 'modernist dichotomy that pits Hollywood and mass culture against forms of high art', our concern is piqued by the limited attention that has been paid to questions of reception and viewer interpretation. A key exception is Eley and Grossman's analysis of *Schindler's List* which, through considering the viewing of the film, hints at the instability of its meanings and the role that audiences play in realising those meanings at a particular historical moment.

They note that the film, even in the previews they saw in the cinema, disrupted their expectations of a Hollywood narrative:

> At first we were nonplussed, then intrigued, by this unidentified Casablanca-like departure from cinema convention, a kind of

stylised World War II reconstruction, with Nazis and cabarets, a conscious evocation. It was only gradually, as the preview exchanged one kind of nostalgia for something else, a different and more sinister iconography, in which Auschwitz was unmistakably present, that we realised: Oh, this must be Spielberg's *Schindler's List*. As we watched, we said to each other: 'Maybe this won't be so bad.' In other words, the arrival of Schindler's List disrupted our anticipated viewing pleasure.

Eley and Grossman's accumulated historical knowledge of the Holocaust and their accumulated experience of Hollywood films were disrupted by *Schindler's List*. The subversion of their viewing pleasure was in part generated by their capacity to use a specifically mnemonic imagination to bring the past represented on screen into productive dialogue with their existing knowledge, producing new meaning in the moment of viewing. In making sense of the film, they also creatively revisited their existing understandings of the Holocaust and the medium in which it is represented. In this productively reordered tension between experience and expectation, the meanings of the Holocaust are neither fixed nor simplified. Going on to discuss their own reading of the film, Eley and Grossman suggest that the film's telling of one very specific story means that it does not self-consciously attempt to provide a 'master-narrative' and in avoiding this, it encourages them to bring this partial account into relation with their existing understandings of the Holocaust; to challenge, rethink and reorganise that knowledge. Indeed, in their account of their own viewing Eley and Grossman comment that 'what was remarkable about *Schindler's List* for us was precisely its openness' in raising rather than closing down questions pertaining to the limits of representation.[70] Anna Reading finds a similar openness in the film *Shoah*, in which she suggests that we are 'invited to imagine and remember the gaps in their discourse, in the unarticulated pain on their faces, the thousands of women and children who could not be interviewed because they did not survive'. This openness is not purely a textual property. It arises in the gap that opens up between viewers' expectations and experiences and those offered by the text. In this liminal but creative space, the mnemonic imagination is at work.

The mnemonic imagination does not involve a simple bivalent movement between the representation of a painful past and what viewers bring to it. We do not read texts in isolation. Our engagement with painful pasts is not performed in atomised moments of reception but in the sense we make of those pasts in the relations between texts. The mnemonic imagination operates by traversing between multiple texts and our responses to them. The ways in which one representation can generate new meaning in the present is in many ways dependent on our accumulated experiences of other representations, for example in Eley and Grossman's reading of *Hitler's Willing Executioners*:

> [O]ne can't help wondering whether Spielberg's haunting 'little girl in the red coat' doesn't somehow reappear in Goldhagen's obsessive invocation of the 'little girl' in the forest, brutally murdered by a German *Familienvater*. It is hard to read *Hitler's Willing Executioners* (or about it), with its occasional and perhaps deliberately cinematic register.[71]

The ways in which they imagine the horror of the little girl's experience derives in part from the way in which Spielberg's representation of the 'little girl in the red coat' arrested their attention in a previous moment of viewing. Similarly, in her interviews with young people about their understanding of the Holocaust, Anna Reading finds that the meanings of the Holocaust emerged through the interconnections they made between representations, for example between books and films, rather than emerging from one text in isolation.[72] The mnemonic imagination allows us to synthesise and accumulate meanings of the past in the present, creating our own historically conscious iconography and lexicon of, in this instance, pain and suffering. In forging imaginative connections between these texts and our own experiences, their meanings emerge as relational, loosening and shifting our horizons of expectation.

Sometimes, when the gulf between the experience and expectations of an audience is completely and radically out of kilter with what is represented, the mnemonic imagination may not be engaged. Only by examining the historical moment of that failed interaction can the causes of it be traced. An example of this is an incident in which a number of black schoolchildren, attending a showing of *Schindler's List* at their local cinema in 1994, were asked to leave after laughing and talking during the screening.[73] Hanlon provides a constructive analysis of the students' response to the film. Film reviewers claimed Spielberg's use of black-and-white was a 'distancing element' that encouraged serious reflection and an almost 'ascetic' response, but for the schoolchildren this aesthetic might well have other connotations. While for some of the audience it may retain a sense of faithfulness to the past by virtue of its association with newsreels, for younger audiences (and indeed some adults) it might mean 'not real, but old, and therefore uninteresting'. The viewing also took place at a historical moment of heightened tension between black and Jewish communities which centred in particular on the lack of recognition of slavery as a historical crime. This was in stark contrast to the substantial funding received by the Holocaust Museum in Washington, DC Students were submerged, at this particular time, in polarised political and racialised discourses which collided with popularly and critically accepted meanings of the film. The compulsory viewing of *Schindler's List* also took place on Martin Luther King Day, a day on which black students might have legitimately expected to have the suffering of their own community addressed. Hanlon notes in his interviews with students that this was specifically raised by them in explaining the unsuitability of the film at that particular moment. In addition, the students' generational experience of film viewing may have provided an added dimension in their failure to engage creatively with the film and bring it into a productive tension with their own experiences and expectations. The popularly sanctioned, reverent response to the film ran counter to students' normal behaviour in a cinema. Hanlon also notes the discomfort students might have felt in the responses they received from other (white) audience members; their self-awareness may well have contributed to their not becoming 'absorbed' in the historical moment of the film. Radical differences in expectations of *how* to consume cultural representations can close down possibilities for the engagement of mnemonic imagining. The students' subject positions and the discourses in which they were immersed at the moment of viewing contributed to their rejection of the film, to their failure in understanding the pasts of others and imagining others' experience in relation to their own. It is the mnemonic imagination which opens us to the past, but the potential for it to be brought into play in the consumption of mediated representations of painful pasts is determined as much by the viewer and the moment of viewing as by the structure and content of the text itself. As Sontag notes, 'no "we" should be taken for granted when the subject is looking at other people's pain'.[74]

Looking at the pain of others via its media representation makes us think not only of others but also of 'we' who are looking, and in this looking across temporal distance, an ethical orientation to the past of others emerges from a triad of conjoining forces: the quality of the mnemonic text, the context in which it is used and understood, and the action of the mnemonic imagination that we bring to bear in making sense of the previous two in combination. Such action draws us in to the partiality of another person's perspective, entering us into a network of mediated meanings in which we ourselves are implicated. In this sense the character of our response is twofold. There is of course recognition of others' experience, which as Charles Taylor suggests, 'is not just a courtesy we owe people. It is a vital human need'.[75] But this recognition involves at its heart an understanding of both sameness and difference: sameness in the sense of recognising possible grounds for commonality with another's past, but at the same time acceptance of its irreducible difference from our own. Inevitably, this has its dangers. The mnemonic imagination can fail and we can become passive consumers of the pain of others, unmoved or unreached by their suffering. In this sense the experience of others is not negotiated with our own; a relational understanding of their past fails and we remain untransformed. This failure can result from the limitations imposed on the mnemonic imagination by retrotypical representations or, as in the case of the schoolchildren's reception of *Schindler's List* discussed earlier, it can result from a radical disjuncture between our contemporary experience, our own narrative self, and the experiences of others represented in the text which our mnemonic imaginations are unable to synthesise. In stark contrast to this, the painful experience of others can be annexed, imitated, or identified and affiliated with too cheaply, in a similar vein to the vicarious thrill or symbolic capital derived from the trauma victim. These self-oriented uses of the other as Other may then lead to, or be associated with, two further interrelated problems: the narcissistic claiming of victimhood as a subject position, and the banal situation in which the 'language of forgiveness has spread in an uncritical manner'.[76]

When it is successful the mnemonic imagination allows us to oscillate between our own experience and that of others delivered to us in textual form, and through that oscillation the experience of others is brought to bear on our own, potentially affecting our own sense of self in the process, at least to the extent that it is absorbed into our own cumulative experience, and becomes part of how we appreciate adversity, harm, tribulation and distress. Although in second-hand remembering 'we are sheltered from the adversity' which causes the suffering of another, our mnemonic imagination allows us to remain open to the effects of their pain.[77] This does not mean that the mnemonic imagination is inherently ethical or moral, for it can be brought to bear on the accounts of perpetrators of violence or abuse just as it can on the accounts of their victims. The action of the mnemonic imagination is nevertheless a precondition for ethical engagement with the past of others, for it requires us to become what Boltanski calls the 'moral spectator' in which we transcend the distance between the other's suffering and our own position as a distant witness of it: 'The spectator represents to himself the sentiments and sensations of the sufferer. He does not identify with him and does not imagine himself to be in the situation'.[78] The mnemonic imagination then pits our own experience in tension with mediated representations of the sufferer's experience, allowing us to make sense of their pain without denying the particularity of their experience.

Painful pasts in their second-hand experience demand more from us than an inwardly directed understanding of the suffering they involve. They also demand outwardly directed action. They demand that we move beyond the easy, even at times facile equation of seeing and sympathy, for as LaCapra suggests, 'any politics limited to witnessing memory, mourning dead victims and honouring survivorship would constitute an excessively limited horizon of action'.[79] The conditions that would make us actively care when confronted with mediated suffering in the past cannot perhaps be definitely prescribed, but that should not stop us from attending to how ethics and praxis may be brought fruitfully together in moving towards a broader horizon. Eschewing the polarisation of ethical value into absolutist and relativist epistemologies is not enough in itself, because we have also to critically gauge the features of, for example, any media representation of painful pasts that sets up certain values and choices as relevant to the way we should or could respond to the temporally distant suffering that is involved. In this respect, Lilie Chouliaraki suggests that an emphasis on pity and emotion 'should be combined with an emphasis on detached reflection, on the question of why *this* suffering is important and what we can do about it'.[80] Seeing moves beyond sympathy only when our own experience is drawn upon to engage with this question and so develop a reflexive identification with the sufferer based upon her or his alterity. The mnemonic imagination is vital in then encouraging viewers or listeners 'to at once act as if they were within the scene of suffering and as if they were speaking out their views on suffering in public'.[81] The aim is not to repeat past suffering, but to respond ethically to it. This involves not the fixing of meaning, but meaning revisited in the relational dynamic between the temporal tenses. It is a matter of remaining faithful to the particularity of people's experience while being able to imagine their pain anew in the continually changing conditions of the present. The mnemonic imagination holds up the promise of our fulfilling the obligations we have to recognise the painful pasts of others, to respond ethically to them, and ensure that in some way or other they inform our future.

Coda

Looking back

Our primary aim in this book has been to reconceive the relationship between memory and imagination. In doing this we have explored the diverse ways in which memory and imagination interact in people's negotiations of the past, from the casual engagement with a photograph of a loved one to the reception of collective pasts represented in popular film or literature. Through reconciling memory and imagination we hope to have provided new ways of thinking about certain difficulties and debates in memory studies. We also hope to have offered useful pointers towards improving our understanding of the mnemonically inscribed contours and fluctuating temporalities of everyday life. In this short tail-piece we want to reflect on the temporal modalities of the mnemonic imagination itself by thinking back over our examination of memory and imagination and where it has taken us, so considering what it offers to memory studies and what it suggests is needed from future research that is conducted in the field.

Our starting point was a concern with the limitations of some of the conventional ways of thinking about memory. It was this which led us on to think, most of all, about the problems posed by the separation of memory and imagination. This separation, sometimes even taking the form of open antagonism, has damaged understanding and debate across a range of significant issues and topics. For example, seeing memory and imagination as sharply divided has resounded in contemporary gender politics. The furore over recovered memory and false memory syndrome, particularly in the United States in relation to child abuse cases, has framed debates over the relationship between imagination and memory as a war between fact and fiction.[1] In this war, meaning

194

is the ultimate casualty. Significant social and political dimensions of the debate surrounding women's sexual abuse in childhood have been displaced to 'successful remembering'.[2] *Inter alia*, this has resulted in a preoccupation with individual cases rather than a consideration of the wider issues of gender and sexuality surrounding women's self-identification – regardless of actual events – as victims of abuse by male authority figures in their childhood. The use of imagination in reconstructing gendered trauma is not considered a legitimate mode of exploration, and stories not conforming to the template of strict recall are discounted as literally *meaning-less*. The stringent parameters of the debate and neglect of imagination as necessary to remembering have limited the potential to rethink women's relationship to their pasts and to familial structures, so denying the possibility of change and transformation in the everyday contexts of their experience.

The damage caused by splitting off memory and imagination from each other are also visible in the domain of cultural production. Memory has been prized over imagination in the search for historical truths because of its presumed guaranteed basis in a past reality. It is this which establishes its apparently unchallengeable claim on what the past means. The result is that some voices are legitimated and others silenced, with the voice of the immediate witness being valued above all others. This is perhaps most markedly seen in criticism of representations of the Holocaust, particularly in the comparative analyses of Claude Lanzmann's *Shoah* (1985) and Steven Spielberg's *Schindler's List* (1994). In contrast to *Shoah*, which was made up of the testimony of sanctioned witnesses with apparently minimal recourse to imagination, *Schindler's List* was frequently criticised for its imaginative, fictionalised rendering of the Holocaust. This deflected attention from the ways in which it productively challenged the debate in contemporary society regarding the memorialisation of the Holocaust and the role it has played in generating new ways of understanding those events from its very specific temporal as well as cultural perspective.[3] The failure to recognise the mutuality of remembering and imagining inevitably ends in a reductive assessment of the ways in which they relate to experience. Experience as a process situated in time is denied, the shifting points in time from which we remember are overlooked, and the value of the imagination in orienting us to possible new futures is rejected. In consequence, the relations between past and present become fixed and determinate.

In order to begin the task of overcoming the separation of memory and imagination we turned to experience as a primary category of analysis. Attending to experience as a plural noun permitted us to lay the conceptual groundwork for seeing remembering as a creative process, and in doing so it helped us to cast off any sense that memory involves a simple reproduction of the past or a straightforward accessing of past experience. Experience as the raw material of memory constitutes the remembering subject through the continuous process of distilling sense, meaning and value out of what it is made to yield, with the act of remembering itself always articulated in the interplay of individual experience and social frames and conventions. The long-term remembering of experience is unstable and error-prone, but also relatively coherent and recognisable to ourselves and others as continuous over time. At the heart of our sense of ourselves in the world is a temporal dynamic of continuity and change. Within this dynamic twofold structure experience unfolds in time, but acts back reflexively on that continuing development. In this sense memory involves both *Erlebnis* as lived experience in time, and *Erfahrung* as cumulative experience mediated and remediated over time in the development of sensibility, dispositions and self-cultivation (*Bildung*). Remembering, in this conception, shuttles us continually back and forth between experience-in-movement as an unfolding process and experience-in-memory as a product of this. It is through this ceaseless shuttle that memory and remembering are creatively involved in the generation of new meanings and understandings of ourselves in the world.

Recognising the complex role of remembering in moving us between past, present and future, in a continual feedback loop of accumulated and accumulating experience, then led us to question how previous experience is reactivated in the present as part of this ongoing temporal transaction. Our response has been that the reactivation of previous experience relies on the conjoined action of memory and imagination. As we discussed in Chapter 2, even when we adopt a reconstructive understanding of memory, it provides an indissoluble link to experience. No matter how selective or continually revised our accumulated experience is, it is always experience that is drawn on in memory whereas, in contrast, imagination does not have to seek reference to experience in the same way. The ways in which we assimilate experience over time and use it as a means for apprehending our own remembered self, orientating ourselves to the future, exploring alternative presents, or thinking about the pasts of others, requires both memory's faithfulness to experience and the imaginative capacity to move beyond this in order to generate new temporally oriented meaning and significance in the present. The mnemonic imagination is a response to this requirement. Its synthesising role allows qualitatively new meaning to be forged from past experience by facilitating the creative treatment of experience within shared frameworks of meaning. At the same time it brings past and future into dialogic relation and allows the space of experience and horizon of expectation to move towards and to inform one another. The mnemonic imagination transforms the past into a resource for the ongoing relational constitution of ourselves as remembered and remembering subjects. This is what we have called the creative action of the mnemonic imagination, and it is this we have sought to convey throughout the various chapters of the book.

The mnemonic imagination in memory studies

We have developed the concept of the mnemonic imagination in order to help us move beyond some of the weaknesses and blind-spots in memory studies. So for instance it enables us to address some of the problems associated with adopting a reconstructive conceptualisation of memory. It is this which now dominates memory studies research. Remembering is now understood as involving the active construction of the past in the present rather than providing a direct conduit to it, with access to past experience being neither stable nor static. Memory studies has nevertheless not addressed, either sufficiently or satisfactorily, the varying relationship of memory to experience. It has also conveniently bypassed the unavoidable fact that the value of memory in its everyday uses relies precisely on a sense of veracity or belief in the truth of our recollections. The difficulty of accommodating the truth claims of memory within a reconstructive conceptualisation of it seems to us to be one of the major reasons why the relationship between memory and imagination has been systematically overlooked. It is by exploring their interaction that we can accommodate the link between memory and experience within a reconstructive framework.

Sue Campbell's consideration of the question of what it is that memory is faithful to is crucial here. She develops the imperative of faithfulness beyond a simple claim to an objectively experienced past by arguing that memory involves firstly, a faithfulness to the narrative self and more specifically to the continuity and coherence of that self, and secondly, a faithfulness to others and to our relations with them. The truth claims of memory refer not to an objectified past but to the reflexively constructed meaning of that past in relation to oneself and others. Faithfulness here is an ethical relation which entails being 'responsive to the concerns of the present', and 'responsive to the ways that other people remember'.[4] This is very much in harmony with the theoretical framework for memory we have tried to develop. It leads us to suggest that the referentiality of memory is confirmed rather than compromised by the imagination since it is the action of the imagination that facilitates and fertilises the ongoing synthesis of experience and its mobilisation of memory-as-product in acts of creating new meaning in the present and for the future. We look backwards in order to see forwards.

The reconciliation of memory and imagination has allowed us consider the past both as persisting in the present and at the same time as being continually reconstructed in the interests of the present. The tension between presentist conceptualisations of memory and those which emphasise the persistence of the past has led to something of an impasse, with studies focusing either on the ways in which memory can be reconstructed and appropriated in relation to the social, personal and political demands of the present, or on the ways in which the past remains impervious or at least resistant to the demands of the present.[5] By prioritising one over the other, the contingency between a remembered past and an imagined future constructed in a unique present is lost. Continuity with the past should not be accounted for at the expense of future change, and likewise changed presents should not subordinate past experience. Using the concept of the mnemonic imagination, we can begin to account for the possibility of both the persistence and constructedness of the past within the same framework. The mnemonic imagination holds the work of memory and imagination in productive tension, each holding the other to account but each also adding to and enhancing what the other provides. The connection to experience, both as process and product, is guaranteed by memory which prevents the action of the imagination floating free of its referential moorings and dissolving memory into ungrounded fantasy. In turn, imagination makes past experience available for ongoing reconstruction and reinterpretation according to specific communicative codes and conventions. The past continues to persist actively in the present not of its own volition but via the mnemonic imagination, yet its meanings and values are always provisional and subject to potential revision.

A further unresolved difficulty in memory studies concerns the distinction between individual and collective memory. The distinction cuts to the core of memory studies as a field of research. and in attempting to deal with this issue there has been a proliferation of typologies which have sought to reconceptualise it in one way or another, whether as private and public memory, communicative and cultural memory, or individual and social memory. The position we have taken is that all memory is social, but can become relatively individualised or collectivised in a continually varying relationship. Following from this we have most frequently used personal and popular as prefixes to distinguish between remembering that is primarily autobiographical and private in nature from that which is publicly shared and rehearsed in terms of both content and performance. At the same time we have sought to avoid any hard-and-fast opposition between autobiographical memory and public memory because, among other reasons, the former may enter into the more public realm of cultural memory, while the latter may affect the most intimate moments of private recollection.

So rather than adopting a twin-track approach to personal and popular memory, the mnemonic imagination allows us to connect personal and public remembering as part of the same mnemonic processes, with each being implicated in the other. The work of the mnemonic imagination produces the synthesis of our first-hand experience with both socially inherited or culturally mediated second-hand experience. First-hand experience is of course always culturally mediated and in various ways and to varying degrees imbricated with what is socially inherited. These are relative distinctions across the range of social and historical experience. In light of this we can then say that, on the one hand, the action of the mnemonic imagination is oriented inwards to the self as the imagination mobilises social frames of memory through which we can marshal our own experience and make it knowable in relation to our own narrative self and meaningful to others. On the other hand, and at the same time, it is oriented outwards to others, facilitating the mobilisation of personal memories through communicative practice into a wider public domain, which we can then in turn imaginatively bring to bear on the processes of gathering together and making sense of our own experience. As Sue Campbell notes in her reading of Diana Taylor's work on the performative strategies associated with publicly remembering the 30,000 disappeared of the Argentinian Dirty War (1976–83), faithful, or what we might call ethical memory, requires 'bringing one's own memories into relation with different aspects of experience at that time'.[6] It is the mnemonic imagination operating in its collective modality that enables this 'bringing into relation' as it opens up the interstitial space between our own experience and that of others in which we remember 'in common' with others.

Over the course of the book we have attempted to demonstrate the value of the concept of the mnemonic imagination in opening up the possibilities of the past, taking it not as inevitable dead weight but as a series of potentially fruitful opportunities for constructing coherent but flexible identities that can endure over time, so opening up our own pasts and the pasts of others as creative resources in voyaging towards our yet-to-be-realised horizons of expectation. This attempt then propelled us towards thinking of how certain forms of what is termed 'nostalgia' can be conceived as a creative engagement with the past, providing the mnemonically oriented means for us somehow to manage disruption and change in the face of their apparent inevitability, and so take our bearings for possibly different futures.

This does not of course mean that the mnemonic imagination is infallible in operation or guaranteed success by any measure. It can be foxed, thwarted and closed down, and we have explored two specific ways in which this might occur: commercialist appropriation, or what we have called retrotyping; and traumatic experience which, for whatever reason, cannot be successfully turned into memory as this is integrated with the relatively coherent life-narrative that is vital for the maintenance of self-identity.

While all memory involves the imaginative synthesis of fragments of experience, retrotyping is a form of attenuated, frozen knowledge of the past that deals only in highly selective fragments and denies the continual, shifting, creative process of their reconstruction both in time and across time. Experience as product in the form of representations of the past becomes detached from any specific temporal mooring or distinct spatial location; these are dissolved into generalities of time and place, and by that move retrotyping gains the amplitude of its sentimentalist appeal. The ways in which the past is recycled to serve historically stereotypical functions elides the processual unfolding and assimilation of experience to which fragments of the past refer and yet develop cumulative meaning with direct reference to time passing. New meanings become intensely difficult to generate from these fragments as they are extricated from experience as process because one of the preconditions for the action of the mnemonic imagination has been removed. The contingent relationship between experience and expectation is closed down and experience as a condition which informs the future is denied. The past is then no longer a creative resource or site of possibility, but a confirmation of comforting views and comfortable assumptions of the past.

The mnemonic imagination is threatened in an altogether different way by past events so radically disruptive that the experiences which constitute them are beyond the capacities of the imagination to bring them faithfully into synthesis with our own narrative identities or communicate them successfully to others. While trauma has become an increasingly fashionable analytical category in memory studies, we have tried to explore more precisely what is involved in the inability to remember unassimilated 'limit' experiences. Where experiences are so far beyond our accumulated experience (both first- and second-hand) the mnemonic imagination is unable to weave experience into an existing tapestry of memories: the expressive frames and forms through which we make the past knowable are inadequate; our experienced past cannot be codified and communicated and so cannot enter the discursive space between our own experience and that of others. Trauma is an engagement with the past in the absence of the mnemonic imagination, and as a result it is not meaningful in a conventional sense. Traumatic pasts are not available as a mnemonic resource for orienting oneself to the future and rethinking the past. This kind of engagement with the past is fragmentary, unpredictable and recalcitrant, manifested only in the form of flashbacks, nightmares, impregnable silences or unbidden physical responses. The process of working through is the arduous task of making these pasts knowable and storyable, and it is here that the mnemonic imagination facilitates and supports movement from a state of trauma into productive engagement with a painful past. The past remains painful, but no longer obstructs the ability to move on.

When actively concerted recollection is, or becomes possible once more, memory and imagination work together as corresponding faculties, and help us alternate between the domains of action marked by experience and expectation and the different horizons they embrace. They do so, in short, through their interaction in the form of the mnemonic imagination. The concept of mnemonic imagination promotes recognition of the interaction of memory and imagination because of its inbuilt refusal to collapse them into one another; instead, while they extend and enhance each other, they also each act as a check and balance on the other. The mnemonic imagination allows experience to fund new temporal meaning in the present and for these meanings to be shared, as for instance across generations or between different social groups. Accordingly, it provides us with new ways of thinking about the relationship between individual and social experience and the possibilities and pitfalls inherent in our epistemological and ethical negotiation both of our own experience and that of others. It is in these ways that the concept helps us overcome some of the current weaknesses and deficiencies in memory studies.

Looking forward

What we have been attempting to develop in this book is a theoretical framework for investigation and analysis in memory studies which centres on the mnemonic imagination. It is the establishment of this concept in particular that has allowed us to reconceive existing analytical categories such as nostalgia and personal and popular memory in order to extend and refine their critical value, and to develop qualitatively new concepts such as retrotyping in order to increase and enhance our analytical capacities in work at the interface of memory and history. Developing such a framework is of course all very well, but the enduring point of it lies in its application. We have tried to apply it in various illustrative ways during the course of the book, but how it is turned to good account in concerted ways is what truly counts. It is to this question that we turn in bringing the book to a close. It is a not simply a narrow question that we pose in relation to our own work, but is instead a question about the kind of work that now needs to be undertaken in memory studies more generally in order to advance our understanding of the temporal dimensions of experience in modernity. For it is now abundantly clear that what is most needed in memory studies is sustained empirical research that will identify how the potentialities of and limitations placed on memory are experienced and performed across the various contexts and varying scales of its manifestation.

As a field, memory studies suffers from a lack of empirical research, and as a consequence of this it has shown little interest in, or concern for, methodological questions relating to the study of memory. This does not mean that no such research is being done (certain notable examples of it have been referred to in this book), but theoretical exposition, the critical refinement of ideas, and textual readings of films or memoirs are activities far more characteristic of memory studies than, say, extensive in-depth interviews with members of various social groups about their everyday practices of remembering. This is perhaps to be expected. The field is still in its early stages and developing our theoretical frameworks and sharpening our conceptual tools are important steps to be taking. These are precisely the steps we have taken in this book. It may be, as well, that the very interdisciplinarity of memory studies has acted as a barrier to the design and implementation of empirical work since it has required that some of the thornier epistemological questions about memory, and the divergent answers to them, be directly addressed and to some degree reconciled. Nevertheless, the field has reached a point in its development where a general move into the complex, messy, unpredictable yet amply rewarding realm of lived experience and practice is now vital if it is, as a viable enterprise, to enter into its majority.

While there is undoubtedly a place for large-scale quantitative assessments of memory processes from individual to global scales, it is the construction of mnemonic meaning and significance through the embedded, at times ephemeral, and often taken-for-granted everyday remembering practices that remains most elusive. Investigating the construction of such meaning and significance doesn't necessarily require long-term anthropological observation in the field, but it does require involvement with the mnemonic landscapes of particular remembering subjects, attention to the minutiae of their experience, and interest in both the form and content of mnemonic communication and representation. Adopting a proximate or close-up ethnographic perspective opens up the possibility for examining remembering as an ongoing lived process, so providing us with a way of apprehending, however imperfectly, its irreducible complexity in a way simply not possible when memory and remembering are separated from one another in procedures of quantification.

The concept of mnemonic imagination places everyday practices of remembering at the heart of debates about the relationship between personal and popular memory. It does so by considering remembering as always including, at the centre of its activities, the relationship between self and others. This relationship is one that is performed in and through practices of remembering. Ethnographic attention to these practices will pave the way towards the development of deeper understandings of the relational qualities of memory, and enable us to address some of the questions posed by Wulf Kansteiner concerning the role of the individual in social and cultural memory:

> If social memory is indeed as malleable as we generally assume, what prevents people from inventing radically idiosyncratic memories, especially in small social settings? Moreover, if social memory exists exclusively in the form of communication between subjects ... would it not make sense to argue that some people have a lot more control over these communications than others? And finally, how and under what circumstances do individuals and collectives escape the gravitational pull of powerful social master narratives and imagine the past in new formats and stories?[7]

The politics of remembering played out in the active navigation and negotiation of the dominant temporal structures and narratives of modernity are observable in our everyday encounters with our own past experience and that of others. Adopting an ethnographic approach allows the productive tensions between mnemonic agency and dominant narratives and power structures to be empirically investigated and not simply dealt with through generalised speculation or inspired guesswork.

As we discussed in Chapter 3, our remembering involves a complex interplay between accumulations of first- and second-hand experience. While second-hand experience can obviously be conveyed via interpersonal communication and narrative, late modernity has witnessed the exponential rise of mediated modes of transmitting second-hand experience. A crucial issue for memory studies is the ways in which mnemonic resources, remembering practices, and the experiential settings in which they are performed are increasingly mediated or remediated. This is widely recognised. The analysis of mediated representations of the past and their encodings in a range of forms and genres has been a mainstay of cultural memory studies. Textual and narrative analysis of one kind or another undoubtedly remains a valuable component activity in the field, but there always comes a point where we need to balance analysis of texts and narratives against analysis of how they are interpreted and understood beyond the point of the semiotician, say, projecting this outwards from the glare of a lone laptop. That may involve extension into various kinds of audience study as one possible direction, opening up a wider range of decodings than are apparent through textual readings alone. Alternatively it could involve exploring how the meaning and significance of past events and experiences are constructed and reconstructed in people's routine reiterative interactions with everyday mnemonic texts and objects. There are various possibilities, but our general point is that a research focus on remembering practices enables us to develop an integrated analysis of both strategies of representation and mundane contexts of usage and understanding.

Ethnographic investigations of remembering practices open up avenues of exploration that have been beyond the scope of this book and have tended to remain beyond the purview of memory studies research more generally. Of particular significance in this regard is the nature of the relationship between different types of memory. In this book we have focused mainly on declarative or reflexive remembering, but this could well be extended into consideration of the ways in which such remembering relates to sensory memory, habit memory and bodily memory. The value of this would lie in developing a more complete understanding of the 'sophisticated taxonomy' of memory as it occurs in our everyday lives.[8] An ethnographic approach has the potential to open up for investigation our multiple modes of accumulating and articulating experience, along with the complex layerings of our varying and shifting remembering practices. This would then perhaps allow us to consider the ways in which physical continuities and embodied habits intersect with, and feed into, the ways in which the past persists in the present as a creative resource. An ethnographic method explicitly guards against these modes of memory being hived off from one another, as unfortunately is often the case in contemporary memory studies research.

So we finish this book in the manner in which we began. As we draw to a close, our concern is primarily with the ways in which we make sense of our intended and unintended experience, in time and across time, as we sift it, assess it, value or devalue it in taking stock of what it has brought us and turning it to use in taking our bearings for the future. Memory studies has so far been extraordinarily successful in providing an intellectual space for theoretical perspectives on remembering that cut across traditional disciplinary lines, but in order to build on this success we need to shift our attention a good deal more to the investigation of everyday practices of remembering, across as broad a social range as we can. This need is imperative because it is within those practices, as time passes and is laid to account, that the mnemonic imagination matters most.

Notes

An Outline of What Lies Ahead

1. Misztal (2003: 115–20).
2. It is worth noting that as far back as Greek mythology, through her alliance with Zeus, Mnemosyne (Memory) gave birth to nine daughters, who were the Muses.
3. John Sutton (2004) provides a handy summary of the conceptual breadth of memory as a label for a variety of cognitive capacities.
4. Rítívoí (2002: 32).

1 Memory and Experience

1. *Plenus rimararum sum, hac atque illac effluo.* Montaigne (1991: 739–40).
2. We have preferred here the translation by J. M. Cohen rather than the more recent one by M. A. Screech. They can be compared in Cohen (1961: 235) and Screech (1991: 907–8). For a short, handy guide to Montaigne, see Burke (1981), and for two recent studies in which discussion of key topics and themes in his work is interwoven with various aspects of his life, see Bakewell (2010) and Frampton (2011). Graham Swift's short, celebratory piece on Montaigne, written as an introduction to the Folio Society's reprint of John Florio's original English translation of the *Essays*, is also recommended (Swift, 2010: 283–94).
3. There are numerous observations to be made of a radical critique of the unitary conception of the subject, but we confine ourselves here to two brief points: firstly, as Daniel Albright (1994: 34) has noted, 'the self that is either too singular or too plural is likely to be diseased', as for example in the cases of the fascistic authoritarian personality and the schizophrenic patient; secondly, there is a world of difference between a pluralised conception of the self and the pathology of multiple personality and other dissociative personality disorders. The transfer of a clinical condition into a cultural topos needs always to be treated with caution.
4. Passerini (1979: 85 and 104).
5. Epstein (1978: 101) has a similar conceptual sense of identity as synthesis in referring to 'the process by which a person seeks to integrate his various statuses and roles, as well as his diverse experiences, into a coherent image of self'. There is a huge literature relating to these issues, but useful sources focused specifically on questions of self and identity are Lasch (1980), Lears (1983), Carrithers (1985), Taylor (1989), Giddens (1991) and Cohen (1994).
6. The term 'oversocialised' derives from a celebrated article by Dennis Wrong, designed to critique the consensual bias in functionalist sociology, and so complement the critique by conflict theorists of the cohesive bias in the over-integrated view of society prevalent in forms of social analysis influenced by functionalism. The article appeared in the *American Journal of*

Sociology in 1961 and is reprinted in Robert Bocock, Peter Hamilton, Kenneth Thompson and Alan Waton (1980) with a useful postscript. The reverse term 'undersocialised' applies in disciplines like psychology and philosophy where individualism has been a prevalent tendency.

7. Mead (1934: 174).
8. Mead (1959: 29).
9. Ribot (1882: 83).
10. Thomson (1994: 216); Green (2008: 93–4).
11. Albright (1994: 33).
12. Ricoeur (1994a: 119–23).
13. Nussbaum (1990: 75).
14. Dewey (1960); see also Jay (2005: 28–39).
15. For these developments, see Jay (2005: Chapters 2–4). It should be noted that the term *Erlebnis* did not enter into common currency until the late nineteenth century, but Schleiermacher can be said to have anticipated its use and paved the way for the emergence of *Lebensphilosophie*.
16. The German term *Bildung* does not have any obvious equivalent in English, but it relates closely to the notion of individual development, especially in the spiritual sense, in the journey from youth to maturity.
17. Giddens (1991: 189). Moretti (1987) regards the *Bildungsroman* as having been exhausted by the final quarter of the nineteenth century, but for a more extended treatment of the genre, see Buckley (1974).
18. Moretti (1987: 46).
19. Tocqueville (1955: 140).
20. Pears (1998: 611).
21. Gadamer (1989: 67).
22. Wordsworth (1969: 213 [Book XI, ll. 258–18]). On the mnemonic significance of spots of time in Wordsworth's conception of the imaginative structures of his life-history, see Hutton (1993: 55–9).
23. For more on Dilthey's and Dewey's conception of this kind of experience, see Pickering (1997: Chapter 4), and Negus and Pickering (2004: Chapter 2).
24. Ireland (2004: 38).
25. Kundera (1991: 351).
26. See Ireland (2004: Chapter 2) on the dialectical aspect of *Erlebnis*. This understanding of experience is close to that held by the social historian E. P. Thompson. For an attempt to rehabilitate a Thompsonian conception of experience, see Pickering (1997).
27. Bell (1996: 89).
28. For more on situated and mediated experience, see Thompson (1995: Chapter 7) and Pickering (2008).
29. Mead (1959: 2).
30. Mead (1938: 616).
31. Emerson (1946: 272 and 283–4).
32. Mead (1959: 30).
33. See, e.g., Hardy (1975), Sarbin (1986), Polkinghorne (1988), Nash (1990), Ricoeur (1990), Bruner (1991), Freeman (1993), Berger (1997) and Brockmeier and Carbaugh (2001).
34. Crites (1971: 297). It should perhaps be noted that along with the shaping influence of narrative structures in particular cultures, the language we

speak directs us in many ways 'to attend to different aspects of experience through grammatically encoding different aspects of experience' (Kövecses, 2006: 335).

35. Crites (1971: 299).
36. Ibid.: 300.
37. Ibid.: 302–3.
38. Ricoeur (1991: 22).
39. Campbell (1997: 110).
40. Lawler (2008: 34–5). Emphases in original.
41. Ricoeur (1991: 24).
42. Kundera (1986: 105). This alternative metaphor, while preferable to that of excavation, may still suggest an unchanging past beneath its changing outer attire. That is not the case with the remembered past because of the continual interchange between remembering and forgetting, and because in any particular instance the remembered past is the cumulative, shifting development of the actively concerted remembering that has preceded it.
43. Locke (1996: 60). In the second edition of the *Essay*, Locke adds a disclaimer acknowledging that talk of ideas being stored in our memories can only be taken as a figurative expression because ideas 'do not remain explicitly in memory over the period from experience to remembering'. This may seem to raise difficulties for his theory of personal identity even though 'the extent to which Locke makes continuity of self dependent on memory' is the subject of considerable dispute (Sutton, 1998: 160, 168). Much depends on how continuity of self is approached. See on this Marya Schechtman's discussion of Locke's memory-based conception of personal identity in relation to the inadequacies of psychological continuity theories. Her version of an alternative story-based approach to self-identity is close to the one we have adopted in this book. As she puts it, autobiographical memory 'links together the different temporal parts of a person's life by providing the unity of a narrative' (1994: 16). In the end, the key to resolving these difficulties depends, for us, on how we conceive of the relationship between memory and imagination.
44. Krell (1990: 3–7), Sutton (2004: 9).
45. See Sutton (2004: 14–20) for a summary of this new consensus.
46. Hobbes, cited in Warnock (1987: 18).
47. Hobbes (1972: 89).

2   The Mnemonic Imagination

1. Lively (1986: 11).
2. Banville (1973: 12).
3. Foster (1838: 8).
4. Husserl (1964: 70).
5. Robinson (2009: 184–5).
6. Ryle (1970: 237).
7. In *The Analysis of Mind*, Bertrand Russell makes a useful point that links with this when he suggests that any distinction between remembered-images and imagined-images is not inherent in the images themselves, but in the relation we have to them based on our experience (2007: 175–6).

8. Warnock (1987: 27).
9. Sartre (1972: 210), emphasis in original.
10. Faulks (1990: 244).
11. See Keightley and Pickering (2007).
12. Warnock (1987: 35).
13. Hacking (1995: 250).
14. Albright (1994: 36).
15. Dilthey (1985: 102).
16. Ibid.: 240.
17. Borges (2000: 95–6).
18. Ibid.: 96.
19. James (1952: 445). On the next page, James went on to quote from Théodule Ribot's *Les Maladies de la Mémoire*: 'Without totally forgetting a prodigious number of states of consciousness, and momentarily forgetting a large number, we could not remember at all. Oblivion, except in certain cases, is thus no malady of memory, but a condition of its health and its life.'
20. See e.g. Douglas (1987: Chapter 7). On the differences between Bartlett's research on remembering and earlier experiments on memory conducted by Ebbinghaus, see Danziger (2008: 137–42, also 127–33).
21. Middleton and Brown (2005: 16).
22. Bartlett (1932: 296).
23. Ibid.: 200.
24. Ibid.
25. Ibid.: 201.
26. Ibid.
27. Middleton and Brown (2005: 16).
28. Ibid: 204.
29. Ibid.
30. Middleton and Brown (2005: 204).
31. Bartlett (1932: 205).
32. Ibid.: 211.
33. Ibid.: 213.
34. Misztal (2003: 118–19).
35. Bartlett (1932: 214).
36. Ibid.: 312.
37. Sutton (2004: 18).
38. Ibid.: 312–14.
39. Ibid.: 296.
40. Ibid.: 212.
41. Ibid.: 20; Shotter (1990: 134).
42. Shotter (1990: 135).
43. While this is the case so far as memory and imagination are concerned, in his study of early modern theories of memory John Sutton (1998) has shown that dynamic views of memory extend further back than is usually acknowledged. He argues convincingly for a distributed, reconstructive model of memory, and against static archival models, as he traces the roots of connectionism and defends it against its critics. For a neat synoptic overview of work taking a situated and distributed approach to memory, see Sutton (2009). Richard Kearney (1998) also offers a wide-ranging survey of different paradigms of

the imagination, from the Ancient Greeks to postmodernism, with the general aim of countering the ways in which imagination has been devalued. The split between memory and imagination originates most of all from the rise of empiricist philosophy in the eighteenth century and the reaction of Romanticism to it in the late eighteenth and early nineteenth centuries.

44. See, for instance, Jan Assmann's discussion of communicative and cultural memory (2008: 109–19).
45. Frosh (2011: 117).
46. Kant (2006: 61).
47. Casey (2000: 184), Kant (2006: 61).
48. Negus and Pickering (2004: 34).
49. Domingues (1997: 486).
50. Hastrup (2007: 195).
51. Kant (2007: 103–4).
52. Ibid.: 104, 149–50.
53. Kearney (1991: 127). Merleau-Ponty's aesthetic theory is based on the sense of art as beginning 'in the least perception, which amplifies into painting and art' (Merleau-Ponty, 1974: 83). See Crowther (1993: Chapter 2) for an outline of Merleau-Ponty's aesthetics.
54. Kearney (1991: 119).
55. Carroll (1994: 79).
56. Tolstoy (1960: 363).
57. Robinson (2009: 47).
58. Ricoeur (1990, vol. 1: ix–x).
59. Ricoeur (1990, vol. 1).
60. Kearney (1998).
61. Ricoeur (2004: 21).
62. Campbell (2006: 362, 365).
63. Ibid.: 365.
64. Ricoeur (1994b: 129).
65. Bergson (2004: 93–4).
66. Barthes (1981). For our reappraisal of Barthes's term '*punctum*', see Pickering and Keightley (2008: 156–9).
67. Ricoeur gives an extended discussion of Bergson's division between these two types of memory. He is careful to characterise this as a polarity rather than a dichotomy, and recognises that memory operates at various points between these poles rather than them being either the one or the other (2004: 26–31).
68. Bergson (1975: 203).
69. Bowie (2008: 27).
70. Domingues (1997).
71. Koselleck (2004: 256).
72. Ibid.: 2.
73. Ibid.: 259.
74. Koselleck (2002: 111).
75. Koselleck (2004: 262).
76. Pickering (2004: 277–8).
77. Koselleck (2004: 262).
78. Koselleck (2004: 262); Pickering (2004: 276).
79. Koselleck (2004: 257).

80. Ibid.: 262.
81. Schinkel (2005: 44).
82. Ibid.: 48.
83. Southgate (2007).
84. Habermas (2001: 132).
85. Pickering (2004: 286).
86. Koselleck (2004: 266–7).
87. Schinkel (2005: 43).
88. This can of course result in an entrenchment of existing prejudices and the emergence of stereotypes of the racial and cultural Other (see Pickering, 2001 for a historical account of stereotypical formation).
89. Pickering (2008: 24).
90. Baudrillard (1983).
91. Kearney (1998: 393).
92. Huyssen (1995: 9).
93. The shift from sympathy to empathy is explored further in Chapter 6, specifically in the section on responding to the pain of others.
94. Stevenson (1911: 154).
95. Ricoeur (1986: 266).
96. Kearney (1991: 159).
97. While we agree on the codependence of ideology and utopia, we do not see them as reducible to the faculty of imagination alone. It seems strange that the reference to the past and ideology are subsumed by Ricoeur into the action of the imagination.
98. As we noted earlier, the critical interrogation of popular reconstructions of the past remains an important activity, but this should not mean that the aesthetics of memory are ignored in preference to the task of demystification and the need analytically to challenge the ideological content of a text or image of officially sanctioned social memory.
99. Middleton and Brown (2010: 241–51).
100. Ibid.: 249.

3 Personal and Popular Memory

1. Casey (1987b: 258–9).
2. Flaubert (1948: 121).
3. Kansteiner (2002: 185).
4. Prager (1998: 97).
5. Hirsch (1997: 22). Postmemory is an important concept and we shall discuss it at greater length in Chapter 6.
6. Hoffman (2005: 34).
7. Karpf (1997: 252). Karpf makes clear that in England at least, parents spoke to their children of their experiences as Holocaust survivors because they were usually denied any other audience in the early post-war period, both among Anglo-Jewish people and in English society more broadly.
8. Fresco (1984: 418, 421–2).
9. Ibid.: 420.
10. Hoffman (2005: 66).

11. Ibid.: 105. The phrase 'smithy of the soul' derives from James Joyce's *Portrait of the Artist as a Young Man* (Levin, 1963: 252).
12. Hoffman (2010: 413–14).
13. Zarecka (1994: 48).
14. Rosenzweig and Thelen (1998: 45).
15. Nora (1989). See Chapter 5 for an extended discussion of this claim.
16. Landsberg (2004).
17. Landsberg (2009: 221–2).
18. Zerubavel (1996: 286).
19. Jedlowski (2001: 36).
20. Halbwachs (1980, 1992). For two overviews of Halbwachs's life and career, see Apfelbaum (2010) and Lewis Coser's Introduction to *On Collective Memory*. Halbwachs should also be credited with helping to undermine biologistic notions of inherited memory, as for example in the concept of 'race memory'.
21. Halbwachs (1992: 43).
22. Halbwachs (1980: 33).
23. The phrase 'socially marked' comes from Ricoeur (2004: 121). Despite this convergence, there were key points of difference between Halbwachs and Bartlett which are attributable to the distinct academic disciplines in which they were primarily working (see Cubitt, 2007: 158–9).
24. Ricoeur (2004: 122).
25. Middleton and Brown (2005: 36).
26. Halbwachs (1980: 48).
27. Middleton and Brown (2005: 39).
28. Ibid.: 52–3. For the localisation of memories, see Halbwachs (1992: 52–3).
29. Halbwachs (1992: 53).
30. Middleton and Brown (2005: 41).
31. Halbwachs (1992: 49).
32. Ibid.: 182–3; 53; see Misztal (2003: 54–5) for an overview of critical perspectives on Halbwachs's conceptualisation of the relationship between individual memories and the social group.
33. Burke (1997: 55).
34. Middleton and Brown (2005: 53).
35. Halbwachs (1992: 76).
36. Ibid.: 77.
37. Ibid.: 81.
38. Ibid.: 76, 81.
39. Ibid.: 38.
40. Ibid.: 172–3.
41. Olick (2008: 156).
42. Halbwachs (1992: 40, 54).
43. Ibid.: 119.
44. Wertsch (2002).
45. Cubitt (2007: 164).
46. Ricoeur (2004: 122).
47. Connerton (1989: 38).
48. Ricoeur (2004: 131).
49. Connerton (1989: 38).
50. Connerton (1989).

51. Assmann (1995: 126).
52. Ibid.: 128–9.
53. Ibid.: 130.
54. Assmann (2010: 111).
55. Assmann (1995: 128).
56. Ibid.: 132.
57. Assmann (2010: 111).
58. Olick (1999: 342).
59. Kuhn (1995/2002: 4–5).
60. Crane (1997).
61. Van Dijck (2007: 1–2).
62. See also Wang and Brockmeier (2002).
63. Van Dijck (2007: 6).
64. Olick (2010: 158–9).
65. Van Dijck (2007: 76).
66. Ibid.
67. Ibid.: 23.
68. Ibid.: 25.
69. Ibid.: 118.
70. Landsberg (2004: 3).
71. Ibid.: 150.
72. Jordan (1965: 40), Greene (1980: 45).
73. Rowe (2011).
74. Frosh (2006: 5).
75. Peters (2009: 40).
76. Olick (2010: 159).
77. Fentress and Wickham (1992: 201).
78. Landsberg (2004: 26).
79. Bergson (2005).
80. Kansteiner (2002: 179–97).
81. Ricoeur (2004: 123).

4   The Reclamation of Nostalgia

1. The first concerted attempt to move beyond this view is Davis (1979).
2. Bevan (2006: 25–6).
3. Gissing (1982: 81–2).
4. As Stuart Tannock (1995: 463) has put it, due to 'the negative connotations of nostalgia, nostalgic narratives viewed as progressive or enabling tend not to be called nostalgic; they may be considered as examples of popular memory or historical consciousness instead'.
5. The song written and composed by Reed, and is available on Document's 1998 CD, *Blind Alfred Reed: The Complete Recorded Works, 1927–29*. Reed died in 1956, apparently from starvation, and is buried in Elgood, West Virginia.
6. Georges Perec, cited in Adair (1986: xv).
7. Chaney (2002: 152).
8. Cited Elliott (2010: 48). Susan Matt refers to the realisation of the impossibility of return as 'a hallmark of modern consciousness' and 'at the heart of

nostalgia' (2007: 469, 485). As well as examining American yearnings for a lost home or past, she traces how this modern perspective on return emerged and developed.

9. Casey (1987a: 366); italics in original.
10. Hofer's introduction of the term into medical terminology was made in his thesis, *Dissertatio Medica de Nostalgia* (Basel, 1688). For an English translation by Carolyn Kiser Anspach, see *Bulletin of the History of Medicine*, 2, 1934. As Starobinski (1966: 84) pointed out, while the observation that 'exiles languished and wasted away far from their native land' was nothing new, what was novel about Hofer's thesis was 'the attention which the candidate paid to it' in the effort to expose it to rational enquiry.
11. Starobinski (1966: 86).
12. Ibid.: 101.
13. Terdiman (1993: 3–5).
14. Roth (1993: 26–7). See also Roth (1989, 1991).
15. Ruml (1946).
16. Elliott (2010: 69).
17. For an insightful treatment of nostalgia as a consequence of the French Revolution, see Fritzsche (2001). As he notes, the French Revolution disrupted Western conceptions of historical continuity to such an extent that there developed a fundamental sense of difference between the modern and non-modern on either side of 1789. The repercussions of the revolution also spread across Europe 'over an entire generation' and created the sense of participating in 'a shared historical process' (pp. 9–11).
18. Gitlin (1980: 233). See Smith (1998) for an overview of late modern temporality in connection with nostalgia and Appadurai (1990) for a more general account of contemporary relations of time, space and culture.
19. Colley (1998: 4).
20. Jameson (1991); cf. Huyssen (1995).
21. Jameson (1969–70: 53).
22. Ibid.: 68. This appears so only because Jameson is nostalgic for the kind of nostalgia he finds in Benjamin's work. He compares contemporary nostalgias to 'the pain of a properly modernist nostalgia' (1991: 19), and as Nicolas Dames (2010: 272) has commented, this is tantamount to saying that nostalgia isn't what it used to be.
23. We take the phrase 'negative certainty' from Bennett (2001: 181).
24. Smith (2000: 507).
25. Fritzsche (2001: 6). The phrase within the Fritzsche quotation is from Adorno and Horkheimer, cited and discussed in Gordon (1997: 19–20).
26. Bonnett (2010: 2351, 2354 et passim); see also Bonnett (2007) and Burchardt (2002). For Spence, see Ashraf (1983); and for Chartism, see, for example, Epstein (1982), Wright (1988), Walton (1999) and Roberts (2003).
27. For example, E. P. Thompson's biography of Morris remains an admirable study of his life and work, but does not deal adequately with Morris's nostalgic imagination (Thompson, 1977/1955). (The same difficulties apply to guild socialism of the late nineteenth/early twentieth century.) Ruth Kinna's study of Morris is far more satisfactory in showing the positive relationship between his Romanticism and his entry into socialism. Significantly, she notes how 'Morris's memory worked on two levels, providing both an

image of the possible future and a theory of action designed to bring this future into being' (2000: 79). For a valuable discussion of Morris's *News from Nowhere* and the relationship between Marxism and utopia, see Levitas (1990: Chapter 5).

28. Frow (1997: 79).
29. Williams (1975).
30. Nostalgia, in Williams's view, is 'universal and persistent' (ibid.: 21).
31. Williams (1975: 11–12; and see Natali (2009).
32. Stafford (1987: 269).
33. Wiener (1981). See also Colls and Dodd (1986), Shaw and Chase (1989; particularly the chapter by William Stafford).
34. Mandler (1997: 155).
35. Ibid.: 160.
36. Marsh (1982: 245). For a slightly later period, see Lowerson (1980) who offers a balanced account of rural nostalgia and its relation to different attitudes to, and uses of, the English countryside in the 1930s.
37. Rosaldo (1993: 69). On the ideological benefits of primitivism for 'civilised' societies, see Pickering (2001: 51–60).
38. Brown (2003: 67).
39. Waters (2000: 192).
40. For post-war slum clearance, see English, Madigan and Norman (1976).
41. Ibid.: 181.
42. Matsuda (1996: 50–1). For the process of Hausmanisation in mid-nineteenth century Paris, see Jordan (2004) and Schwartz (1998: 16–26).
43. For an example of anti-nostalgia critique that ignores the mnemonic value of such places, seeing them only in the pejorative sense of 'little worlds', see Boys (1989).
44. Cashman (2006: 146–48). See also Cashman (2002). The kind of community and its everyday rhythms for which the Derg Valley inhabitants of County Tyrone are nostalgic is wonderfully evoked by John MaGahern in his last novel, *That They May Face the Rising Sun.*
45. Cashman (2006: 154–5).
46. Moody (1984: 161).
47. Drake (2003: 190).
48. *The Sunday Times* (5 April 1998).
49. Stauth and Turner (1988: 510).
50. See Pickering and Green (1987) for more on this.
51. Ladino (2007).
52. Boym (2001: 41–2, 49).
53. Bonnett (2010: 2354). For this tendency in others, see also Davis (1979: 16–29) and Legg (2005).
54. Hamilton (2007/8: 71). Patrick Wright is a fine example of a writer whose work operates with a sense of these different forms of nostalgia working dialectically rather than dichotomously. See especially *On Living in an Old Country*, in which he deals with the ideological role of national history while also demonstrating the value of historical experience for so-called ordinary people, and recognising that everyday nostalgia 'as a critical and subversive potential' (1985: 26).
55. Field (2008: 114–16); emphases in original.

56. Tannock (1995: 459).
57. Ibid.: 454.
58. Rítívoí (2002: 29).

5   The Foreclosure of Mnemonic Imagining

1. Oliver (2001: 135–6).
2. Pickering (1987: 40) et passim.
3. Leiss, Kline and Jhally (1986: 210).
4. Chaney (1996: 106).
5. Appadurai (2000: 77).
6. Ibid.: 78.
7. Jameson (1991: Chapter 9).
8. Nora (1996, vol. 1: xvii). The *Lieux de Mémoire* project resulted in a seven-volume publication appearing between 1984 and 1992, edited by Nora and combining essays by nearly 120 French scholars. Only a third of these have been translated into English and published as the three-volume *Realms of Memory* between 1996 and 1998.
9. Judt (2008: 203–4). The *Guide Michelin* (green) divides tourist sites into three categories: interesting, worth a detour, worth a journey.
10. Nora (1996: 2).
11. Ibid.
12. Nora (1989: 13).
13. Ibid.: 7. As we have seen since the inauguration of Nora's monumental project, there is little evidence for the separation of history and memory in the Balkans. His thesis was conceived very much through a natio-centric optic.
14. Nora (1996, vol. 1: 8).
15. Ibid.: 1, and see 6–7.
16. Pickering and Green (1987: 9), and see in general for discussion of the vernacular milieux Nora associates with lived memory and traditional forms of community.
17. See Crane (1994) and Heffernan (1995) for two case-study examples of this. Matsuda (1996) is a more extended study which offers ingenious and illuminating analysis of conflicting forms of memory in late nineteenth-century France.
18. Nora (1996, vol. 1: 8).
19. Savage (1994: 146).
20. Nora (2002: 4).
21. Gillis (1994: 15).
22. Hess (2002: 41).
23. Legg (2005: 493).
24. Wood (1994: 146).
25. Tacchi (2003: 283).
26. Ibid.: 287–8, and see Seremetakis (1994).
27. Battaglia (1995: 93).
28. Cited in Schwarz (2010: 53). Schwarz usefully compares Nora to J. H. Plumb (1969) and Carl Schorske (1980), each of whom respectively claims the end of memory, the end of the past, and the end of history.

29. The phrase 'vicarious experience and fake sensations' is taken from Clement Greenberg's 1939 essay 'Avant-Garde and Kitsch', a classic example of mass cultural criticism (Greenberg, 1964: 102).
30. The autobiographical texts we have in mind are Lively (1994) and Shaw (1979).
31. Grossman (2007), and for the heavy-handed tactics sometimes used in pursuing payment, see Grossman (2008).
32. Frosh (2003: 8).
33. Ibid.: 157–66; emphasis in original.
34. Boym (2001: 339).
35. *The Independent* (2 May 2006). The excerpt from Dvořák is commonly referred to now as 'the Hovis music', as for example in requests to Classic FM.
36. De Baubeta (2000: 104). The two examples we cite are from here.
37. Ibid.: 106.
38. Fritzsche (2002: 81).
39. The 2005 BBC programme featured the English war veteran Harry Patch in an encounter with a German veteran from the First World War, Charles Kuentz. For Patch, see Patch (2008) and Parker (2009). For his obituary see *The Guardian* (27 July 2009). The celebrated Monroe image derives from the movie *The Seven Year Itch* (1955), directed by Billy Wilder.
40. Guehenno (1995: 29).
41. Cubitt (2007: 245–6).
42. See Doane and Hodges (1987) for an argument to this effect.
43. Hobsbawm (1994: 3).
44. Jameson (1991).
45. Rich (1982: 59).
46. On these temporalities of forgetting, see Connerton (2009: 40–98).
47. Le Goff (1992: 95).
48. Hutton (2011: 103).
49. Huyssen (1995: 5).
50. Ibid.: 7–9, 100.
51. Huyssen (2000a: 27–8, 35).
52. Retrotyping therefore should not become associated with a mode of evaluative analysis that is oriented entirely or even in the main to the cultural text through which regressive nostalgic feelings or associations are constructed, rather than to the uses made of such a text. Identifying retrotyping through its occurrence in cultural texts remains a limitation until it is also identified in individual practices of remembering or in individual responses to objects and texts of popular memory.
53. Confino and Fritzsche (2002: 4).

6 Creative Memory and Painful Pasts

1. Myers understood the relation of this condition to hysteria but coined the new term in order to avoid stigmatising British soldiers with what was perceived as a female affliction (Showalter, 1997: 72).
2. Stone (1985: 249).

3. On the variation of cause and consequences in cases of war neuroses, see Bourke (1999: 246–48).
4. Winter (2006: 52–3, 58).
5. Erickson (1951: 37).
6. Stereotypically, such men were considered as in conformity with the ideals of masculinity and manliness, whereas those suffering from shell-shock were often considered enfeebled, effeminate, and a threat to the proper distinction between men and women (see Feudtner, 1992; also Bourke, 2000: 59–60). In George Mosse's summary, war 'was the supreme test of manliness, and those who were the victims of shell-shock had failed this test' (Mosse, 2000: 104).
7. Fussell (2000: 29–35).
8. Calvino (1993: 85).
9. Leys (2000: 86). See Chapters 3 and 6 of her book for discussion of responses to war neuroses in the two world wars.
10. Herman (1992: 181).
11. See Chapter 4, pp. 52–4.
12. Leydesdorff (1994: 15).
13. James (1894).
14. For one version of this distinction, see Bridgers (2005). We perhaps need also to acknowledge that the resilient handling of wartime experience may for some have derived from the excitement and satisfaction felt in combat. In response to this, Joanna Bourke (2000: 57) has noted that the 'emphasis on emotional breakdown and psychiatric illness has obscured the fact that most men coped remarkably well with the demands being made upon them in wartime'. While accepting this, we should also note that, at least in certain cases, soldiers may react differently to traumatic experience because of earlier psychic disturbances of one kind or another which are exacerbated by combat (Herman, 1992: 13–32; Leys, 2000: 18–22).
15. Janoff-Bulman (2004).
16. Vaughan (1987: 224–5).
17. Thackeray (1899: 87).
18. Freud (1955–74, 12: 147–56). Freud's paper on this was first published in 1914.
19. Laplanche and Pontalis (1973: 488).
20. Caruth (1995: 4 and 8).
21. LaCapra (1994: 174).
22. Jacobs (2008: 211) refers to 'traumatised societies' in an article on the representation of women at Auschwitz, and Zylinska (2005: 76) talks of 'screen trauma' in discussing the media theatricalisation of the events of 9/11. The first of these usages suggests the possibility of mass trauma, which is simply a contradiction in terms, while the second suggests not only that trauma can be communicated, but also that audiences can be traumatised by the representations of traumatic events in film or television. This implies a crude transmission model of mass communication and direct media effects, both of which have been largely discredited in media studies (the only potential exception being the exposure of media violence to young children).
23. Misztal (2003: 141).

24. We use the term 'metaphor' here as a meta-category to include such figures of speech as metonym, synecdoche, simile, allegory and symbol, as well as metaphor as a more specific device of comparative substitution.
25. Radstone (2005: 143).
26. Colvin (2003: 159).
27. Ibid.:166.
28. There are other cases where the applicability of psychological and/or psychoanalytic terms for collective experiences and memories needs to be called into question and interrogated, but these are beyond the bounds of our discussion here.
29. Radstone (2005: 147).
30. Neal (1998: 4–5).
31. Ibid.: 4.
32. Alexander (2004: 9–10).
33. Gerner (2006: 105).
34. Three key texts responsible for making such theory fashionable are Felman and Laub (1992) and Caruth (1995, 1996).
35. Caruth (1991: 7).
36. Deresiewicz (2004: 37).
37. Hoffman (2010: 406).
38. Appignanesi (2000: 6).
39. Benjamin (1970: 257).
40. Pierre Janet, cited in van der Kolk and van der Hart (1995: 170–71) and Leys (2000: 111).
41. Auerhahn and Laub (1998).
42. Although our focus in this chapter is on second-generation Holocaust survivors, the transmission of memory to the subsequent generation has been explored by Anna Reading (2003).
43. Hoffman (2005: 33–4).
44. Hoffman (2010: 411).
45. Ibid.: 4.
46. Hoffman (1998: 280).
47. Hoffman (1998: 274).
48. Hirsch (2008: 106–7; Hoffman (2010: 414).
49. See Rothberg and Spiegelman (1994) for a more detailed analysis of Maus.
50. Levine (2002: 319).
51. Numerous analyses of Maus have been written. See, for example, Staub (1995), Young (1998), Levine (2002), Elmwood (2004) and Hirsch (2008).
52. Rothberg and Spiegelman (1994).
53. Hoffman (2005: 173).
54. Metz (1972: 9–25).
55. Levine (2002).
56. Benjamin (1970: 257).
57. Hirsch (2008: 114).
58. Ricoeur (2004: 131–2).
59. Shandler (1999: xi).
60. Sontag (2003).
61. Sontag (1977).
62. Zelizer (1998: 203).

63. Huyssen (1995).
64. Sontag (2003: 111).
65. Ibid.: 89.
66. Landsberg (1997: 81).
67. Landsberg (2004: 145).
68. Landsberg (1997: 67).
69. Huyssen (2000). See Hansen (1996) for an excellent and more detailed analysis of this debate.
70. Eley and Grossmann (1997: 46).
71. Eley and Grossmann (1997: 56).
72. Reading (2003: 157).
73. Hanlon (2009).
74. Sontag (2003: 6).
75. Taylor (1994).
76. LaCapra (1998: 182–3); Ricoeur (2004: 469).
77. Boltanski (1999: 36).
78. Ibid.: 38.
79. LaCapra (1998: 198).
80. Chouliaraki (2006: 13).
81. Ibid.: 178, 214.

Coda

1. Campbell (2003).
2. Ibid.: 17.
3. See, for example, McNab (2005), and see Hansen (1996) for further consideration of *Shoah* and *Schindler's List* as Holocaust representations.
4. Campbell (2006: 377).
5. For an overview of presentism in memory studies, see Misztal (2003); for an excellent discussion of research which emphasises the persistence of the past, see Mihelj (2012).
6. Taylor (2002).
7. Kansteiner (2010: 3).
8. Sutton (2009a: 65).

Bibliography

Adair, Gilbert (1986) *Myths and Memories*, London: Fontana.

Albright, Daniel (1994) 'Literary and Psychological Models of the Self' in Ulric Neisser and Robyn Flush (eds) *The Remembering Self: Construction and Accuracy in the Self-Narrative*, Cambridge and New York: Cambridge University Press, 19–40.

Alexander, Jeffrey (2004) 'Toward a Theory of Cultural Trauma' in Jeffrey C. Alexander, Ron Eyerman, Bernhard Giesen, Neil J. Smelser, Piotr Sztompka (eds) *Cultural Trauma and Collective Identity*, Berkeley, CA and London: University of California Press, 1–30.

Apfelbaum, Erika (2010) 'Halbwachs and the Social Properties of Memory' in Susannah Radstone and Bill Schwarz (eds) *Memory: Histories, Theories, Debates*, New York: Fordham University Press, 77–92.

Appadurai, Arjun (1990) 'Disjuncture and Difference in the Global Cultural Economy', *Public Culture*, 2(2): 1–24.

Appadurai, Arjun (2000) *Modernity at Large*, Minneapolis and London: University of Minnesota Press.

Appignanesi, Lisa (2000) *Losing the Dead: A Family Memoir*, London: Vintage.

Ashraf, P. Mary (1983) *The Life and Times of Thomas Spence*, Newcastle upon Tyne: Frank Graham.

Assmann, Jan (1995) 'Collective Memory and Cultural Identity', *New German Critique*, 65, Spring–Summer: 125–33.

Assman, Jan (2008) 'Communicative and Cultural Memory' in Erll Astrid and Nunning Ansgar (eds) *Cultural Memory Studies: An International and Interdisciplinary Handbook*. Berlin, Walter de Gruyter.

Assmann, Jan (2010) 'Communicative and Cultural Memory' in Astrid Erll and Ansgar Nunning, *Cultural Memory Studies: An International and Interdisciplinary Handbook*, Berlin and New York: Walter de Gruyter, pp. 109–19.

Auerhahn, Nanette C. and Laub, Dori (1998) 'Intergenerational Memory of the Holocaust' in Yael Danieli (ed.) *International Handbook of Multigenerational Legacies of Trauma*, New York: Plenum Press, pp. 21–42.

Bakewell, Sarah (2010) *How to Live, or A Life of Montaigne in One Question and Twenty Attempts at an Answer*, London: Chatto & Windus.

Banville, John (1973) *Birchwood*, London: Secker and Warburg.

Barthes, Roland (1981) *Camera Lucida*, New York: Hill and Wang.

Bartlett, Frederick (1932) *Remembering: A Study in Experimental and Social Psychology*, Cambridge: Cambridge University Press.

Battaglia, Debbora (1995) 'On Practical Nostalgia: Self-Prospecting among Urban Trobianders' in Debbora Battaglia (ed.) *Rhetorics of Self-Making*, London: University of California Press, 77–96.

Baudrillard, Jean (1983) *Simulations*, Los Angeles: Semiotext(e).

Bell, Daniel (1996 [1976]) *The Cultural Contradictions of Capitalism*, New York: Basic Books.

Benjamin, Walter (1970) *Illuminations*, London: Jonathan Cape.
Bennett, Oliver (2001) *Cultural Pessimism: Narratives of Decline in the Postmodern World*, Edinburgh: Edinburgh University Press.
Berger, Asa (1997) *Narratives in Popular Culture, Media and Everyday Life*, London: Sage.
Bergson, Henri (1975) 'Intellectual Effort' in *Mind-Energy* (trans. H. Wildon Carr), Westport, CT: Greenwood, 186–230.
Bergson, Henri (2004 [1912]) *Matter and Memory*, London: Dover Publications.
Bergson, Henri (2005 [1907]) *Creative Evolution*, USA: Barnes and Noble Books.
Bevan, Robert (2006) *The Destruction of Memory: Architecture at War*, London: Reaktion Books.
Bocock, Robert, Peter Hamilton, Kenneth Thompson and Alan Waton (eds) (1980) *An Introduction to Sociology: A Reader*, Brighton: Harvester Press.
Boltanski, Luc (1999) *Distant Suffering: Morality, Media and Politics*, Cambridge: Cambridge University Press.
Bonnett, Alastair (2007) 'Radical Nostalgia', *History Today*, 57(2): 41–2.
Bonnett, Alastair (2010) 'Radicalism, Antiracism, and Nostalgia: The Burden of Loss in the Search for Convivial Culture', *Environment and Planning A*, 42(10): 2351–69.
Borges, Jorge Luis (2000 [1944]) 'Funes, His Memory' in *Fictions* (trans. Andrew Hurley), London: Penguin.
Bourke, Joanna (1999) *An Intimate History of Killing*, London: Granta.
Bourke, Joanna (2000) 'Effeminacy, Ethnicity and the End of Trauma: The Sufferings of "Shell-Shocked" Men in Great Britain and Ireland, 1914–39', *Journal of Contemporary History*, 35(1): 57–69.
Bowie, Malcolm (2008) 'Remembering the Future' in Harriet Harvey Wood and A. S. Byatt (eds) *Memory: An Anthology*, London: Chatto and Windus, 13–27.
Boym, Svetlana (2001) *The Future of Nostalgia*, New York: Basic Books.
Boys, Jos (1989) 'Right Up Your Street', *Marxism Today*, September: 49.
Bridgers, Lynn (2005) *Contemporary Varieties of Religious Experience*, Lanham, MD: Rowman and Littlefield.
Brockmeier, Jens and Carbaugh, Donal (eds) (2001) *Narrative and Identity: Studies in Autobiography, Self and Culture*, Amsterdam: John Benjamins.
Brown, Michael (2003) *Who Owns Native Culture?* Cambridge, MA: Harvard University Press.
Bruner, Jerome (1991) 'The Narrative Construction of Reality', *Critical Inquiry*, 18, Autumn: 1–21.
Buckley, Jerome (1974) *Season of Youth: The Bildungsroman from Dickens to Golding*, Cambridge, MA: Harvard University Press.
Burchardt, Jeremy (2002) *Paradise Lost: Rural Idyll and Social Change in England since 1800*, London and New York: I. B. Tauris.
Burke, Peter (1981) *Montaigne*, Oxford, Melbourne and Toronto: Oxford University Press.
Burke, Peter (1997) *Varieties of Cultural History*, Cambridge: Polity.
Calvino, Italo (1993) *The Road to San Giovani*, London: Sage.
Campbell, John (1997) 'The Structure of Time in Autobiographical Memory', *European Journal of Philosophy*, 5(2): 105–18.
Campbell, Sue (2003) *Relational Remembering: Rethinking the Memory Wars*, Lanham ML and Oxford UK: Rowman & Littlefield.

Campbell, Sue (2006) 'Our Faithfulness to the Past: Reconstructing Memory Value', *Philosophical Psychology*, 19(3), June: 361–80.

Carrithers, Michael (ed.) (1985) *The Category of the Person*, Cambridge: Cambridge University Press.

Carroll, Lewis (1994 [1871]) *Through the Looking Glass*, London: Penguin.

Caruth, Cathy (1991) 'Introduction to Psychoanalysis, Trauma and Culture', *American Imago*, 48(1): 1–12.

Caruth, Cathy (ed.) (1995) *Trauma: Explorations in Memory*, Baltimore: Johns Hopkins University Press.

Caruth, Cathy (1996) *Unclaimed Experience: Trauma, Narrative, and History*, Baltimore: Johns Hopkins University Press.

Casey, Edward (1987a) 'The World of Nostalgia', *Man and World*, 20(4): 361–84.

Casey, Edward (1987b) *Remembering: A Phenomenological Study*, Bloomington and Indianapolis: Indiana University Press.

Casey, Edward (2000) *Imagining: A Phenomenological Study*, Bloomington: Indiana University Press.

Cashman, Ray (2002) *Wakes, Ceilis, and Characters: Commemoration and Identity in County Tyrone, Northern Ireland*, Unpublished Ph.D. dissertation, Indiana University.

Cashman, Ray (2006) 'Critical Nostalgia and Material Culture in Northern Ireland', *Journal of American Folklore*, 119(472): 137–60.

Chaney, David (1996) *Lifestyles*, London and New York: Routledge.

Chaney, David (2002) *Cultural Change and Everyday Life*, Basingstoke: Palgrave Macmillan.

Chouliaraki, Lilie (2006) *The Spectatorship of Suffering*, London; Thousand Oaks, CA and New Delhi: Sage.

Cohen, Anthony (1994) *Self-Consciousness: An Alternative Anthropology of Identity*, London and New York: Routledge.

Colley, Ann C. (1998) *Nostalgia and Recollection in Victorian Culture*, Basingstoke and New York: Palgrave Macmillan.

Colls, Robert and Dodd, Philip, (eds) (1986) *Englishness: Politics and Culture 1880–1920*, London: Croom Helm.

Colvin, Christopher J. (2003) '"Brothers and Sisters, Do not be Afraid of Me": Trauma, History and the Therapeutic Imagination in the New South Africa' in Katherine Hodgkin and Susannah Radstone *Contested Pasts: the Politics of Memory*, London: Routledge, pp. 153–67.

Confino, Alon and Fritzsche, Peter (eds) (2002) *The Work of Memory: New Directions in the Study of German Society and Culture*, Urbana and Chicago: University of Illinois Press.

Connerton, Paul (1989) *How Societies Remember*, Cambridge: Cambridge University Press.

Connerton, Paul (2009) *How Modernity Forgets*, Cambridge and New York: Cambridge University Press.

Crane, Susan (1994) 'Memory, Distortion, and History in the Museum', *History and Theory*, 36(4): 44–63.

Crane, Susan (1997) 'Writing the Individual Back into Collective Memory', *American Historical Review*, 102(5), December: 1372–85.

Crites, Stephen (1971) 'The Narrative Quality of Experience', *Journal of the American Academy of Religion*, 34(3): 291–311.

Crowther, Paul (1993) *Art and Embodiment: From Aesthetics to Self-Consciousness*, Oxford: Clarendon Press.

Cubitt, Geoffrey (2007) *History and Memory*, Manchester and New York: Manchester University Press.

Dames, Nicholas (2010) 'Nostalgia and its Disciplines', *Memory Studies*, 3(3), July: 269–75.

Danziger, Kurt (2008) *Marking the Mind: A History of Memory*, Cambridge and New York: Cambridge University Press.

Davis, Fred (1979) *Yearning for Yesterday*, New York and London: The Free Press/ Collier Macmillan.

De Baubeta, Patricia Anne Odber (2000) 'Bread, the Staff of Advertising', *Paremia*, 9: 103–10.

Deresiewicz, William (2004) *Jane Austen and the Romantic Poets*, New York: Columbia University Press.

Dewey, John (1960) *The Quest for Certainty*, New York: Putnam.

Dilthey, Wilhelm (1985) *Poetry and Experience, Selected Works, Vol. V*, Princeton, NJ: Princeton University Press.

Doane, Janice and Devon Hodges. (1987) *Nostalgia and Sexual Difference: The Resistance to Contemporary Feminism*, New York and London: Methuen.

Domingues, José Maurício (1997) 'Social Memory, Social Creativity and Collective Subjectivity', *Theory and Methods*, 36(3): 469–92.

Douglas, Mary (1987) *How Institutions Think*, London: Routledge and Kegan Paul.

Drake, Philip. (2003) '"Mortgaged to Music": New Retro Movies in 1990s Hollywood Cinema' in Paul Grainge (ed.) *Memory and Popular Film*, Manchester and New York: Manchester University Press, pp. 183–201.

Eley, Geoff and Grossmann, Atina (1997) 'Watching Schindler's List: Not the Last Word', *New German Critique*, 71(Spring/Summer): 41–62.

Elliott, Richard (2010) *Fado and the Place of Longing: Loss, Memory and the City*, Farnham, UK and Burlington, VT: Ashgate.

Elmwood, Victoria A. (2004) '"Happy, Happy, Ever After": The Transformation of Trauma between the Generations in Art Spiegelman's Maus: A Survivor's Tale', *Biography*, 27(4): 691–720.

Emerson, Ralph Waldo (1946) *The Portable Emerson*, New York: The Viking Press.

English, John, Madigan, Ruth and Norman, Peter (1976) *Slum Clearance: The Social and Administrative Context in England and Wales*, London: Croom Helm.

Epstein, A. L. (1978) *Ethos and Identity: Three Studies in Ethnicity*, London: Tavistock.

Epstein, James (1982) *The Chartist Experience*, London: Macmillan.

Erickson, Erik (1951) *Childhood and Society*, London: Imago.

Faulks, Sebastian (1990) *The Girl at the Lion d'Or*, London: Vintage.

Felman, Shoshana and Laub, Doris (1992) *Testimony: Crises of Witnessing in Literature, Psychanalysis, and History*, New York: Routledge.

Fentress, James and Wickham, Chris (1992) *Social Memory*, London. Blackwell.

Feudtner, Chris (1992) 'Minds The dead Have Ravished', *History of Science*, 31(4): 377–420.

Field, Sean (2008) 'Imagining Communities: Memory, Loss, and Resilience in Post-Apartheid Cape Town' in Paula Hamilton and Linda Shopes (eds) *Oral History and Public Memories*, Philadelphia: Temple University Press, 107–24.

Flaubert, Gustave (1948 [1857]) *Madame Bovary* (trans. Gerard Hopkins), London: Hamish Hamilton.

Foster, John (1838) *Essays in a Series of Letters to a Friend*, London: Samuel Holdsworth.

Frampton, Saul (2011) *When I Am Playing With My Cat, How Do I Know She Is Not Playing With Me? Montaigne and Being in Touch With Life*, London: Faber & Faber.

Freeman, Mark (1993) *Rewriting the Self: History, Memory, Narrative*, London and New York: Routledge.

Fresco, Nadine (1984) 'Remembering the Unknown', *International Review of Psychoanalysis*, 11: 417–27.

Freud, Sigmund (1955–74) *The Standard Edition of the Complete Psychological Works of Sigmund Freud*, London: Hogarth Press.

Fritzsche, Peter (2001) 'Spectres of History: On Nostalgia, Exile, and Modernity', *The American Historical Review*, 106(5), December: 1–40.

Fritzsche, Peter (2002) 'How Nostalgia Narrates Modernity' in Alon Confino and Peter Fritzsche (eds) *The Work of Memory: New Directions in the Study of German Society and Culture*, Illinois: University of Illinois Press. pp. 62–85.

Frosh, Paul (2003) *The Image Factory*, Oxford and New York: Berg.

Frosh, Paul (2006) 'Telling Presences: Witnessing, Mass Media, and the Imagined Lives of Strangers', *Critical Studies in Media Communication*, 23(4): 265–84.

Frosh, Paul (2011) 'Television and the Imagination of Memory: *Life on Mars*' in Motti Neiger, Oren Meyers and Eyal Zandberg (eds) *On Media Memory: Collective Memory in a New Media Age*, Basingstoke and New York: Palgrave Macmillan, pp. 117–31.

Frow, John (1997) *Time and Commodity Culture*, Oxford: Clarendon.

Fussell, Paul (2000) *The Great War and Modern Memory*, Oxford and New York: Oxford University Press.

Gadamer, Hans-Georg (1989) *Truth and Method*, London: Sheed & Ward.

Gerner, Kristian (2006) 'Open Wounds? Trianon, the Holocaust and the Hungarian Trauma' in Conny Mithander, John Sundholm and Maria Holmgren Troy (eds) *Collective Traumas: Memories of War and Conflict in 20th Century Europe*, Brussels: Peter Lang, 79–110.

Giddens, Anthony (1991) *Modernity and Self-Identity*, Stanford, CA: Stanford University Press.

Gillis, John R. (1994) 'Memory and Identity: The History of a Relationship' in John R. Gillis (ed.) *Commemorations: The Politics of National Identity*, Princeton, NJ: Princeton University Press, pp. 3–26.

Gissing, George (1982 [1903]) *The Private Papers of Henry Ryecroft*, Brighton: Harvester.

Gitlin, Todd (1980) *The Whole World is Watching: Mass Media in the Making and Unmaking of the New Left*, Berkeley, Los Angeles and London: University of California Press.

Gordon, Avery (1997) *Ghostly Matters: Haunting and the Sociological Imagination*, Minneapolis: University of Minnesota Press.

Green, Anna (2008) *Cultural History*, Basingstoke and New York: Palgrave Macmillan.

Greenberg, Clement (1964) 'Avant-Garde and Kitsch' in Bernard Rosenberg and David Manning White (eds) *Mass Culture: The Popular Arts in America*, New York and London: Collier-Macmillan, pp. 98–110.

Greene, Graham (1980 [1938]) *Brighton Rock*, Harmondsworth: Penguin.

Grossman, Wendy (2007) 'A Picture Paints a Thousand Invoices', *The Guardian*, 1 February, available at http://www.guardian.co.uk/technology/2007/feb/01/ copyright.newmedia (accessed on 6 june 2012).

Grossman, Wendy (2008) 'Is a Picture Really Worth £1000?' *The Guardian*, 27 November, available at http://www.guardian.co.uk/technology/2008/ nov/27/internet-photography?INTCMP=SRCH (accessed on 6 june 2012).

Guehenno, Jean-Marie (1995) *The End of the Nation-State* (trans. Victoria Elliott), Minneapolois: University of Minnesota Press.

Habermas, Jürgen (2001) *The Postnational Constellation*, Cambridge: Polity.

Hacking, Ian (1995) *Rewriting the Soul: Multiple Personality and the Sciences of Memory*, Princteon, NJ: Princeton University Press.

Halbwachs, Maurice (1980) *The Collective Memory*, New York: Harper & Row Colophon Books.

Halbwachs, Maurice (1992) *On Collective Memory* (trans./ed. Lewis A. Coser), Chicago: The University of Chicago Press.

Hamilton, Carrie (2007/8) 'Happy Memories', *New Formations*, 63, Winter: 65–81.

Hanlon, Dennis (2009) 'Does Anyone Have the Right to Say, "I Don't Care"?: Resistance and Reverence at Schindler's List', *Film & History: An Interdisciplinary Journal of Film and Television Studies*, 39(1): 53–65.

Hansen, Miriam Bratu (1996) *'Schindler's List* is not *Shoah*: The Second Commandment, Popular Modernism and Public Memory', *Critical Enquiry* 22(2): 292–312.

Hardy, Barbara (1975) *Tellers and Listeners: The Narrative Imagination*, London: The Athlone Press.

Hastrup, Kirsten (2007) 'Performing the World: Agency, Anticipation and Creativity' in Elizabeth Hallam and Tim Ingold. (eds) *Creativity and Cultural Improvisation*, Oxford and New York: Berg, 193–206.

Heffernan, Michael (1995) 'Forever England: The Western Front and the Politics of Remembrance in Britain', *Ecumene*, 2(3): 293–323.

Herman, Judith (1992) *Trauma and Recovery*, New York: Basic Books.

Hess, Jonathan (2002) 'Memory, History and the Jewish Question' in Confino and Peter Fritzsche (eds) *The Work of Memory: New Directions in the Study of German Society and Culture*, Illinois: University of Illinois Press, pp. 62–85

Hirsch, Marianne (1997) *Family Frames: Photography, Narrative and Postmemory*, Cambridge, MA: Harvard University Press.

Hirsch, Marianne (2008) 'The Generation of Postmemory', *Poetics Today*, 29(1): 103–28.

Hobbes, Thomas (1972 [1651]) *Leviathan*, Harmondsworth: Penguin.

Hobsbawm, Eric (1994) *Age of Extremes*, London: Michael Joseph.

Hoffman, Eva (1998) *Lost in Translation*, London: Vintage.

Hoffman, Eva (2005) *After Such Knowledge*, London: Vintage.

Hoffman, Eva (2010) 'The Long Afterlife of Loss' in Susannah Radstone and Bill Schwarz (eds) *Memory: Histories, Theories, Debates*, New York: Fordham University Press, 406–15.

Husserl, Edmund (1964) *The Phenomenology of Internal Time-Consciousness*, Bloomington: Indiana University Press.

Hutton, Patrick (1993) *History as an Art of Memory*, Hanover and London: University Press of New England.

Hutton, Patrick (2011) 'How the Old Left has Found a New Place in the Memory Game', *History and Theory*, 50, February: 98–111.

Huyssen, Andreas (1995) *Twilight Memories: Marking Time in a Culture of Amnesia*, New York and London: Routledge.

Huyssen, Andreas (2000a) 'Present Pasts: Media, Politics, Amnesia', *Public Culture*, 12(1): 21–38.

Huyssen, Andreas (2000b) 'Of Mice and Mimesis: Reading Spiegelman with Adorno', *New German Critique*, 81(August 2000): 65–82.

Ireland, Craig (2004) *The Subaltern Appeal to Experience*, Montreal, London and Ithaca: McGill-Queen's University Press.

Jacobs, Janet (2008) 'Gender and Collective Memory: Women and Representation at Auschwitz', *Memory Studies*, 1(2), May: 211–25.

James, William (1894) 'Professor Wundt and Feelings of Innervation', *Psychological Review*, 1(May 2002): 70–3.

James, William (1952 [1891]) *The Principles of Psychology*, Chicago, London and Toronto: William Benton/Encyclopaedia Britannica.

Jameson, Fredric (1969–70) 'Walter Benjamin, or Nostalgia', *Salmagundi*, 9–12: 52–68.

Jameson, Fredric (1991) *Postmodernism or, the Cultural Logic of Late Capitalism*, Durham: Duke University Press.

Janoff-Bulman, Ronnie (2004) 'Posttraumatic Growth: Three Explanatory Models', *Psychological Inquiry*, 15(1): 30–4.

Jay, Martin (2005) *Songs of Experience: Modern American and European Variations on a Universal Theme*, Berkeley, Los Angeles and London: University of California Press.

Jedlowski, Paulo (2001) 'Memory and Sociology', *Time and Society*, 10(1): 29–44.

Jordan, David P. (2004) 'Haussmann and Haussmanisation: The Legacy for Paris', *French Historical Studies*, 27(1): 87–113.

Jordan, John (ed.) (1965) Percy Bysshe Shelley, *A Defence of Poetry*/Thomas Love Peacock, *The Four Ages of Poetry*, Indianapolis: Bobbs-Merrill.

Judt, Tony (2008) *Reappraisals*, London: William Heinemann.

Kansteiner, Wulf (2002) 'Finding Meaning in Memory: A Methodological Critique of Collective Memory Studies', *History and Theory*, 41(2): 179–97.

Kansteiner, Wulf (2010) 'Memory, Media and *Menschen*: Where is the Individual in Collective Memory Studies?' *Memory Studies*, 3(1): 3–4.

Kant, Emmanuel (2006) *Anthropology from a Pragmatic Point of View*, Cambridge: Cambridge University Press.

Kant, Emmanuel (2007 [1781]) *Critique of Pure Reason*, London: Penguin.

Karpf, Anne (1997) *The War After: Living with the Holocaust*, London: Minerva.

Kearney, Richard (1998) *The Wake of Imagination*, London: Routledge.

Kearney, Richard (1991) *Poetics of Imagining: From Husserl to Lyotard*, London: HarperCollins.

Keightley, Emily and Pickering, Michael (2007) 'Les Deux Voies du Passé: Le Ressouvenir, Entre Progrès et Perte', *Cahiers de Recherche Sociologique*, 44, September: 83–96.

Kinna, Ruth (2000) *William Morris: The Art of Socialism*, Cardiff: University of Wales Press.

Koselleck, Reinhart (2002) *The Practice of Conceptual History*, Stanford, CA: Stanford University Press.

Koselleck, Reinhart (2004) *Futures Past: On the Semantics of Historical Time*, New York: Columbia University Press.

Kövecses, Zoltán (2006) *Language, Mind and Culture*, Oxford: Oxford University Press.

Krell, David Farrell (1990) *Of Memory, Reminiscence and Writing*, Bloomington and Indianapolis: Indiana University Press.

Kuhn, Annette. (1995/2002) *Family Secrets: Acts of Memory and IMagination*. London and New York, Verso.

Kundera, Milan (1986 [1973]) *Life is Elsewhere*, London and Boston: Faber & Faber.

Kundera, Milan (1991) *Immortality*, London: Faber & Faber.

LaCapra, Dominick (1994) *Representing the Holocaust: History, Theory, Trauma*, Ithaca and London: Cornell University Press.

LaCapra, Dominick (1998) *History and Memory after Auschwitz*, Cornell University Press.

Ladino, Jennifer (2007) 'Longing for Wonderland: Nostalgia for Nature in Post-Frontier America', *Iowa Journal of Cultural Studies*, 5, available at http://www.uiowa.edu/~ijcs/nostalgia/ladino.htm (accessed on 16 May 2012).

Landsberg, Alison (1997) 'America, The Holocaust and the Mass Culture of Memory: Towards a Radical Politics of Empathy', *New German Critique*, 71, Spring–Summer: 63–86.

Landsberg, Alison (2004) *Prosthetic Memory: The Transformation of American Remembrance in the Age of Mass Culture*, New York and Chichester, West Sussex: Columbia University Press.

Landsberg, Alison (2009) 'Memory, Empathy, and the Politics of Identification', *International Journal of Politics Culture and Society*, 22(2): 221–9.

Laplanche, Jean and Pontalis, J-B. (1973) *The Language of Psychoanalysis*, New York: Norton.

Lasch, Christopher (1980) *The Culture of Narcissism*, London: Abacus.

Lawler, Steph (2008) 'Stories and the Social World' in Michael Pickering (ed.) *Research Methods for Cultural Studies*, Edinburgh: Edinburgh University Press, pp. 32–51.

Le Goff, Jacques (1992) *History and Memory*, New York and Oxford: Columbia University Press.

Lears, T. J. Jackson (1983) 'From Salvation to Self-realization: Advertising and the Therapeutic Roots of the Consumer Culture, 1880–1930' in Richard Wightman Fox and T. J. Jackson Lears (eds) *The Culture of Consumption: Critical Readings in American History, 1880–1980*, New York: Pantheon Books.

Legg, Stephen (2005) 'Contesting and Surviving Memory: Space, Nation, and Nostalgia in *Les Lieux de Mémoire*', *Environment and Planning D: Society and Space*, 23(4): 481–504.

Levin, Harry (ed.) (1963) *The Essential James Joyce*, Harmondsworth: Penguin.

Levine, Michael G. (2002) 'Necessary Stains: Spiegelman's MAUS and the Bleeding of History', *American Imago*, 59(3): 317–41.

Levitas, Ruth (1990) *The Concept of Utopia*, New York and London: Philip Allan.

Leydesdorff, Selma (1994) *How We Lived With Dignity: The Jewish Proletariat of Amsterdam, 1900–1940*, Detroit, MI: Wayne State University Press.

Leys, Ruth (2000) *Trauma: A Genealogy*, Chicago and London: University of Chicago Press.

Liess, William, Kline, Stephen and Jhally, Sut (1986) *Social Communication in Advertising*, London: Methuen.

Lively, Penelope (1986) *Going Back*, Harmondsworth: Puffin.

Lively, Penelope (1994) *Oleander, Jacaranda*, London: Viking.

Locke, John (1996 [1689]) *An Essay Concerning Human Understanding*, (ed.) Kenneth P. Winkler, Indianapolis: Hackett Publishing Company.

Lowerson, John (1980) 'Battles for the Countryside' in Frank Gloversmith (ed.) *Class, Culture and Social Change*, Brighton: Harvester, pp. 258–80.

MaGahern, John (2003) *That They May Face the Rising Sun*, London: Faber & Faber.

Mandler, Peter (1997) 'Against Englishness: English Culture and the Limits to Rural Nostalgia, 1850–1940', *Transactions of the Royal Historical Society*, 6(7): 155–75.

Marsh, Jan (1982) *Back to the Land: The Pastoral Impulse in Victorian England from 1880 to 1914*, London, Melbourne and New York: Quartet Books.

Matsuda, Matt (1996) *The Memory of the Modern*, New York and Oxford: Oxford University Press.

Matt, Susan J. (2007) 'You Can't Go Home Again: Homesickness and Nostalgia in U.S. History', *The Journal of American History*, 94(2): 469–97.

McNab, Geoffrey (2005) 'Schindler's List? Kitsch', available at http://www.guardian. co.uk/books/2005/aug/23/edinburghfilmfestival2005.edinburghfilmfestival (accessed on 9 February 2012).

Mead, George Herbert (1934) *Mind, Self and Society*, Chicago: University of Chicago Press.

Mead, George Herbert (1938) *The Philosophy of the Act*, Chicago: University of Chicago Press.

Mead, George Herbert (1959) *The Philosophy of the Present*, La Salle, IL: Open Court Publishing Co.

Merleau-Ponty, Maurice (1974) *The Prose of the World*, London: Heinemann.

Metz, Johannes B. (1972) 'The Future in the Memory of Suffering', *Concilium*, 76: 9–25.

Middleton, David and Brown, Steven D. (2005) *The Social Psychology of Experience: Studies in Remembering and Forgetting*, London: Sage.

Middleton, David and Brown, Steven D. (2010) 'Experience and Memory: Imaginary Futures in the Past' in Astrid Erll and Ansgar Nünning (eds) *A Companion to Cultural Memory Studies*, Berlin and New York: De Gruyter, pp. 241–52.

Mihelj, Sabina (2012, under review) 'The Persistence of the Past: Memory, Generation and "the Iron Curtain"', *Contemporary European History*.

Misztal, Barbara (2003) *Theories of Social Remembering*, Maidenhead and Philadelphia: Open University Press.

Montaigne, Michel de (1961) *Essays* (trans. J. M. Cohen), Harmondsworth: Penguin.

Montaigne, Michel de (1991) *The Complete Essays* (trans. M. A. Screech), London and New York: Penguin.

Moody, Harry (1984) 'Reminiscence and the Recovery of the Public World' in Marc Kaminsky (ed.) *The Uses of Reminiscence*, New York: Haworth Press, 157–67.

Moretti, Franco (1987) *The Way of the World: The Bildungsroman in European Culture*, London: Verso.

Mosse, George (2000) 'Shell-Shock as a Social Disease', *Journal of Contemporary History*, 35(1): 101–8.

Nash, Cristopher (1990) *Narrative in Culture: The Uses of Storytelling in the Sciences, Philosophy and Literature*, London and New York: Routledge.

Natali, Marcos Piason (2009) 'History and the Politics of Nostalgia', *Iowa Journal of Cultural Studies*, 5, available at http://www.uiowa.edu/~ijcs/nostalgia/nostfel. htm, (accessed on 15 May 2012).

Neal, Arthur (1998) *National Trauma and Collective Memory: Major Events in the American Century*, New York and London: M. E. Sharpe.

Negus, Keith and Pickering, Michael (2004) *Creativity, Communication and Cultural Value*, London, Thousand Oaks and New Delhi: Sage.

Nora, Pierre (1989) 'Between Memory and History: Les Lieux de Mémoire', *Representations*, 26(Spring): 7–25.

Nora, Pierre (1996–8) *Realms of Memory: Rethinking the French Past*, Three vols, New York: Columbia University Press.

Nora, Pierre (2002) 'Reasons for the Current Upsurge in Memory', *Eurozine*, available at www.eurozine.com/articles/2002-04-19-nora-en.html (accessed on 17 June 2011).

Nussbaum, Martha (1990) *Love's Knowledge*, New York and Oxford: Oxford University Press.

Olick, Jeffrey (1999) 'Collective Memory: The Two Cultures', *Sociological Theory*, 17(3), November: 333–48.

Olick, Jeffrey (2008) 'From Collective Memory to the Sociology of Mnemonic Practices and Products' in Erll, Astrid and Nunning, Ansgar (eds) *Cultural Memory Studies: An International and Interdisciplinary Handbook*. Berlin, Walter de Gruyter, pp. 151–61.

Olick, Jeffrey (2010) 'From Collective Memory to the Sociology of Mnemonic Practices' in Astrid Erll and Ansgar Nünning (eds) *A Companion to Cultural Memory Studies*, Berlin and New York: De Gruyter, pp. 151–62.

Oliver, Kelly (2001) *Witnessing*, Minneapolis and London: University of Minnesota Press, Oxford University Press.

Parker, Peter (2009) *The Last Veteran: Harry Patch and the Legacy of War*, London: Fourth Estate.

Passerini, Louise (1979) 'Work Ideology and Consensus under Italian Fascism', *History Workshop Journal*, 8, Autumn: 82–108.

Patch, Harry with van Emden, Richard (2008) *The Last Fighting Tommy*, London: Bloomsbury.

Pears, Iain (1998) *An Instance of the Fingerpost*, London: Vintage.

Peters, John Durham (2009) 'Witnessing' in Paul Frosh and Amit Pinchevski (eds) *Media Witnessing: Testimony in the Age of Mass Communication*, Basingstoke and New York: Palgrave Macmillan, pp. 23–48.

Pickering, Michael (1987) 'The Past as a Source of Aspiration: Popular Song and Social Change' in Michael Pickering and Tony Green (eds) *Everyday Culture*, Milton Keynes and Philadelphia: Open University Press, pp. 39–69.

Pickering, Michael (1997) *History, Experience and Cultural Studies*, Basingstoke and New York: Palgrave Macmillan.

Pickering, Michael (2001) *Stereotyping: The Politics of Representation*, Basingstoke and New York: Palgrave Macmillan.

Pickering, Michael (2004) 'Experience as Horizon: Koselleck, Expectation and Historical Time', *Cultural Studies*, 18(2/3): 271–89.

Pickering, Michael (2008) 'Experience and the Social World' in Michael Pickering (ed.) *Research Methods for Cultural Studies*, Edinburgh: Edinburgh University Press, 17–31.

Pickering, Michael and Green, Tony (1987) 'Towards a Cartography of the Vernacular Milieu' in Michael Pickering and Tony Green (eds) *Everyday Culture*, Milton Keynes and Philadelphia: Open University Press, pp. 1–38.

Pickering, Michael and Keightley, Emily (2008) 'Echoes and Reverberations: Photography and Phonography as Historical Forms' in S. Nicholas, T. O'Malley and K. Williams (eds) *Reconstructing the Past: History in the Mass Media, 1890–2005*, London and New York: Routledge, pp. 153–68.

Plumb, John Harold (1969) *The Death of the Past*, London: Macmillan.

Polkinghorne, Donald (1988) *Narrative Knowing and the Human Sciences*, Albany: SUNY Press.

Prager, Jeffrey (1998) *Presenting the Past: Psychoanalysis and the Sociology of Misremembering*, Cambridge, MA and London: Harvard University Press.

Radstone, Susannah (2005) 'Reconceiving Binaries: the Limits of Memory', *History Workshop Journal*, 59(Spring): 134–50.

Reading, Anna (2003) *The Social Inheritance of the Holocaust: Gender, Culture and Memory*, Basingstoke: Palgrave Macmillan.

Ribot, Théodule (1882) *Diseases of Memory*, London: K. Paul & Trench.

Rich, Adrienne (1982) *A Wild Patience Has Taken Me This Far: Poems 1978–81*, New York and London: W. W. Norton.

Ricoeur, Paul (1986) *Lectures on Ideology and Utopia*, New York and Guildford: Columbia University Press.

Ricoeur, Paul (1990) *Time and Narrative*, Three vols, Chicago: University of Chicago Press.

Ricoeur, Paul (1991) 'Life in Quest of Narrative' in David Wood (ed.) *On Paul Ricoeur: Narrative and Interpretation*, London and New York: Routledge.

Ricoeur, Paul (1994a) *Oneself as Another*, Chicago and London: University of Chicago Press.

Ricoeur, Paul (1994b) 'Imagination in Discourse and Action' in Gillian Robinson and John F. Rundell (eds) *Rethinking Imagination: Culture and Creativity*, London: Routledge, pp. 118–135.

Ricoeur, Paul (2004) *Memory, History and Forgetting*, Chicago: University of Chicago Press.

Rítívoí, Andrea Decíu (2002) *Yesterday's Self: Nostalgia and the Immigrant Identity*, Lanham, Boulder, New York and Oxford: Rowman & Littlefield.

Roberts, Stephen (2003) *The People's Charter*, London: The Merlin Press.

Robinson, Marilynne (2009) *Gilead*, London: Virago.

Rosaldo, Renato (1993) *Culture and Truth: The Remaking of Social Analysis*, London: Routledge.

Rosenzweig, Roy and Thelen, David (1998) *The Presence of the Past: Popular Uses of History in American Life*, New York and Chichester, West Sussex: Columbia University Press.

Roth, Michael (1989) 'Remembering Forgetting: Maladies de la Mémoire in Late Nineteenth Century France', *Representations*, 26(Spring): 49–68.

Roth, Michael (1991) 'Dying of the Past: Medical Studies of Nostalgia in Nineteenth Century France', *History and Memory*, 3(1): 5–29.

Roth, Michael (1993) 'Returning to Nostalgia' in Suzanne Nash (ed.) *Home and its Dislocations in Nineteenth Century France*, Albany: State University of New York, pp. 25–44.

Rothberg, Michael and Spiegelman, Art (1994) '"We Were Talking Jewish": Art Spiegelman's "Maus" as "Holocaust" Production', *Contemporary Literature*, 35(4): 661–87.

Rowe, Dorothy (2011) 'The Missing Pot of Gold', *Guardian Review*, 15 April, www. guardian.co.uk/books/2011/apr/15/zero-degrees-of-empathy-baron-cohen-review, (accessed on 22 May 2012).

Ruml, Beardsley (1946) 'Some Notes on Nostalgia', *Saturday Review of Literature*, 22 June, pp. 7–9.

Russell, Bertrand (2007 [1921]) *The Analysis of Mind*, London: Allen & Unwin Limited.

Ryle, Gilbert, (1970 [1949]) *The Concept of Mind*, Harmondsworth: Penguin.

Sarbin, Theodore (ed.) (1986) *Narrative Psychology: The Storied Nature of Human Conduct*, New York: Praeger.

Sartre, Jean Paul (1972) *The Psychology of Imagination*, London: Routledge.

Savage, Kirk (1994) 'The Politics of Memory: Black Emancipation and the Civil War Monument' in John R. Gillis (ed.) *Commemorations: The Politics of National Identity*, Princeton, NJ: Princeton University Press, pp. 127–49.

Schechtman, Marya (1994) 'The Truth about Memory', *Philosophical Psychology*, 7(1): 3–18.

Schinkel, Anders (2005) 'Imagination as a Category of History: An Essay Concerning Koselleck's Concepts of *Erfahrungsraum* and *Erwartungshorizont*', *History and Theory*, 44(1): 42–54.

Schorske, Carl (1980) *Fin-de-Siècle Vienna: Politics and Culture*, London: Weidenfeld and Nicolson.

Schorske, Carl (1998) *Fin-de-Siècle Vienna*, London: Weidenfeld and Nicolson.

Schwarz, Bill (2010) 'Memory, Temporality, Modernity' in Susannah Radstone and Bill Schwarz (eds) *Memory: Histories, Theories, Debates*, NY: Fordham University Press, pp. 41–60.

Schwartz, Vanessa R. (1998) *Spectacular Realities: Early Mass Culture in Fin-de-Siècle Paris*, Los Angeles and London: University of California Press.

Serematakis, C. Nadia (1994) 'The Memory of the Senses, Part One: Marks of the Transitory' in C. Nadia Serematakis (ed.) *The Senses Still: Perception and Memory as Material Culture in Modernity*, London: University of Chicago Press, pp. 1–18.

Shandler, Jeffrey (1999) *While America Watches: Televising the Holocaust*, Oxford and New York: Oxford University Press.

Shaw, Charles (1979 [1903]) *When I Was A Child*, Sussex: Caliban Books.

Shaw, Christopher and Chase, Malcom (eds) (1989) *The Imagined Past: History and Nostalgia*, Manchester and New York: Manchester University Press.

Shotter, John (1990) 'The Social Construction of Remembering and Forgetting' in David Middleton and Stephen D. Brown (eds) *Collective Remembering*, London: Sage, pp. 120–38.

Showalter, Elaine (1997) *Hystories*, New York: Columbia University Press.

Smith, Jason Scott (1998) 'The Strange History of the Decade: Modernity, Nostalgia and the Perils of Periodisation', *Journal of Social History*, 32(2): 263–85.

Smith, Kimberly (2000) 'Mere Nostalgia: Notes on a Progressive Paratheory', *Rhetoric and Public Affairs*, 3(4): 505–27.

Sontag, Susan (1977) *On Photography*, New York: Farrar, Straus and Giroux.

Sontag, Susan (2003) *Regarding the Pain of Others*, London: Penguin.

Southgate, Beverley (2007) 'Memories into Something New: Histories for the Future', *Rethinking History*, 11(2): 187–99.

Stafford, William (1987) *Socialism, Radicalism, and Nostalgia: Social Criticism in Britain, 1775–1830*, Cambridge and New York: Cambridge University Press.

Stafford, William (1989) '"This Once Happy Country": Nostalgia for Pre-modern Society' in Christopher Shaw and Malcom Chase (eds) *The imagined past: history and nostalgia*, Manchester and New York: Manchester University Press, pp. 33–46.

Starobinski, Jean (1966) 'The Idea of Nostalgia', *Diogenes*, 14: 81–103.

Staub, Michael E. (1995) 'The Shoah Goes On And On: Remembrance and Representation in Art Spiegelman's Maus', *History and Memory*, 20(3): 33–46.

Stauth, George and Turner, Bryan S. (1988) 'Nostalgia, Postmodernism and the Critique of Mass Culture', *Theory, Culture and Society*, 5(2–3), June: 509–26.

Stevenson, Robert Louis (1911) *Across the Plains*, London: Chatto & Windus.

Stone, Martin (1985) 'Shell-Shock and the Psychologists' in W. F. Bynum, Roy Porter and Michael Shepherd (eds) *The Anatomy of Madness*, London: Tavistock, Three vols, II, pp. 242–71.

Sutton, John (1998) *Philosophy and Memory Traces: Descartes to Connectionism*, Cambridge and New York: Cambridge University Press.

Sutton, John (2004) 'Memory', Stanford Encyclopedia of Philosophy, available at http://plato.stanford.edu/entries/memory (accessed on 29 June 2007).

Sutton, John (2009a) 'The Feel of the World: Exograms, Habits, and the Confusion of Types of Memory' in Andrew Kania (ed.) *Memento*, Abingdon and New York: Routledge, pp. 65–86.

Sutton, John (2009b) 'Remembering' in Philip Robbins and Murat Aydede (eds) *The Cambridge Handbook of Situated Cognition*, Cambridge and New York: Cambridge University Press, pp. 217–35.

Swift, Graham (2010) *Making an Elephant*, London: Picador.

Tacchi, Jo (2003) 'Nostalgia and Radio Sound' in Michael Bull and Les Back (eds) *The Auditory Culture Reader*, Oxford and New York: Berg, pp. 281–95.

Tannock, Stuart (1995) 'Nostalgia Critique', *Cultural Studies*, 9(3): 453–64.

Taylor, Charles (1989) *Sources of the Self*, Cambridge: Cambridge University Press.

Taylor, Charles (1994) 'The Politics of Recognition' in Amy Gutman (ed.) *Multiculturalism: Examining the Politics of Recognition*, Princeton, NJ: Princeton University Press, pp. 25–73.

Taylor, Diana (2002) '"You Are Here": The DNA of Performance', *The Drama Review*, 46(1), Spring: 149–69.

Terdiman, Richard (1993) *Present Past: Modernity and the Memory Crisis*, Ithaca, NY: Cornell University Press.

Thackeray, William Makepeace (1899) *The Memoirs of Barry Lyndon* in his *The Works of William Makepeace Thackeray*, 13 volumes, Vol. 4, London: Smith, Elder & Co.

Thompson, E. P. (1977/1955) *William Morris: Romantic to Revolutionary*, London: Merlin Press.

Thompson, John B. (1995) *The Media and Modernity*, Cambridge: Polity.

Thomson, Alistair (1994) *Anzac Memories: Living with the Legend*, Melbourne: Oxford University Press.

Tocqueville, Alexis de (1955) *The Old Regime and the French Revolution* (trans. Stuart Gilbert), New York: Doubleday.

Tolstoy, Leo (1960) *Anna Karenina*, Harmondsworth: Middlesex.

Van der Kolk, Bessel A. and van der Hart, Onno. (1995) 'The Intrusive Past: The Flexibility of Memory and the Engraving of Trauma', In Cathy Caruth (ed.) *Trauma: Explorations in Memory*, Baltimore: The Johns Hopkins University Press, pp. 158–82.

Van Dijck, José (2007) *Mediated Memories in the Digital Age*, Stanford: Stanford University Press.

Vaughan, Edwin Campion (1987) *Some Desperate Glory*, London: Leo Cooper in association with Frederick Warne Ltd.

Walton, John (1999) *Chartism*, London: Routledge.

Wang, Qi and Brockmeier, Jens (2002) 'Autobiographical Remembering as Cultural Practice: Understanding the Interplay between Memory, Self and Culture', *Culture and Psychology*, 8(1): 45–64.

Warnock, Mary (1987) *Memory*, London: Faber and Faber.

Waters, Chris (2000) 'Autobiography, Nostalgia, and the Changing Practices of Working-Class Selfhood' in George K. Behlmer and Fred M. Leventhal (eds) *Singular Continuities: Tradition, Nostalgia, and Identity in Modern British Culture*, Stanford, CA: Stanford University Press, pp. 178–95.

Wertsch, James V. (2002) *The Voices of Collective Remembering*, Cambridge: Cambridge University Press.

Wiener, Martin J. (1981) *English Culture and the Decline of the Industrial Spirit, 1850–1980*, Cambridge: Cambridge University Press.

Williams, Raymond (1975) *The Country and the City*, St Albans: Paladin.

Winter, Jay (2006) *Remembering War: The Great War Between Memory and History in the Twentieth Century*, New Haven and London: Yale University Press.

Wood, Nancy (1994) 'Memory's Remains: Les Lieux de Mémoire', *History and Memory*, 6(1), Spring–Summer: 123–49.

Wordsworth, William (1969 [1805]) *The Prelude*, London and New York: Oxford University Press.

Wright, David Gordon (1988) *Popular Radicalism: The Working-Class Experience, 1780–1880*, London: Longman.

Wright, Patrick (1985) *On Living in an Old Country*, London: Verso.

Wrong, Dennis H. (1961) 'The Oversocialised Conception of Man', *American Sociological Review*, 26(2): 184–93.

Young, James E. (1998) 'The Holocaust as Vicarious Past: Art Spiegelman's "Maus" and the Afterimages of History', *Critical Inquiry*, 24(3): 666–99.

Zarecka, Iwona Irwin (1994) *Frames of Remembrance*, New Brunswick and London: Transaction.

Zelizer, Barbie (1998) *Remembering to Forget: Holocaust Memory Through the Camera's Eye*, Chicago: University of Chicago Press.

Zerubavel, Eviatar (1996) 'Social Memories: Steps to a Sociology of the Past', *Qualitative Sociology*, 19(3): 283–99.

Zylinska, Joanna (2005) *The Ethics of Cultural Studies*, London and New York: Continuum.

Index